MAKING

PEACE

A Reading/Writing/Thinking
Text on Global Community

MAKING PEACE

A Reading/Writing/Thinking Text on Global Community

Elaine Brooks

Brooklyn College, City University of New York

Len Fox

Brooklyn College, City University of New York

CAMBRIDGE
UNIVERSITY PRESS

PUBLISHED BY THE PRESS SYNDICATE OF THE UNIVERSITY OF CAMBRIDGE
The Pitt Building, Trumpington Street, Cambridge CB2 1RP, United Kingdom

CAMBRIDGE UNIVERSITY PRESS
The Edinburgh Building, Cambridge CB2 2RU, UK   http: //www.cup.cam.ac.uk
40 West 20th Street, New York, NY 10011-4211, USA   http: //www.cup.org
10 Stamford Road, Oakleigh, Melbourne 3166, Australia

First published by St. Martin's Press, Inc. 1995

Reprinted 1999

Printed in the United States of America

Library of Congress Cataloging-in-Publication Data Available

ISBN 0-521-65780-6 Student's Book
ISBN 0-521-65779-2 Instructor's Manual

Acknowledgments are given on page(s) 278–279.

To Len, a good colleague and friend who has always supported and encouraged me.

E. B.

To Ruth Fox, a consummate peacemaker.

L. F.

Preface

PEOPLE SOMETIMES THINK of peace education as speaking against war and against the proliferation of weapons of war such as nuclear armaments. This is one aspect of peace education, which Betty Reardon calls "negative peace education." But peace education can be defined much more broadly. Reardon defines it as preparing students for "efforts to achieve human dignity for all people and to realize a viable global society on an ecologically healthy planet".[1] In other words, peace education involves developing in young people not just the desire to avoid war, but also the desire to build a more peaceful world—one with peaceful relations among people, among nations, and between human beings and the natural environment. The goal of *Making Peace* is to encourage in students the desire to build such a world, while at the same time helping them to improve their reading and writing skills.

We believe that *Making Peace* is unique in its focus on critical thinking about peace education—about how we, as individuals and in collaboration with one another, can increase the possibility for a more peaceful world by thinking about what such a world would be like, what conditions would have to exist for such a world to emerge, and what we could do to help create it.

The text is intended for two audiences: (1) advanced ESL students, including international students studying English in their own country and immigrant students learning in an English-dominant environment, and (2) native speakers of English who wish to improve their reading, writing, and critical thinking skills (for example, in basic skills or general education diploma courses). The book's theme is of concern to anyone living in today's world,

---

[1]B. Reardon, *Comprehensive Peace Education* (New York: Teachers College Press, Columbia University, 1988).

and the activities are meant to encourage intelligent and innovative thinking about issues that affect us all.

Overview of the Text

Making Peace is divided into six *thematic parts:* (1) working for a healthy environment; (2) developing peaceful relations between men and women; (3) educating families and children for a more peaceful world; (4) promoting greater cross-cultural understanding, (5) exploring spiritual values, and (6) working for a better world. Each part contains four *chapter readings* offering students information and ideas that may be new to them but that provide opportunities to make connections to what students already know or have experienced of the world. Students will thus not only practice and improve their reading/writing/thinking abilities, they will also have a chance to discuss, think, write, and learn about values that will make them more informed, more active citizens in the struggle to create a better, more peaceful world. *Making Peace* is accompanied by an *Instructor's Manual*, which is discussed in detail below.

THE READINGS

As the text contains many readings, instructors may not be able to cover all of them in a typical semester. Instead, two or three readings from each part may be used, or the class may focus on certain parts in greater depth.

THE ACTIVITIES

Accompanying each reading are numerous activities that encourage students to think critically about the topics discussed in the selection and to link the reading to the overall theme of the book and to other selections. The activities also give students the opportunity to practice various strategies involved in the processes of reading and writing, and to develop their language skills through communication with their classmates.

The *prereading* activities lead students into the reading process by helping them to think about and prepare for their reading of the selection. The *postreading* activities take students through the stages of the writing process as they explore what they have read through discussion and their own writing. The activities are organized in a way that allows instructors unable to cover all of them to focus on selected stages of the reading and writing processes.

Getting Ready to Read

The three prereading activities give students a context for thinking about the selection before they actually read it. In *Thinking about the Title*, students are encouraged to do just that, either on their own or through class discussion. The *Key Vocabulary/Concepts* activity lists terms from the reading so that students can share their knowledge of those concepts with each other and thereby prepare for the reading. This activity is meant to generate class discussion and should therefore be done with the whole class. Instructors may choose to focus student discussion on only a selected number of terms, depending on the needs of the class. The *Prereading Questions* are meant to spark students' interest in what they are about to read by asking them to think about issues related to the overall theme of the selection. This activity may be done individually or in small groups, or the entire class can share responses.

Thinking about the Reading

The chapter readings are followed by numerous activities that test students' reading comprehension and guide them through the writing process. In the first postreading activity, *True/False Questions*, students must refer to the relevant sections of the reading to determine the correct answers. (An answer key for this exercise is provided in the *Instructor's Manual*.) The *Comprehension Questions* are more demanding; they require students to write correct responses in their own words rather than simply copying answers from the reading. By paraphrasing parts of the reading, students gain a better understanding of what they have read. The Comprehension Questions are preceded by a sample question and answer, while Appendix A provides additional guidance on answering such questions. (Sample answers to the comprehension questions in Appendix A are given in the *Instructor's Manual*.) Teachers are encouraged to discuss, model, and practice paraphrasing with students.

In the *Outline* activity, students must read the indicated paragraphs of the selection in order to complete the missing parts of the outline. In so doing, they learn to read more fluently by focusing not on individual words but on the main points of a selection. (The *Instructor's Manual* contains sample completed outlines.) Next, using their completed outline, students are asked in the *Summary* exercise to write a synopsis of the reading. In addition to providing writing practice, this activity tests students' understanding of what they have read. Appendix B gives detailed guidance on how to write a summary and provides a model.

Making Connections

In this set of activities, students are given opportunities to make meaningful connections between what they have read and their own experience or other sources. Students write about their personal response to the selection in *Reacting to the Reading*, either in class or at home in a journal or log for small- or large-group discussion later on.

Instructors may assign or allow students to select one or both exercises in *Finding Related Sources*. By exploring other sources related to the reading (finding relevant pictures or texts or interviewing someone, for example), students get into the habit of learning independently and using English outside the classroom.

Getting Ready to Write

The *Prewriting Activities* help students to generate ideas for writing—through freewriting, clustering, listing, and cubing. By overcoming the frustration and difficulties typically associated with this early writing stage, students can begin to develop confidence in their ability to think and write. This activity is closely tied to Appendix C, which explains and models the various prewriting techniques. It is suggested that students practice freewriting first, then proceed to clustering, listing, and cubing as they develop their prewriting skills. Students should work on the prewriting activities individually and then share their ideas with the class.

The *Discussion and Composition Questions* focus on issues raised in the reading that are related to world peace and other topics. What a more peaceful world would be like and how we might achieve that goal are among the many questions focusing on peacemaking topics. In addition to stimulating thought about peacemaking and other issues, the questions enable students to practice using various rhetorical modes—to describe, compare, argue, explain, solve, and so forth—in their writing and discussion.

Students then choose one of the questions as their writing topic for the following activity, *Planning to Write*. Since it is important for students to write about a topic that interests them, an effort has been made to provide numerous topics. In addition, instructors may opt to allow students to generate their own questions about the reading and to choose the writing topic. Since the text is intended for both high intermediate and advanced ESL students, the instructor could decide to assign either a paragraph- or an essay-length writing. Students can consult Appendixes D and E for guidelines on how to write a paragraph or an essay as well as for sample writings. The Planning to

Write activity also asks students to devise a writing plan by identifying the topic and listing what they plan to write about it. The actual paragraph or essay writing may be done at home or in class, individually or collaboratively—in short, in whatever manner the instructor considers most appropriate. In any case, a major goal of the writing is to allow students to reflect critically on the readings, on related issues tied to world peace, and on their own lives and experiences.

Revising and Editing Your Writing

After students write the first draft of their paragraph or essay, they work through the revising stage by consulting the *Revision Checklist* in Appendix F. Here students may work on identifying problems of content and organization in either their own or a classmate's writing. Other possible activities include class discussion of revision strategies, reading of the paragraphs or essays in small groups, and individual conferences with students to identify problem areas. A second draft is then written, incorporating the revisions. As students gain practice in revision, they will also learn how to evaluate their own writing critically.

Once students are satisfied with the content, development, and organization of their paragraph or essay (which may require more than one subsequent draft), they proceed to the editing stage. The *Editing Checklist* in Appendix G provides helpful guidelines for editing and proofreading. Here, again, students may work on their own or a classmate's writing to gain practice at spotting and correcting particular types of errors. In order to develop beginning editing skills, students may, for example, be asked to underline subjects and verbs to check for verb form errors or to underline noun phrases (subjects or objects of verbs and objects of prepositions) to check for errors involving articles or singular/plural forms. This will make students more aware of the kinds of writing errors they tend to make as well as of how to correct such errors.

Research Assignments

Use of the *Research Topics* that appear at the end of each part is optional. Instructors may choose not to assign these topics if time constraints or students' skill levels pose difficulties. However, the topics and accompanying assignments should be used whenever possible and appropriate. They are especially valuable to students in academic settings, who will need to learn how to conduct research for other courses. When assigning the formal research paper, with title page, endnotes, and bibliography, instructors should use a process approach. This includes explaining in depth the various steps of the research assignment (choosing a topic, preparing a preliminary outline, conducting research, preparing a final outline, and so on) and providing appropriate models. If, instead, the instructor wishes to assign one or two research-related tasks, students could engage in library research on a topic or read and summarize one of the books listed in *Suggested Further Reading* (near the end of the text). Additional research assignments are given in Appendix H.

Acknowledgments

We would like to thank the teachers who have chosen to use this book with their students for joining in our effort to combine the teaching of language skills with education for a more peaceful world. We are particularly grateful to Anita Wenden for introducing us to peace education through her inspiring work in this area.

We also thank our excellent editor at St. Martin's Press, Naomi Silverman, for her support, helpful suggestions, and comradeship; our project editor, Talvi Laev; our copy editor, Wendy Polhemus-Annibell; and our photo researcher, Barbara Salz. Finally, we thank the following reviewers for their comments: John Hedgcock, University of Houston; Ila Jean Kragthorpe, Moorpark College; Richard A. Nuzzo, Community College of Southern Nevada; Jan Peterson, Edmonds Community College; and Anita Wenden, York College, CUNY.

Elaine Brooks
Len Fox

Contents

xiii

MAKING
PEACE

A Reading/Writing/Thinking
Text on Global Community

IN THE PAST CENTURY, we humans have taken pride in our "mastery" of nature. We have viewed ourselves as conquerors of the skies and the oceans. We have devised ways of using the natural resources of the earth for great profit. In recent years, however, we have begun to realize that we are not the masters of the natural world, but a part of it. We have also begun to understand that if we do not treat the natural world with greater respect, our very existence as a species may be threatened.

The readings in Part I discuss aspects of the current state of the world that are causes for concern. In "The Illusion of Progress," Lester R. Brown addresses the careless consumption of natural resources and the economic decline in the Third World. "Land Hunger in Asia," by Paul Harrison, presents case studies illustrating the oppressive social conditions in Bangladesh. Helen Caldicott, an antinuclear weapons and antiwar activist, advises us in "Eradicate Nuclear Weapons from the Face of the Earth" to spend our money on more important things than producing weapons. Finally, in "Picturing a Sustainable Society," Lester R. Brown, Christopher Flavin, and Sandra Postel suggest how we could develop a "sustainable world" by shifting our focus from short-term profits to the long-term good of humanity.

1

The Illusion of Progress

LESTER R. BROWN

Lester R. Brown is a senior researcher at the Worldwatch Institute, which every year since 1984 has produced a volume about the *State of the World*. Each year, this book updates information on poverty, over-population, air and water quality, agricultural land, and other world conditions. A respected sourcebook, it is consulted by the United Nations and other organizations concerned about protecting our world environment. The following reading is an excerpt from the first chapter of *State of the World, 1990*.

Getting Ready to Read

THINKING ABOUT THE TITLE

What is the meaning of the word *illusion*? What does the word *progress* mean? How might the idea of progress be an illusion?

KEY VOCABULARY/CONCEPTS

Discuss with your classmates what you know about some of the following words and concepts.

progress	ozone layer	grasslands
global economic production	greenhouse effect	acid rain
population growth	global warming	forests
modern technology	foreign debt	deforestation
accounting	infant death rates	air pollution
natural resources	croplands	

Before reading the selection, ask yourself and/or discuss with your class-mates the following questions.

1. What effects does our modern way of living have on the environment (air, water, atmosphere, and so on)?
2. Should we change what we are doing in order to protect the environment? Why or why not?

For about four-fifths of human beings born since World War II, life has   1
seemed to be a time of continuous economic progress. The global economic production is about five times larger than it was in 1950. The increase in economic growth every ten years has been similar to the increase from the beginning of civilization until 1950.

World food production has also increased a great deal. This was a result   2
of increased demand caused by population growth and rising wealth, and was made possible by modern technology. The world's grain harvest is 2.6 times larger than it was in 1950. No other generation of human beings has seen such large gains in production.

Such gains would seem to be a cause for celebration, but instead there is   3
a sense of illusion, a feeling that not so much progress has been made. One reason for this is that our system of national accounting used to measure progress considers the loss in value of factories and equipment, but does not consider the using up of natural resources. Since mid-century, the world has lost nearly one-fifth of the topsoil from its croplands, a fifth of its tropi-cal rain forests, and tens of thousands of its plant and animal species.

During this same period, atmospheric carbon dioxide (CO_2) levels have   4
increased by 13 percent, causing hotter summers. The protective ozone layer in the stratosphere has decreased by 2 percent worldwide and far more over Antarctica. Dead lakes and dying forests have resulted from industrial-ization. Historians in the twenty-first century may admire our economic performance—but regret the environmental consequences.

Throughout our lifetimes, economic trends have shaped environmental   5
trends, often affecting the earth's natural resources and systems in ways not clear at the time. Now, as we enter the nineties, the reverse is also beginning to happen: environmental trends are beginning to shape economic trends.

Environmental damage to the planet is beginning to affect harvests of   6
food. The effects of losing 24 billion tons of topsoil each year are being felt in some of the world's major food-producing regions. Recent studies indi-

cate that air pollution is damaging crops in both auto-centered economies of the West and coal-burning economies of the East. Meteorologists cannot yet be certain, but the hotter summers and decreased rainfall of the eighties may be early indications of the greenhouse effect.

Environmental damage undoubtedly was a cause of slower growth in world grain production during the eighties. The doubling of grain output mentioned above occurred between 1950 and 1984; since then, there has been no significant increase. The 1989 estimated harvest (1.67 billion tons) was up only 1 percent from that of 1984, which means that grain output per person is down nearly 7 percent. 7

Large amounts of previously stored food have been used up. In some areas, people have consumed less food. Although five years is not long enough to indicate a long-term trend, this does show that the world's farmers are finding it more difficult to keep up with growth in population. 8

Nowhere is this more clear than in Africa, where the combination of high population growth and damage to croplands is decreasing grain production per person. A drop of 20 percent in production from 1967 has changed the continent into a grain importer, caused an increase in the region's foreign debt, and left millions of Africans hungry and physically weakened. In a 1989 report, World Bank economists described the continuation of recent trends as a "nightmare scenario." 9

In both Africa and Latin America, food consumption per person is lower today than it was when the decade began. Infant death rates—a good indicator of malnutrition—appear to have increased in many countries in Africa and Latin America, reversing the previous trend of decrease. Nations in which there are data to indicate this rise in infant death rate include Brazil, the Dominican Republic, El Salvador, Ghana, Madagascar, Mexico, Peru, Uruguay, and Zambia. 10

The Earth's Declining Productivity

Three biological systems—croplands, forests, and grasslands—support the world economy. Except for fossil fuels and minerals, they supply all the raw materials for industry; except for seafood, they provide all our food. Forests are the source of fuel, lumber, paper, and many other products. Grasslands provide meat, milk, leather, and wool. Croplands supply food, feed for animals, and countless raw materials for industry, such as fiber and vegetable oils. 11

Common to all these biological systems is the process of photosynthesis, 12
the ability of plants to use solar energy to combine water and carbon dioxide to produce carbohydrates. Although an estimated 41 percent of photo-
synthetic activity takes place in the oceans, it is the 59 percent occurring
on land that supports the world economy. And it is the loss of photosynthesis as a result of environmental damage that is hurting many national
economies.

The biological activity that supplies most of our food and raw materials 13
takes place on the nearly one-third of the earth's surface that is land, some
13 billion hectares. According to a U.N. Food and Agriculture Organization
study for 1986, 11 percent of this—nearly 1.5 billion hectares—is used to
produce crops. About 25 percent is pasture, providing grass for domesti-
cated animals and wild grass-eating animals. A somewhat larger area (31
percent) is in forests, including open forest or savannahs only partly covered
with trees. The remaining 33 percent of the world's land supports little biological activity. It is either wasteland, essentially desert, or has been paved
over or built on.

The share of land planted to crops increased from the time agriculture 14
began until 1981, but since then the area of new land has been less than the
area that has become useless or has been changed to nonfarm uses. The
grasslands area has decreased since the mid-seventies, as over-use has
changed some of it to desert. The forest areas have been decreasing for centuries, but the rate of loss increased at mid-century and even more from
1980 onward. The combined area of these three biologically productive categories is decreasing while the remaining categories—wasteland and that
covered by human settlements—are increasing.

Not only is the biologically productive land area decreasing, but on part 15
of it, productivity is falling. In forests, for example, output is being lowered
by air pollution and acid rain. Evidence of this damage in industrial countries is clear. In the United States, it can be found throughout much of the
country, and in Europe it is found from the Atlantic coast in the West to
Siberia in the East.

Recalculating Economic Progress

Looking at the basic biological systems just discussed, the world is not 16
doing very well. Yet economic indicators show the world is prospering. Despite a slow start at the beginning of the eighties, global economic output

increased by more than a fifth during the decade. The economy grew, trade increased, and millions of new jobs were created. How can biological indicators show the opposite of economic indicators?

The answer is that the economic indicators have a basic fault: they show no difference between resource uses that sustain progress and those uses that will hurt it. The main measure of economic progress is the gross national product. In simple terms, this totals the value of all goods and services produced and subtracts loss in value of factories and equipment. Developed a half-century ago, GNP helped establish a common way among countries of measuring change in economic output. For some time, this seemed to work reasonably well, but serious weaknesses are now appearing. As indicated earlier, GNP includes loss in value of factories and equipment, but it does not consider the loss of natural resources, including nonrenewable resources such as oil or renewable resources such as forests.

This basic fault can produce a misleading sense of national economic health. According to GNP, for example, countries that overcut forests actually do better than those that sustain their forests: the trees cut down are counted as income but no subtraction is made for using up the forests, a natural resource. The advantage is short-lived, however, as overcutting eventually destroys the resource entirely, leading to the end of the forest products industry.

To show the fault in GNP accounting, economist Robert Repetto and his colleagues at the World Resources Institute recalculated the GNP of Indonesia, including the using up of natural resources. Considering only loss of oil, soil, and forest, [they] showed that Indonesia's economic growth rate from 1971 to 1984, originally reported at 7 percent, was in reality only 4 percent. GNP not only overstates progress, it may indicate progress when there is actually decline. In Repetto's revised system of national economic accounting, loss of natural resources is counted just as is loss of value of factories and equipment.

Including changes in natural resources represents an improvement in national economic accounting. But if this system is to be a basis for making policy in a time when environmental issues are so important, it will have to go one step further and consider the environmental effects of economic activity. For example, the loss of forests that counted as a loss in Indonesia's economy also contributed to the buildup of CO_2 around the world, thus increasing global warming. How much will it cost to deal with the climate change due to deforestation in Indonesia?

17

18

19

20

Or consider the oil produced in Indonesia, which Repetto subtracted from the country's natural resources. To what extent is it contributing to the serious air pollution problem in Jakarta and to the respiratory illnesses among the people who live there? How much is the Indonesian oil burned in the Netherlands contributing to the air pollution and acid rain destroying lakes in Scandinavia and forests in [the former] West Germany? It is certainly true that data on the costs of lost forest productivity in Europe or of global warming are not very good. But is that a good reason to ignore them entirely rather than to try to make some estimates and include them in the national economic accounts? The results are so important that it would be better to include some estimate. ☐

Thinking about the Reading

TRUE/FALSE QUESTIONS

In the space provided, write T if the sentence is true, and F if the sentence is false, based on your reading of the preceding selection.

_____ 1. Our system of national accounting considers loss of natural resources as a negative factor.

_____ 2. In Africa and Latin America today people eat more food than they did ten years ago.

_____ 3. Croplands, forests, and grasslands supply raw materials, food, and fuel.

_____ 4. Photosynthesis is the process by which plants produce carbon dioxide.

_____ 5. According to our current way of accounting, countries that overcut forests are doing better economically than countries that keep the same number of trees.

COMPREHENSION QUESTIONS

In answering the following comprehension questions, *paraphrase* the selection—that is, restate it in your own words without copying phrases of more than three or four words from the reading. (See Appendix A for more on how to answer comprehension questions.) Here is an example:

Sample question:
How has the world made progress since World War II?

Sample answer (words and phrases from the reading are italicized):
The world has made progress because *global economic production* has increased a lot and more *food* has also been produced. *Modern technology* has allowed this to occur.

Here are the questions:

1. What are some negative effects of environmental damage?
2. How have croplands, forests, and grasslands been damaged in recent years?
3. What does GNP measure?
4. In addition to loss of natural resources, what should we consider in evaluating a country's economy?

OUTLINE

Complete the following outline of Brown's essay by listing the topics he discusses in the space provided.

Paragraph(s) 1–2: Global economic progress since World War II
   3–4: _____
   5–8: Negative effects of environment on economy.
   9–10: _____
11–13: Importance of croplands, forests, grasslands
14–16: _____
17–18: GNP does not account for loss of natural resources
19–21: _____

SUMMARY

Use the preceding outline to write a summary of the reading. In the first sentence of your summary, mention the title, the author, and the main topic of the selection. Paraphrase the writer's points in your own words. (See Appendix B for more on how to write a summary.)

Making Connections

REACTING TO THE READING

Write about your personal reaction to Brown's essay. Possible topics include your agreement or disagreement with a specific issue; a relevant personal experience; an idea that is new to you; a related idea from another source (such as a book, a movie, or a television program); or why you like (or dislike) the selection.

FINDING RELATED SOURCES

1. Find a picture related to one of the following topics: global environmental damage, economic progress, or another topic discussed in the selection. In writing, describe the picture and relate your thoughts and feelings about it. Discuss your picture and writing with your classmates.
2. Find a passage in a book, magazine, or newspaper that is related to the selection. In writing, summarize the passage and describe how it relates to Brown's essay. Discuss the passage and your writing with your classmates.

Getting Ready to Write

PREWRITING ACTIVITIES

Using the topic *global environmental damage* or another topic from the reading, spend 10 minutes on one of the following prewriting activities: freewriting, clustering, listing, or cubing. (See Appendix C.) Then discuss your prewriting with your classmates.

DISCUSSION AND COMPOSITION QUESTIONS

Choose one or more of the following questions to discuss with your classmates in preparation for writing.

On Peacemaking Issues

1. How is the state of the world environment related to the goal of achieving world peace?
2. What other issues raised in the reading are related to the goal of achieving world peace? How are they related?

3. What have you personally observed about world or local environmental damage?
4. Describe a place where people do (or do not) protect the local environment.
5. Compare two places in relation to how much the people protect the surrounding environment.
6. In what ways are we presently polluting the environment?
7. Why are we polluting the environment?
8. What are we presently doing to protect the environment?
9. What more could we do to protect the environment?
10. Do you think we will achieve a cleaner environment (either throughout the world or in a particular place) in the future? Why or why not?
11. What could you do (by yourself or with others) to help create a cleaner environment locally and/or globally?

On Related Issues

12. Do you believe in "progress"? Discuss.
13. Has the world become a better place since the 1950s? Why or why not?
14. Does the government of the United States or of your native country take good care of the environment? Why or why not?
15. Discuss the advantages and/or disadvantages of industrialization.
16. Describe one particular kind of damage to the environment and the problem it causes (for example, air pollution, water pollution, nuclear waste, global warming, acid rain, or loss of forests, croplands, or grasslands).

PLANNING TO WRITE

Choose one of the preceding Composition Questions as your writing topic. Begin to plan your paragraph or essay by identifying the topic and listing your thoughts about that topic.

Example: Has the world become a better place since the 1950s? Why or why not? (See Appendixes D and E for more on how to write paragraphs and essays, as well as for a response to the preceding sample question.)

Topic: Has the world become a better place?
—More things are being produced.
—A better quality of life has not resulted.

Then write the first draft of your paragraph or essay.

Revising and Editing Your Writing

REVISING YOUR WRITING

Use the Revision Checklist in Appendix F (p. 271) to evaluate the first draft of your (or your classmate's) writing in terms of content and organization. After deciding how your paragraph or essay can be improved, write a second draft incorporating the changes. On the checklist identify the areas in which you had difficulty so you can double-check these areas in later writings.

EDITING YOUR WRITING

After you are satisfied with content and organization, use the Editing Checklist in Appendix G (p. 272) to reevaluate your (or your classmate's) writing. On the checklist identify the areas in which you had difficulty so you can double-check these areas in later writings.

2

Land Hunger in Asia

PAUL HARRISON

Paul Harrison traveled in eleven countries in the Third World from 1975 to 1980 to do research for his book *Inside the Third World*. In the following selection, taken from that book, he tells us about "the growing poverty of the landless" in areas of Asia such as Bangladesh, and the governments' inefficiency in solving the problem.

Getting Ready to Read

THINKING ABOUT THE TITLE

We usually think of hunger as a desire for food, but in this selection the writer is referring to a hunger for land. Many people in the world, and in Asia in particular, depend on their land for food production. Unfortunately, many people are losing their land for various reasons, thus finding it harder and harder to survive.

KEY VOCABULARY/CONCEPTS

Discuss with your classmates what you know about some of the following words and concepts.

the colonial experience	laws of supply and demand	interest on loans
commercialization	disaster	fertilizer
self-sufficient villages	flood	irrigation
world market	cyclone	exploitation
the landless	drought	mortgage

tenants	subsistence	moneylenders
rent	the homeless	legal fees
wage	bank loan	sharecroppers

PREREADING QUESTIONS

Before reading the selection, ask yourself and/or discuss with your class-mates the following questions.

1. What examples of poverty have you seen or read about?
2. Why does poverty exist?

T he colonial experience brought to traditional societies all over the world a new sickness, as deadly culturally as the smallpox in the blankets given to American Indians:* that sickness was commercialization and the cash economy. Self-sufficient villages were often forced to grow cash crops to get money to pay colonial taxes. Roads and railways allowed the world market to get into the farthest areas and to start to tear apart the traditional ways. This process is now going faster due to the commercial opportunities of growing food markets and to the opportunities for profit from new technology. Gresham's law of economics says that a less valuable means of purchase will always replace a more valuable one wherever it is introduced. In the same way, the need for cash is replacing traditional morality throughout Asia and Africa. Payment in wages is replacing payment in goods. That would not matter so much if the wages were fair or sufficient. But they are not. Poverty is increasing in Asia. Most of this poverty is found in the rural areas, among those with no land or not enough land to feed themselves. The growing poverty of the landless follows from population growth and the failure of governments to create enough employment in rural areas. If the people are tenants, there are more of them wanting land than there is land available, therefore rents go up and the money left for the tenants' own needs goes down. If they are workers, there are more of them seeking jobs than there are jobs available. Therefore wages go down. Those are the simple laws of supply and demand.

Nowhere in Asia have these problems gone so far as in Bangladesh, whose situation illustrates the deadly process going on in Asian society. Liv-

*In contemporary speech, "Native American" is frequently used instead of "American Indian."

ing in a tiny 55,593 square miles, an area slightly bigger than highly indus-
trialized England (population, 46 million), there are some 85 million people, nine-tenths of whom live on the land. Water is Bangladesh's greatest
friend—and her greatest enemy. Two of Asia's mightiest rivers, the Ganges
and the Brahmaputra, deliver here the rich minerals washed down from the
rocks of the Himalayas, making the soil fertile for agriculture. Yet for four
months of the year much of the land is under water and cannot grow any
kind of crop, and over the drowned field, men ride on barges that have not
changed in style since ancient times. Going upwind, six standing men pull
on big oars. Going downwind, the barges ride on sails made from cloth
bags. The houses barely keep above the waters.

Land hunger has become a serious problem. At Bangladesh's low yield of   3
half a ton of rice per acre, a man would need about 1.8 acres of land to feed
the average-sized family of six. At least two-thirds of the households have
less than that: 11 percent have no land at all, not even for a house, while
another 47 percent own less than an acre, and the average size of their land
is just 0.23 acres. Two things could have helped despite the increase in
population: the use of new land for agriculture, and an increase in food
production. But the area of croplands has not increased over the last decade, and crop yields have risen by only 5 percent while population has
grown by 25 percent.

People need land so much that they have settled in areas of the delta and   4
islands which may be flooded or hit by cyclones several times a year. They
build only weak houses, knowing the houses will be destroyed before long.
If they get a warning of a cyclone or a tidal wave, they will climb onto their
roofs and tie themselves and their family down, hoping that the rushing
waters will carry them away and put them down safely. Bangladesh's violent
rivers every year eat away large pieces of land, leaving their owners homeless and poor. In other places, the waters pull back, leaving new pieces of
land known as chars. These become the cause of fights for possession, generally won by the rich man who can bring the biggest group of armed relatives, supporters, and hired thugs.

The great extent of landlessness in Bangladesh today is a new thing. Al-   5
most every landless peasant you meet either once owned more land himself,
or his father did. Dividing land among children has made the size of plots
smaller. As these become too small for subsistence, the owner becomes vul-
nerable. If he cannot find enough outside work—or if he suffers from dis-

ease or some other problem—he will have to mortgage his land to get money, and risk losing it. Or he will have to sell it off piece by piece to get temporary help, risking long-term ruin for short-term survival.

Abdurrashid Ali Khan is a small fifty-year-old from Sivalaya district. He has the misfortune of having four daughters, who can bring in no money and will each cost perhaps $120 to marry off. Khan's father had just enough land to live off—one and a half acres. But he had three sons, and on his death, the land was divided equally between them, giving each one just half an acre. Unable to find enough work to meet his family's needs, Khan was forced to sell his land, piece by piece, in order to stay alive. Now he owns only the land his house is built on, and sharecrops (works and keeps a share of the crop) one acre and a cow.

Selling land is the result of the economics of poverty in Bangladesh. The average family of six members needs five pounds of rice per day for a survival diet of only 1,700 calories per person. Total requirement = 1800 pounds of rice per year. The average peasant's land of 0.23 acres would yield only 200 pounds of rice or less. Annual deficit = at least 1600 pounds of rice. Cash needed to buy it, at present market prices of 1.5 to 2 taka per pound = 2,400 to 3,000 taka ($160 to $200). Add 30 percent for other necessities such as fuel and only enough clothing to hide your nakedness. Family income needed for survival = 3,000 to 4,000 taka. If the average peasant is lucky enough to find eight months work a year, at the daily wage of around ten taka per day, he cannot expect a cash income of more than 2000 taka. Annual deficit = between 1,000 and 2,000 taka. Now the price of one acre of land in Bangladesh in 1978 was around 30,000 taka. To meet his deficit, therefore, the average peasant landowner would need to sell from 0.03 to 0.06 acre, or between one-eighth and one-quarter of his entire land, each year. And that was in 1978, after three or four years of good harvests and rising incomes.

In the first half of the seventies, a series of disasters added to the troubles of peasant farmers, although they were only a larger form of what can hit any poor man at any time. In November 1970, a 125-mile-per-hour cyclone killed about 200,000 people and made a million or more homeless. Civil war followed in March 1971, killing about a half million people and causing damage of about $1.2 billion. Drought [water shortage] in the 1972–1973 growing season cut the harvest from an expected 11.8 million tons to 9.8 million tons. In 1974, famine [food shortage] came after serious floods: from 50,000 to 500,000 people died, another 1.3 million tons of grain were lost, and $3.5 billion of damage was done. All these events came to the unfortunate Bangladeshis as if they were cursed by God, increasing the pressure to sell and mortgage land. Farmers' crops were smaller at the same time as opportunity for agricultural labor was reduced. So land sales went from 94,100 in 1971 to 453,200 in 1974, dropping slightly to 378,700 in 1976. In the six years after 1971, 761,000 acres were sold. If the sales were mainly among owners of less than an acre, this suggests that the poor farmers sold off half their land in those difficult years.

Middle-income peasants—earning enough money to support themselves   9
on two to five acres of land, and composing around 20 percent of the rural population—may not have been harmed, though it must be remembered that when the middle-income peasant dies leaving more than one son, his sons will become poor peasants.

The winners in this chess game, picking up the poor pawns as they fall,   10
have been the rich peasants, which in land-hungry Bangladesh means those 6 percent of rural households with more than five acres each, who owned 43 percent of the land in 1977. Many of this class had been rent collectors for the Hindu landlords who worked with the British. When the Hindus left at the division of India in 1947, these Bangladeshi big fish illegally seized the farms and have since taken other state land. Population increase and natural disasters have enabled them to increase their holdings by buying up the land sold by the poor. Thus in much of non-communist Asia, at one end, smallholdings are being divided and landlessness is increasing. At the other, the wealthier peasants are accumulating more and more land.

This accumulation of land gives economic, social and political power,   11
which the landlords have used to increase their advantages. They control government services—and use them to exploit the poor. Fertilizer, usually in short supply, is sold by government officials to whoever can pay most— which is not the poor. Bank loans go to the wealthier peasants. One group of twenty-six almost landless sharecroppers in Savar district found it impossible to get a bank loan—either they did not have enough land for collateral, or the land titles were in their fathers' or grandfathers' names because they couldn't afford the fees to change the records, or they could not afford to take a day off work to go to town, or to pay a bribe to a bank official to get a loan. So the poor had to borrow from the rich, at the rate of 250 percent interest a year. Though the lending of money for interest is against Moslem

beliefs, the landlords get around this by accepting a required "gift" in rice, equal to the sum demanded.

Tubewells [sources of water] have become another means of oppression. The government has been building these in large numbers for groups of wealthy landlords forming themselves into cooperatives. The cooperatives then charge high rates for the use of the tubewell water. The annual cost of running a typical tubewell to irrigate around 200 acres was 15,600 taka—this includes 4,200 in wages for the guard and pump attendant, who would probably be members of the landlords' families. The local co-op was charging water rates of 110 taka per acre, thus making a profit of 6,600 taka a year (about $440) which was divided up among the fifteen co-op members. In ways like this, the money the government puts into local development, which is supposed to be for the common good, only increases inequality and exploitation.

Finally, the wealthy landlords buy favors from the police and judges. I once asked a Bangladeshi lawyer if the police were usually on the side of the rich. "Not usually," he answered, "Always." This unfairness of the legal system leads to a third process, besides sale and division, that is taking land away from the poor: that is taking land by force or by fraud.

Hassan Ali, a thirty-five-year-old farmer from Savar district, mortgaged one-sixth of an acre of land, worth around 4,000 taka, for a 1,200 taka loan. The moneylender, a wealthy local landlord, made him sign a piece of paper, on which he wrote in a debt of 1,400 taka. When Hassan had collected enough money to repay the landlord, with interest, the landlord refused to take repayment and insisted on keeping the land instead. Hassan was forced to go to court and had to sell more land to pay 500 taka (about $32) in bribes. But the landlord had more money and won the case, thus getting the land at less than one-third of its market value.

Mohamed Ayubali, a landless worker from crowded Comilla district, still remembers with anger how his father was cheated of his land twelve years ago. A wealthy landlord had sent some thugs to take away part of a neighbor's land, and Ayubali senior had helped to fight them off. The landlord then accused Ayubali's father of injuring his cattle. The police came to the house, pushed him, to force him to defend himself, then arrested him for fighting with them. While Ayubali senior was in jail, the police took possession of his land. He had to sell his land to pay legal fees, but died of a heart attack before the case was settled.

12

13

14

15

Thinking about the Reading

TRUE/FALSE QUESTIONS

In the space provided, write T if the sentence is true and F if the sentence is false, based on your reading of the preceding selection.

_____ 1. Self-sufficient villages in Bangladesh were doing better before colonialism.

_____ 2. Water is always a friend to people in Bangladesh.

_____ 3. From 1970 to 1976, a series of disasters caused many deaths and increased homelessness in Bangladesh.

_____ 4. The government tubewell projects have greatly helped the poor.

_____ 5. The police in Bangladesh are fair to the poor.

COMPREHENSION QUESTIONS

In answering the following comprehension questions, *paraphrase* the selection—that is, restate it in your own words without copying phrases of more than three or four words from the reading. (See Appendix A for more on how to answer comprehension questions.) Here is an example:

Sample question:
What has caused the growing poverty of the landless in Asia?

Sample answer (words and phrases from the reading are italicized):
Poverty has increased among *the landless in Asia* because the *population* has increased and the governments have not created jobs in *rural areas.*

Here are the questions:

1. Why do most peasants in Bangladesh have less land than their grandparents did?
2. Explain what is meant by the "economics of poverty" in Bangladesh.
3. How do wealthy landowners exploit the poor in Bangladesh?
4. Give one example of an unfair legal practice in Bangladesh.

OUTLINE

Complete the following outline of Harrison's essay by listing the topics he discusses in the space provided.

Paragraph(s) 1: Increasing poverty in Asia

    2: _____

    3: Land hunger

    4: _____

    5: Causes of land shortage

    6: _____

    7: The economics of poverty

  7–8: _____

    9: The situation facing middle-income peasants

  10: _____

  11: How the rich exploit the poor

  12: _____

13–15: Examples of the unfair legal system

SUMMARY

Use the preceding outline to write a summary of the reading. In the first sentence of your summary, mention the title, the author, and the main topic of the selection. Paraphrase the writer's points in your own words. (See Appendix B for more on how to write a summary.)

Making Connections

REACTING TO THE READING

Write about your personal reaction to the reading. Some possible topics include your agreement or disagreement with a specific issue; a relevant personal experience; an idea that is new to you; a related idea from another source (such as a book, a movie, or a television program); or why you like or dislike the selection.

FINDING RELATED SOURCES

1. Find a picture related to one of the following topics: poverty, exploitation of the poor, or another topic discussed in the selection. In writing, describe the picture and relate your thoughts and feelings about it. Discuss your picture and writing with your classmates.

2. Interview someone you know about poverty, exploitation of the poor, or another topic discussed in the selection. Ask that person to describe his or

her thoughts, feelings, and experiences in relation to the topic. Take notes during the interview. Then, using your notes, write a summary of the interview that includes your reaction as well. Discuss the interview and your summary with your classmates.

Getting Ready to Write

PREWRITING ACTIVITIES

Using the topic *poverty* or another topic from the reading, spend 10 minutes on *one* of the following prewriting activities: freewriting, clustering, listing, or cubing. (See Appendix C.) Then discuss your prewriting with your classmates.

DISCUSSION AND COMPOSITION QUESTIONS

Choose one or more of the following questions to discuss with your classmates in preparation for writing.

On Peacemaking Issues

1. Is poverty related to world peace? Discuss.
2. What other issues raised in the reading are related to the goal of achieving world peace?
3. Describe the kinds of poverty you have seen or read about.
4. Describe the characteristics of one particular place where poverty exists (or does not exist).
5. Compare the degree of poverty in two different places (or in one place at different periods of time, such as the past and present).
6. Why does poverty exist?
7. How could we solve the problem of poverty?
8. Would people's values have to change in order for us to solve the problem of poverty? Discuss.
9. What are we presently doing to attack world poverty?
10. Do you think we will solve the problem of poverty in the future? Why or why not?
11. What could you do (by yourself or with others) to help eliminate poverty?

On Related Issues

12. Why does Abdurrashid Ali Khan consider it a "misfortune" to have four daughters? Would you consider this a misfortune? Discuss.
13. Describe the ways in which some rich people exploit the poor.
14. Why have the poor people in Bangladesh not revolted against those who exploit them?
15. Tell about an example of a case involving an unfair legal system.
16. Is the legal system of the United States (or of your native country) fair? Why or why not?
17. Compare Harrison's views on world poverty with Brown's in "The Illusion of Progress."

PLANNING TO WRITE

Choose one of the preceding Composition Questions as your writing topic. Begin to plan your paragraph or essay by identifying the topic and listing your thoughts about that topic.

Example: What are some of the causes of crime in a particular area?

Topic: Causes of crime in U.S. inner cities
—Poor education
—Lack of jobs
—Racism
—Lack of good low-income housing

Then write the first draft of your paragraph or essay. (See Appendixes D and E for more on how to write paragraphs and essays.)

Revising and Editing Your Writing

REVISING YOUR WRITING

Use the Revision Checklist in Appendix F (p. 271) to evaluate the first draft of your (or your classmate's) writing in terms of content and organization. After deciding how your paragraph or essay can be improved, write a second draft incorporating the changes. On the checklist identify the areas in which you had difficulty so you can double-check these areas in later writings.

EDITING YOUR WRITING

After you are satisfied with content and organization, use the Editing Checklist in Appendix G (p. 272) to reevaluate your (or your classmate's) writing. On the checklist identify the areas in which you had difficulty so you can doublecheck these areas in later writings.

3

Eradicate Nuclear Weapons from the Face of the Earth

HELEN CALDICOTT

Helen Caldicott is a founder of Physicians for Social Responsibility and a devoted anti–nuclear armaments activist. In the following selection from *Women on War* (1986), a collection of writings by women aimed at increasing awareness of the horrors of war and at encouraging action for peace, Caldicott speaks out against the production of weapons.

Getting Ready to Read

THINKING ABOUT THE TITLE

Why might men and women feel differently about war? Might women have more negative feelings about war than men do, or vice versa?

KEY VOCABULARY/CONCEPTS

Discuss with your classmates what you know about some of the following words and concepts.

blinding flash	priority	carcinogen
march	industrial conversion	toxic chemicals
conservative	medical expertise	endemic disease
the Pentagon	birth-control techniques	luxury

arms race	reforestation	affluence
weapon	equitable distribution	nuclear disarmament
terminal illness	illiteracy	preventive medicine

PREREADING QUESTIONS

Before reading the selection, ask yourself and/or discuss with your class-mates the following questions.

1. What have you seen or read about war?
2. What are the effects of war?
3. Why do wars occur?

. . . What happened was that at 8:15 a.m. a plane, a single plane, appeared overhead, and the Japanese were pleased—they thought the plane had been shot down and the pilot was escaping. Another parachute opened adjacent to the first, and a little boy was reaching up to catch a red dragon fly on his hand against the blue sky . . . and there was a blinding flash and he disappeared . . . and so did tens of thousands of other human beings. About a hundred thousand people were killed with that bomb. . . . The bomb dropped on Hiroshima was equivalent to about 13,000 tons of TNT. That's a small bomb. . . .

When I had my first baby, I knew I'd die to save that life. Now I had never felt like that about any other human life before; it was a profound revelation for me. If we can mobilize that instinct that women have to save their babies, across the world, we may survive. So I started the Women's Party for Survival and we're having a march on Mother's Day in Washington, wearing our Sunday best, even Republican ladies, everybody—because this is a very conservative issue. The ultimate *conservative* issue. . . . The baby is our symbol . . . we thought of an action called Babies Against the Pentagon and that abbreviates to BAP. What we can do, when the Senate is debating the arms race, is to release hundreds of naked toddlers into the Senate chamber.

. . . We're on a terminally ill planet, you know that, and we are about to destroy ourselves. . . . What I'm really saying to you is that if you love this planet, and I'm deeply in love with it, and you watch the spring come and you watch the magnolias flower and the wisteria come out, and you smell a rose—you will realize that you're going to have to change the priorities of your life—if you love this planet.

After World War II, America took the initiative and quickly converted its economy to peacetime uses. . . . The American corporations that are involved in the arms race are run by very intelligent people who will quickly perceive that the people of America will not allow the wartime economic system to continue. . . . They will put their heads together and will be motivated to design equipment that will be used to the benefit of people both in the United States and internationally.

The world urgently needs adequate production and equitable distribution of food. It needs vast production of medicines and vaccines, and redistribution of medical expertise and medical supplies to the millions of suffering people in the Third World. Adequate distribution of birth-control techniques is required to prevent an increase in global population growth from 4.5 billion now to 6 billion in 2000. Reforestation of many areas of the world is a mandatory priority, since trees currently are used to provide fuel for the poor countries, and trees recycle carbon dioxide to produce oxygen. The riches of the sea must be equitably distributed among all nations of the earth and must not be mined only by those few Western nations that currently possess the technology and expertise to do so. All the world's natural resources must be shared and used for the benefit of the family of man and not hoarded and wasted on production of weapons. Millions of the world's people must be delivered from their situation of illiteracy and poverty—a vicious cycle that perpetuates endemic overpopulation and hunger.

The air and water of . . . large parts of the world are fast becoming irretrievably polluted with carcinogenic and mutagenic poisons produced by industry to make profits. There are 4.5 million known toxic chemicals, and 375,000 new ones are produced annually. Most have never been adequately tested for carcinogenicity, and most are released to the environment, often illegally. Many of these chemicals are by-products of industries that produce plastic throwaway materials we don't need (and, of course, weaponry).

. . . [The United States] needs to tighten its belt. My husband and I visited Cuba. . . . Before the revolution, malaria, hookworm, tuberculosis, and gastrointestinal disease were endemic there. Cuba now has one of the best medical schemes in the world—so good that Dr. Julius Richmond, . . . a Surgeon General of the United States, visited Cuba to develop ideas for America's healthcare system. Prerevolutionary illiteracy was about 40 percent; now it is almost negligible. (There are over 40 million, and some say many more, illiterate people in the United States.) The education programs are excellent. Nevertheless, life is still spare. There is no choice of clothes in the shops—one type of shoe, one type of trouser . . . and limited variety of food. The government has helped its people enormously, and the people are grateful. We returned to Christmas in America with the stores just dripping with luxury and affluence. We knew that if America redefined its priorities, it could help to feed many of the world's people. Americans do not have a God-given right to be the wealthiest people in the world to the detriment of millions of others. These poor countries are now developing their own nuclear weapons, and they are justifiably angry. Who will they drop them on?

Men are very smart—so smart they have learned to destroy themselves. 8 They could with a little effort and ingenuity develop a global economic system (excluding the production and sales of weapons) that would benefit the Western corporations, as well as all the countries of earth. For several years, the Third World has been pleading for such a move, but the selfish Western nations have refused to cooperate or to contemplate ways to alleviate the plight of the poor—even in their own lands. Yet it is obvious that the global situation is all interconnected and relevant to prevention of nuclear war.

All such a scheme would take is creative initiative with the right motiva- 9 tions. If people see that in the end, they, too, will benefit as wealth is equitably shared around the world, thus making the world a safer place, they will become enthusiastic about such an endeavor. This is not pie-in-the-sky talk; it is pragmatic and ultimately reasonable and rational. It will take place only if the people in the wealthy Western democracies educate themselves about the plight of mankind and decide for their own well-being that they and their politicians will create solutions. . . . Conversion of a corporation from war to peace can be achieved not just by decisions of the corporate heads, but also by initiative from the workers. In England, the Lucas Aerospace Industry used to make parts for missiles. After many years, the workers became concerned with the global implications of their work. They called in some consultants and asked, "With our technical skills, what can we make that would benefit mankind?" So the consultants designed electric cars, dialysis machines, and mass-transit systems. The workers then took these plans to the management and said, "We are not going to make missiles anymore. We are going to make equipment." Management was surprised but was influenced. . . . Other workers and high technologists have begun to leave the military industry because of profound moral concern.

They have formed an organization called High Technologists for Social Responsibility. . .

. . . True happiness lies in helping one another. No other generation has inherited this enormous responsibility. We have been given the privilege of saving all past and all future generations, all animals, all plants. Think of the enormous variety of delicate butterflies; think of the gorgeous birds of the earth, of the endless designs of fish in the sea; think of the beautiful exotic flowers with their gorgeous and seductive perfumes; think of the proud lions and tigers and of the wondrous prehistoric elephants and hippo-potamuses; think of what we are about to destroy. . . . Rapid nuclear dis-armament is the ultimate issue of preventive medicine. It is the ultimate parenting issue. It is the ultimate Republican and ultimate Democratic and ultimate Socialist issue. It is the ultimate patriotic issue. Above all, it is the ultimate spiritual issue. . . . We are the curators of life on earth; we hold it in the palms of our hands. Can we evolve spiritually and emotionally in time to control the overwhelming evil that our advanced and rational intellect has created? We will know the answer to this question in our life-time. □

Thinking about the Reading

TRUE/FALSE QUESTIONS

In the space provided, write T if the sentence is true and F if the sentence is false, based on your reading of the preceding selection.

———— 1. Republican women marched against war.
———— 2. American military companies cannot convert to peacetime uses.
———— 3. All nations of the earth profit from the riches of the sea.
———— 4. Most chemicals produced by industry are adequately tested to see if they are carcinogenic.
———— 5. Men could develop a global economic system that would be good for all nations.

COMPREHENSION QUESTIONS

In answering the following comprehension questions, *paraphrase* the selec-tion—that is, restate it in your own words without copying phrases of more

28   *The State of the World*

than three or four words from the reading. (See Appendix A for more on how to answer comprehension questions.) Here is an example:

Sample question:
How are babies related to war?

Sample answer (words and phrases from the reading are italicized):
Since women have an *instinct* to *save their babies*, they do not want the babies to be *killed by a war*.

Here are the questions:

1. According to Caldicott, what are some things that the world needs?
2. What did Caldicott see in Cuba before the revolution?
3. What did she see after the revolution?
4. What happened at the Lucas Aerospace Industry?

OUTLINE

Complete the following outline of Caldicott's essay by listing the topics she discusses in the space provided.

Paragraph(s) 1: The effects of the atomic bomb
2: _____
3: An ill planet
4: _____
5: The world's needs
6: _____
7: Progress in Cuba
8: _____
9: An example: Lucas Aerospace
10: _____

SUMMARY

Use the preceding outline to write a summary of the reading. In the first sentence of your summary, mention the title, the author, and the main topic of the selection. Paraphrase the writer's points in your own words. (See Appendix B for more on how to write a summary.)

Making Connections

Write about your personal reaction to the reading. Some possible topics include your agreement or disagreement with a specific issue; a relevant personal experience; an idea that is new to you; a related idea from another source (such as a book, a movie, or a television program); or why you like or dislike the selection.

FINDING RELATED SOURCES

1. Find a picture related to one of the following topics: war, the world's needs, or another topic discussed in the selection. In writing, describe the picture and relate your thoughts and feelings about it. Discuss your picture and writing with your classmates.
2. Interview someone you know about war, the world's needs, or another topic discussed in the selection. Ask that person to describe his or her thoughts, feelings, and experiences in relation to the topic. Take notes during the interview. Then, using your notes, write a summary of the interview that includes your reaction as well. Discuss the interview and your summary with your classmates.

Getting Ready to Write

PREWRITING ACTIVITIES

Using the topic *war* or *the world's needs*, or another topic from the reading, spend 10 minutes on *one* of the following prewriting activities: freewriting, clustering, listing, or cubing. (See Appendix C.) Then discuss your prewriting with your classmates.

DISCUSSION AND COMPOSITION QUESTIONS

Choose one or more of the following questions to discuss with your classmates in preparation for writing.

On Peacemaking Issues

1. What experiences have you had in relation to war?
2. What other issues raised in the reading are related to the goal of achieving world peace?
3. Describe a specific place where a war is occurring or has recently occurred. What were (or are) the effects of this war?
4. What are the causes of war?
5. What could we do to avoid war?
6. What are people currently doing in a particular place or throughout the world to avoid or to end war?
7. Do you think we will ever have a world without war? Why or why not?
8. What could you do (by yourself or with others) to work against war?

On Related Issues

9. Was the United States justified in dropping atom bombs on Japan at the end of World War II? Why or why not?
10. Are women more opposed to war than men are? Why or why not?
11. Do Western nations help the Third World? Discuss.
12. How could Western nations better help Third World nations?
13. Do you think Western nations will help the Third World more in the future? Why or why not?
14. Do you agree with Caldicott that "We have been given the privilege of saving all past and all future generations"? If so, will we succeed? Discuss.
15. Compare Caldicott's role as political activist with that of Rigoberta Menchu in "Political Activity" (see Chapter 24).
16. Compare Caldicott's views on women and war with I. F. Stone's views on men and war in "Machismo in Washington" (see Chapter 8).

PLANNING TO WRITE

Choose one of the preceding Composition Questions as your writing topic. Begin to plan your paragraph or essay by identifying the topic and listing your thoughts about that topic.

Example: Do you think Western nations will help the Third World more in the future? Why or why not?

Topic: Western nations will help Third World nations more in the future.
   —Western nations are not economically self-sufficient.
   —A stronger Third World will mean better business.

Then write the first draft of your paragraph or essay. (See Appendixes D and E for more on how to write paragraphs and essays.)

Revising and Editing Your Writing

REVISING YOUR WRITING

Use the Revision Checklist in Appendix F (p. 271) to evaluate the first draft of your (or your classmate's) writing in terms of content and organization. After deciding how your paragraph or essay can be improved, write a second draft incorporating the changes. On the checklist identify the areas in which you had difficulty so you can doublecheck these areas in later writings.

EDITING YOUR WRITING

After you are satisfied with content and organization, use the Editing Checklist in Appendix G (p. 272) to reevaluate your (or your classmate's) writing. On the checklist identify the areas in which you had difficulty so you can doublecheck these areas in later writings.

4

Picturing a Sustainable Society

LESTER R. BROWN, CHRISTOPHER FLAVIN, AND SANDRA POSTEL

Like Lester R. Brown, Christopher Flavin and Sandra Postel are senior researchers for the Worldwatch Institute. In the following selection, reprinted from *State of the World, 1990*, the authors urge us to change our behavior in order to develop a "global community that can last."

Getting Ready to Read

THINKING ABOUT THE TITLE

A "sustainable" society is one in which each generation's way of life allows for the next generation to enjoy the same quality of life. Is our present society sustainable?

KEY VOCABULARY/CONCEPTS

Discuss with your classmates what you know about some of the following words and concepts.

development organization	environmental organization	equitable world economy
responsibility	climate change	pollution
sustainability	overcutting forests	materialism
fossil fuels	nuclear waste	consumerism

throwaway society   population growth   haves/have-nots

intergenerational   energy-saving   birthrate
equality   technology

PREREADING QUESTIONS

Before reading the selection, ask yourself and/or discuss with your class-mates the following questions.

1. What would a sustainable society be like?
2. Why haven't we made greater efforts to develop a sustainable society?

Societies everywhere are slowly coming to understand that they are not   1
only destroying their environments but hurting their futures. In response,
governments, development organizations, and people all over the world
have begun to try to change dangerous trends. So far, there has been much
disorganized activity—a new pollution law here, a larger environmental organization there—but we need an overall sense of what we wish to achieve.

Building a more environmentally safe future requires a vision of how it   2
should be. If not fossil fuels to power society, then what? If forests are no
longer to be cut down to grow food, then how is a larger population to be
fed? If a throwaway society leads to pollution and wasting resources, how
can we satisfy our needs? In sum, if the present course of action is unwise,
what picture of the future can we use to guide ourselves toward a global
community that can last?

A sustainable society is one that satisfies its needs without hurting future   3
generations. Part of this definition is the responsibility of each generation to
ensure that the next one gets equal natural and economic resources. This
idea of intergenerational equity, deeply moral in character, is often not followed by our present society.

In fact, there are no models of sustainability. For the past several decades,   4
most developing nations have worked to be like the automobile-centered,
fossil-fuel-driven economies of the industrial West. But from the local problems of pollution to the global danger of climate change, it is now clear that
these societies cannot continue to work in the same way; in fact, they are
quickly causing their own destruction.

Efforts to understand sustainability often look at what it is not. Obvi-   5
ously, an economy that is rapidly changing the climate on which its food-
producing ability depends is not sustainable. Neither is one that over-cuts

the forests that provide its fuel and timber. But this negative definition leads one to just react to problems, trying to repair the results of our destructive behavior.

The World Bank, for example, now tries to understand the environmental effects of projects it is thinking about funding. Not one of its member countries, however, has an overall plan of action for the purpose of achieving sustainability, which should be used to decide what kinds of investments are needed. The United States has had a similar policy for the last 20 years. Its National Environmental Policy Act requires the government to study the environmental effects of proposed government actions. But this, too, is a defensive approach, one that tries to avoid negative effects rather than working positively toward a sustainable economy.   6

In thinking about a vision of an environmentally safe society, we have started with some basic ideas. The first is that if the world is to achieve sustainability, it will need to do so within the next 40 years. If we have not succeeded by then, environmental damage and economic problems will be making each other worse, leading to serious social problems. Our vision of the future therefore looks to the year 2030.   7

Second, new technologies will of course be developed: Forty years ago, for example, some energy-saving technologies now on the market did not even exist. Under the pressure of finding a way to slow global warming, scientists are likely to develop new energy technologies, some of which may be difficult to imagine at the moment. In order to be conservative, however, the future we describe here is based only on existing technologies and possible improvements in them.   8

Our third idea is that the world economy of 2030 will not be powered by coal, oil, and natural gas. It is now accepted that continuing dependence on fossil fuels will cause dangerous changes in climate. The most recent scientific studies indicate that keeping the climate the same depends on cutting annual global carbon production to some 2 billion tons per year, about one-third the present level. Considering population growth, the world in 2030 will need to have per person carbon production that is one-eighth the level in Western Europe today.   9

The choice then becomes whether to make solar or nuclear power the basis of energy systems. We believe societies will not accept nuclear power because of its many economic, social, and environmental disadvantages. Though supported by many political leaders during the sixties and seventies, the nuclear industry has been slowing down for over a decade. Only 94   10 plants are presently being constructed, and most will be completed in the next few years. Meanwhile, there are few worldwide plans for new plants. The accidents at Three Mile Island and Chernobyl and the failure to develop a safe way to store nuclear wastes have turned governments and citizens away from nuclear power.

It is of course possible that scientists could develop new nuclear technologies that are more economical and less dangerous. Yet this would not solve the waste problem. Nor would it answer growing concern about going from using nuclear energy to developing nuclear weapons. Trying to prevent this in a plutonium-based economy with thousands of nuclear factories would probably be impossible. Therefore, societies are more likely to choose solar-based energy systems.

The fourth idea is about population size. Present United Nations estimates say that the world will have 9 billion people by 2030. This number is based on an expected doubling or tripling of the populations of Ethiopia, India, Nigeria, and many other countries where the population is already too large. Either these societies will start to encourage smaller families and bring birth rates down, or rising death rates from hunger and malnutrition will stop population growth.

The humane way to sustainability by the year 2030 therefore requires a significant drop in birth rates. More countries must do as China has done, and as Thailand is doing: cut their population growth rates in half within a few years.

As of 1990, thirteen European countries have stable or decreasing populations; by 2030, most countries should be in that situation. For the world as a whole, human numbers should then total well below 9 billion. We expect a population of at most 8 billion that will either be stable or decreasing slowly—toward a number the earth can support comfortably and continuously into the future.

The last idea is that the world in 2030 must have a more equitable and secure economy. Unless Third World debt can be decreased so that there is more equal exchange of capital from industrial to developing countries, developing countries will not have the resources to invest in sustainability.

In the end, individual values are what cause social change. Progress towards sustainability thus depends on our deepening our sense of responsibility to the earth and to future generations. Without re-thinking our personal desires and motivations, we will never achieve an environmentally healthy global community. . . .

The basic changes we have discussed cannot occur without changes in
the social, economic, and moral character of human societies. During the
move to sustainability, political leaders and citizens will have to change their
goals and hopes to change their definition of success, and to change their
way of life for the benefit of future generations. ¹⁷

Given the difficulty of these changes, many people may not want to
move in this direction. But given the choice of fixing your house or
having it fall down around you, you would not question the need to do
the job. ¹⁸

Progress toward a sustainable society cannot occur without a change of
values. Throughout history, philosophers and religious leaders have spoken
against materialism as a way to a better life. Yet societies have continued to
think of quality of life as equal to consuming more goods. Personal self-
worth is considered as equal to personal possessions just as social progress
is seen as equal to GNP [gross national product] growth. ¹⁹

Because of the waste of resources that it creates, materialism cannot continue in a sustainable world. As the public begins to understand the need to
consume less, it will not be considered admirable to own new cars and
clothes. This change, however, will be hard to make, since consumerism is
so much a part of our society. Yet we can greatly benefit from using in other
ways the energy presently used for planning, producing, advertising, buying, consuming, and throwing away material goods. Much energy would go
into forming better human relationships, stronger communities, and more
cultural activities such as music and the arts. ²⁰

As people become less interested in acquiring material goods, there will
be less distance between haves and have-nots, which will eliminate many
social problems. Nations will have more common concerns and will realize
the importance of shared values, democratic principles, freedom to create
new things, respect for human rights, and acceptance of diversity. Having
to cooperate in trying to repair the world, people may be less interested in
war. ²¹

Fortunately, much is pushing us toward a sustainable society. As economist Herman Daly and religious leader John Cobb write, "People can be
attracted by new ways of ordering their lives as well as driven by the recognition of what will happen if they do not change." ²²

The opportunity to build a lasting world will pass us by if we do not start
to do it soon. To begin, we only need to stop resisting all the reasons to
build a sustainable society. ²³

Thinking about the Reading

In the space provided, write T if the sentence is true and F if the sentence is false, based on your reading of the preceding selection.

_____ 1. Our society pursues the goal of "intergenerational equality."
_____ 2. Our dependence on fossil fuels creates a lot of pollution.
_____ 3. To keep the world climate the same, we must continue to produce the same amount of carbon.
_____ 4. Using nuclear energy could lead to producing more nuclear bombs.
_____ 5. Social change is not related to individual values.

COMPREHENSION QUESTIONS

In answering the following comprehension questions, *paraphrase* the selection—that is, restate it in your own words without copying phrases of more than three or four words from the reading. (See Appendix A for more on how to answer comprehension questions.) Here is an example:

Sample question:
What kind of a vision must we have to build a sustainable world in the future?

Sample answer (words and phrases from the reading are italicized):
We must develop a society that does not depend on *fossil fuels*, that does not cut down its *forests*, and that does not *throw away* great quantities of unnecessary goods.

Here are the questions:

1. What is wrong with the World Bank's policy on judging the environmental effects of its projects?
2. Why should societies not depend on nuclear energy for power?
3. How would the world benefit from a more equitable economy?
4. What is more important than acquiring material possessions?

OUTLINE

Complete the following outline of the reading by listing the topics it discusses in the space provided.

Paragraph(s) 1–2: The need for a new vision of the future

     3: _____

     4: Present societies are not sustainable

     5: _____

     6: An overall global plan is needed

   7–9: _____

10–11: Solar versus nuclear energy

12–14: _____

    15: An equitable world economy

    16: _____

17–19: A change of values

19–20: _____

21–23: A better future

SUMMARY

Use the preceding outline to write a summary of the reading. In the first sentence of your summary, mention the title, the authors, and the main topic of the selection. Paraphrase the writers' points in your own words. (See Appendix B for more on how to write a summary.)

Making Connections

REACTING TO THE READING

Write about your personal reaction to the reading. Some possible topics include your agreement or disagreement with a specific issue; a relevant personal experience; an idea that is new to you; a related idea from another source (such as a book, a movie, or a television program); or why you like or dislike the selection.

FINDING RELATED SOURCES

1. Find a picture related to one of the following topics: a sustainable society, a throwaway society, materialism, or another topic discussed in the selection. In writing, describe the picture and relate your thoughts and feelings about it. Discuss your picture and writing with your classmates.

2. Locate a passage in a book, magazine, or newspaper that is related to the selection. In writing, summarize the passage and describe how it relates to the reading. Discuss the passage and your writing with your classmates.

Getting Ready to Write

PREWRITING ACTIVITIES

Using the topic *a sustainable society* or another topic from the reading, spend 10 minutes on *one* of the following prewriting activities: freewriting, clustering, listing, or cubing. (See Appendix C.) Then discuss your prewriting with your classmates.

DISCUSSION AND COMPOSITION QUESTIONS

Choose one or more of the following questions to discuss with your classmates in preparation for writing.

On Peacemaking Issues

1. How is a sustainable society related (or not related) to the goal of achieving world peace?
2. What other issues raised in the reading are related to the goal of achieving world peace? How are they related?
3. Have you personally observed efforts to achieve a sustainable world? If so, tell about them.
4. Compare two places in relation to their residents' efforts to create a sustainable society.
5. Why do people tend not to work toward creating a sustainable society?
6. What could people do to achieve the goal of a sustainable society?
7. Do you think people will make a greater effort to create a sustainable society in the future? Why or why not?
8. What could you do (by yourself or with others) to help build a sustainable society?

On Related Issues

9. Describe your vision of a sustainable society.
10. Are people today concerned about the well-being of future generations? Discuss.
11. Are you concerned about the well-being of future generations? Discuss.

12. What must we stop doing if we wish to create a sustainable society?
13. In your opinion, which energy source will future generations depend on—fossil fuels, nuclear power, or solar power? Why?
14. Do you think the future will bring a more equitable world economy? Why or why not?
15. Will the importance of materialism decrease in the future? Discuss.

PLANNING TO WRITE

Choose one of the preceding Composition Questions as your writing topic. Begin to plan your paragraph or essay by identifying the topic and listing your thoughts about that topic.

Example: Will the importance of materialism decrease in the future? Explain your view.

Topic: A materialistic society can be changed.
　　—People need to understand the unimportance of materialism.
　　—People need to understand the social problems caused by materialism.

Then write the first draft of your paragraph or essay. (See Appendixes D and E for more on how to write paragraphs and essays.)

Revising and Editing Your Writing

REVISING YOUR WRITING

Use the Revision Checklist in Appendix F (p. 271) to evaluate the first draft of your (or your classmate's) writing in terms of content and organization. After deciding how your paragraph or essay can be improved, write a second draft incorporating the changes. On the checklist identify the areas in which you had difficulty so you can doublecheck these areas in later writings.

EDITING YOUR WRITING

After you are satisfied with content and organization, use the Editing Checklist in Appendix G (p. 272) to reevaluate your (or your classmate's) writing. On the checklist identify the areas in which you had difficulty so you can doublecheck these areas in later writings.

PART I: RESEARCH TOPICS

Choose one of the following topics on the state of the world for research. Refer to Appendix H for specific assignments. In addition, you may find it helpful to consult the list of Suggested Further Reading (at the end of this book) for sources related to your topic.

global environmental damage

economic progress

environment (in a particular place)

poverty

economic exploitation

colonialism

crime

revolution

unjust legal practices

overpopulation

birth control

medical technology

political activism

a political organization

linguistic barriers

cultural and social barriers

class structure

war

military conversion

nuclear weapons

economic aid to the Third World

a Third World country

PART II

MEN AND

WOMEN

SOME OF THE MOST basic human relationships are those formed between men and women—as husbands and wives, as mothers and fathers, as colleagues, as friends. Yet sometimes these fundamental relationships can contain conflicts and confrontations of a kind not unlike those observed among strangers or adversaries.

The selections in Part II address these conflicts among men and women, their potential sources, and various approaches to resolving them. In "Where I Come from Is Like This," Paula Gunn Allen shares her perspective as a Native American woman. Carola Hansson and Karin Liden give us a glimpse into the daily life of a single working mother in the former Soviet Union in "Liza and Family." Ashley Montagu's "American Men Don't Cry" and I. F. Stone's "Machismo in Washington" show us some of the consequences of gender stereotyping.

5

Where I Come from Is Like This

PAULA GUNN ALLEN

Paula Gunn Allen is a Laguna Pueblo/Sioux woman. In the following selection, taken from *The Sacred Hoop: Recovering the Feminine in American Indian Traditions* (1986), she discusses ways in which images of women in her Native American culture differ from those in mainstream American culture.

Getting Ready to Read

THINKING ABOUT THE TITLE

How would you describe where you come from? Why might you wish to describe this to someone?

KEY VOCABULARY/CONCEPTS

Discuss with your classmates what you know about some of the following words and concepts.

American Indian	good sense	mother-right
traditional	reconcile	destiny
harmonize	tribal	mythic
role/image	integration	adversarial
madonna	autonomous	creation
characteristic	female prototype	passive

whore	witch	goddess
dualistic	belief	contradictory
segregation	perception	male-dominant
power	ritual	"weak sister"
impose	balance	

PREREADING QUESTIONS

Before reading the selection, ask yourself and/or discuss with your classmates the following questions.

1. What images of women do you have from your own culture?
2. Do these images of women differ from those of the dominant culture in your country? Why or why not?
3. What advantages or disadvantages do women in your culture have?
4. From your observation or experience, what advantages or disadvantages do women of a different culture have?

Modern American Indian* women, like their non-Indian sisters, are deeply engaged in the struggle to redefine themselves. In their struggle they must reconcile traditional tribal definitions of women with industrial and postindustrial non-Indian definitions. Yet while these definitions seem to be more or less mutually exclusive, Indian women must somehow harmonize and integrate both in their own lives.

An American Indian woman is primarily defined by her tribal identity. In her eyes, her destiny is necessarily that of her people, and her sense of herself as a woman is first and foremost prescribed by her tribe. The definitions of woman's roles are as diverse as tribal cultures in the Americas. In some she is devalued, in others she wields considerable power. In some she is a familial/clan adjunct, in some she is as close to autonomous as her economic circumstances and psychological traits permit. But in no tribal definitions is she perceived in the same way as are women in western industrial and postindustrial cultures.

In the west, few images of women form part of the cultural mythos, and these are largely sexually charged. Among Christians, the madonna is the female prototype, and she is portrayed as essentially passive: her contribution is simply that of birthing. Little else is attributed to her and she certainly

---

*In contemporary speech, *Native American* is frequently used instead of *American Indian*.

possesses few of the characteristics that are attributed to mythic figures among Indian tribes. This image is countered (rather than balanced) by the witch-goddess/whore characteristics designed to reinforce cultural beliefs about women, as well as western adversarial and dualistic perceptions of reality.

The tribes see women variously, but they do not question the power of femininity. Sometimes they see women as fearful, sometimes peaceful, sometimes omnipotent and omniscient, but they never portray women as mindless, helpless, simple, or oppressed. And while the women in a given tribe, clan, or band may be all these things, the individual woman is provided with a variety of images of women from the interconnected supernatural, natural, and social worlds she lives in.   4

As a half-breed American Indian woman, I cast about in my mind for negative images of Indian women, and I find none that are directed to Indian women alone. The negative images I do have are of Indians in general and in fact are more often of males than of females. All these images come to me from non-Indian sources, and they are always balanced by a positive image. My ideas of womanhood, passed on largely by my mother and grandmothers, Laguna Pueblo women, are about practicality, strength, reasonableness, intelligence, wit, and competence. I also remember vividly the women who came to my father's store, the women who held me and sang to me, the women at Feast Day, at Grab Days,* the women in the kitchen of my Cubero home, the women I grew up with; none of them appeared weak or helpless, none of them presented herself tentatively. I remember a certain reserve on those lovely brown faces; I remember the direct gaze of eyes framed by bright-colored shawls draped over their heads and cascading down their backs. I remember the clean cotton dresses and carefully pressed hand-embroidered aprons they always wore; I remember laughter and good food, especially the sweet bread and the oven bread they gave us. Nowhere in my mind is there a foolish woman, a dumb woman, a vain woman, or a plastic woman, though the Indian women I have known have shown a wide range of personal style and demeanor.   5

My memory includes the Navajo woman who was badly beaten by her Sioux husband; but I also remember that my grandmother abandoned her Sioux husband long ago. I recall the stories about the Laguna woman beaten regularly by her husband in the presence of her children so that the children   6

*A Laguna ritual in which women throw food and small items, such as pieces of cloth, to those attending.

would not believe in the strength and power of femininity. And I remember the women who drank, who got into fights with other women and with the men, and who often won those battles. I have memories of tired women, partying women, stubborn women, sullen women, amicable women, selfish women, shy women, and aggressive women. Most of all I remember the women who laugh and scold and sit uncomplaining in the long sun on feast days and who cook wonderful food on wood stoves, in beehive mud ovens, and over open fires outdoors.

Among the images of women that come to me from various tribes as well as my own are White Buffalo Woman, who came to the Lakota long ago and brought them the religion of the Sacred Pipe which they still practice; Tinotzin the goddess who came to Juan Diego to remind him that she still walked the hills of her people and sent him with her message, her demand and her proof to the Catholic bishop in the city nearby. And from Laguna I take the images of Yellow Woman, Coyote Woman, Grandmother Spider (Spider Old Woman), who brought the light, who gave us weaving and medicine, who gave us life. Among the Keres she is known as Thought Woman who created us all and who keeps us in creation even now. I remember Iyatiku, Earth Woman, Corn Woman, who guides and counsels the people to peace and who welcomes us home when we cast off this coil of flesh as huskers cast off the leaves that wrap the corn. I remember Iyatiku's sister, Sun Woman, who held metals and cattle, pigs and sheep, highways and engines and so many things in her bundle, who went away to the east saying that one day she would return. . . .

My mother told me stories all the time, though I often did not recognize them as that. My mother told me stories about cooking and childbearing; she told me stories about menstruation and pregnancy; she told me stories about gods and heroes, about fairies and elves, about goddesses and spirits; she told me stories about the land and the sky, about cats and dogs, about snakes and spiders; she told me stories about climbing trees and exploring the mesas; she told me stories about going to dances and getting married; she told me stories about dressing and undressing, about sleeping and waking; she told me stories about herself, about her mother, about her grandmother. She told me stories about grieving and laughing, about thinking and doing; she told me stories about school and about people; about darning and mending; she told me stories about turquoise and about gold; she told me European stories and Laguna stories; she told me Catholic stories and Presbyterian stories; she told me city stories and country stories; she told me political stories and religious stories. She told me stories about living and stories about dying. And in all of those stories she told me who I was, who I was supposed to be, whom I came from, and who would follow me. In this way she taught me the meaning of the words she said, that all life is a circle and everything has a place within it. That's what she said and what she showed me in the things she did and the way she lives.

Of course, through my formal, white, Christian education, I discovered   9
that other people had stories of their own—about women, about Indians, about fact, about reality—and I was amazed by a number of startling suppositions that others made about tribal customs and beliefs. According to the un-Indian, non-Indian view, for instance, Indians barred menstruating women from ceremonies and indeed segregated them from the rest of the people, consigning them to some space specially designed for them. This showed that Indians considered menstruating women unclean and not fit to enjoy the company of decent (nonmenstruating) people, that is, men. I was surprised and confused to hear this because my mother had taught me that white people had strange attitudes toward menstruation: they thought something was bad about it, that it meant you were sick, cursed, sinful, and weak and that you had to be very careful during that time. She taught me that menstruation was a normal occurrence, that I could go swimming or hiking or whatever else I wanted to do during my period. She actively scorned women who took to their beds, who were incapacitated by cramps, who "got the blues."

As I struggled to reconcile these very contradictory interpretations of   10
American Indians' traditional beliefs concerning menstruation, I realized that the menstrual taboos were about power, not about sin or filth. My conclusion was later borne out by some tribes' own explanations, which, as you may well imagine, came as quite a relief to me.

The truth of the matter as many Indians see it is that women who are at   11
the peak of their fecundity are believed to possess power that throws male power totally out of kilter. They emit such force that, in their presence, any male-owned or -dominated ritual or sacred object cannot do its usual task. For instance, the Lakota say that a menstruating woman anywhere near a yuwipi man, who is a special sort of psychic, spirit-empowered healer, for a day or so before he is to do his ceremony will effectively disempower him. Conversely, among many if not most tribes, important ceremonies cannot be held without the presence of women. Sometimes the ritual woman who empowers the ceremony must be unmarried and virginal so that the power

she channels is unalloyed, unweakened by sexual arousal and penetration by a male. Other ceremonies require tumescent women, others the presence of mature women who have borne children, and still others depend for empowerment on postmenopausal women. Women may be segregated from the company of the whole band or village on certain occasions, but on certain occasions men are also segregated. In short, each ritual depends on a certain balance of power, and the positions of women within the phases of womanhood are used by tribal people to empower certain rites. This does not derive from a male-dominant view; it is not a ritual observance imposed on women by men. It derives from a tribal view of reality that distinguishes tribal people from feudal and industrial people.

I remember my mother moving furniture all over the house when she 12 wanted it changed. She didn't wait for my father to come home and help—she just went ahead and moved the piano, a huge upright from the old days, the couch, the refrigerator. Nobody had told her she was too weak to do such things. In imitation of her, I would delight in loading trucks at my father's store with cases of pop or fifty-pound sacks of flour. Even when I was quite small I could do it, and it gave me a belief in my own physical strength that advancing middle age can't quite erase. My mother used to tell me about the Acoma Pueblo women she had seen as a child carrying huge ollas (water pots) on their heads as they wound their way up the tortuous stairwell carved into the face of the "Sky City" mesa, a feat I tried to imitate with books and tin buckets. ("Sky City" is the term used by the Chamber of Commerce for the mother village of Acoma, which is situated atop a high sandstone table mountain.) I was never very successful, but even the attempt reminded me that I was supposed to be strong and balanced to be a proper girl.

Of course, my mother's Laguna people are Keres Indian, reputed to be 13 the last extreme mother-right people on earth. So it is no wonder that I got notably nonwhite notions about the natural strength and prowess of women. Indeed, it is only when I am trying to get non-Indian approval, recognition, or acknowledgment that my "weak sister" emotional and intellectual ploys get the better of my tribal woman's good sense. At such times I forget that I just moved the piano or just wrote a competent paper or just completed a financial transaction satisfactorily or have supported myself and my children for most of my adult life. □

Thinking about the Reading

TRUE/FALSE QUESTIONS

In the space provided, write T if the sentence is true and F if the sentence is false, based on your reading of the preceding selection.

_____ 1. Although American Indian women perform diverse roles in tribal culture, perceptions of women differ from those of women in non-Indian cultures.

_____ 2. In western culture, images of women focus on their sexuality.

_____ 3. Femininity in Indian culture is rarely seen as powerful.

_____ 4. The stories about life that Allen learned from her mother were confirmed when she began her formal schooling.

_____ 5. Allen believes that the roles played by men and women in tribal rituals are related to a balance of power.

COMPREHENSION QUESTIONS

In answering the following comprehension questions, *paraphrase* the selection—that is, restate it in your own words without copying phrases of more than three or four words from the reading. (See Appendix A for more on how to answer comprehension questions.) Here is an example:

Sample question:
What must American Indian women try to reconcile in their efforts to redefine themselves?

Sample answer (words and phrases from the reading are italicized):
In their efforts to *redefine themselves* as women, American Indian women *must reconcile traditional tribal roles* with those offered in modern non-Indian societies.
Here are the questions.

1. According to Allen, what is a primary difference in the way women in tribal culture and in non-Indian cultures are perceived?
2. Where did Allen find negative images of Indian women?
3. How did Allen develop her understanding of womanhood?
4. What sometimes causes Allen to forget her "tribal woman's good sense"?

OUTLINE

Complete the following outline of Allen's essay by listing the topics she discusses in the space provided.

Paragraph(s) 1: Need to integrate two traditions

2: _____

3: Limitations of western women's roles

4: _____

5–7: Images of tribal women

8: _____

9–10: Discovery of contradictory views through formal education

11: _____

12: Learning to be strong and balanced

13: _____

SUMMARY

Use the preceding outline to write a summary of the reading. In the first sentence of your summary, mention the title, the author, and the main topic of the selection. *Paraphrase* the writer's points in your own words. (See Appendix B for more on how to write a summary.)

Making Connections

REACTING TO THE READING

Write about your personal reaction to the reading. Some possible topics include your agreement or disagreement with a specific issue; a relevant personal experience; an idea that is new to you; a related idea from another source (such as a book, a movie, or a television program); or why you like or dislike the selection.

FINDING RELATED SOURCES

1. Interview someone you know about images of women, images of men, or another topic discussed in the selection. Here are some sample questions:

How do you see yourself as a woman/man?

Is it important for people to think about their roles as women/men? Why or why not?

Take notes during the interview. Then, using your notes, write a summary of the interview that includes your reaction as well. Discuss the interview and your summary with your classmates.

2. Locate a passage in a book, magazine, or newspaper that is related to the selection. In writing, summarize the passage and describe how it relates to the reading. Discuss the passage and your writing with your classmates.

Getting Ready to Write

PREWRITING ACTIVITIES

Using the topic *images of women* or *images of men*, or another topic from the reading, spend 10 minutes on *one* of the following prewriting activities: freewriting, clustering, listing, or cubing. (See Appendix C.) Then discuss your prewriting with your classmates.

DISCUSSION AND COMPOSITION QUESTIONS

Choose one or more of the following questions to discuss with your classmates in preparation for writing.

On Peacemaking Issues

1. What issues raised in the reading are related to the goal of achieving world peace?
2. How are images of women and of men related to world peace? Discuss.
3. Do you believe most people have a "definition of self"? How is a "definition of self" related to world peace? Discuss.

On Related Issues

4. If images of women and images of men vary, why do gender stereotypes still exist in the world? Is it important for people to examine stereotypes? Explain.
5. Describe a kind of stereotype that exists in a particular place and explain why it exists there. Do you think the stereotype will be reexamined in the future? Why or why not?
6. What particular stereotype are you most concerned about? Could you (on your own or with others) do anything to change this stereotype? If so, what? If not, why?

7. Describe present-day relations between females and males in your culture.

8. Does femininity have its own special power? Discuss.

9. Discuss a movie or book that tells a story about women and/or men. What happens in the movie or book? What is its message?

10. Tell about an example of stereotyping that you saw or read about. Was the stereotype reinforced or destroyed? Explain why.

11. Are men more powerful than women? Why or why not?

12. Describe someone you know who is happy with life despite his or her refusal to fulfill the role (or roles) expected by society or a particular culture.

13. Do you live according to the role (or roles) expected of you as a woman or man in your culture? Discuss.

PLANNING TO WRITE

Choose one of the preceding Composition Questions as your writing topic. Begin to plan your paragraph or essay by identifying the topic and listing your thoughts about that topic.

Example: Do you live according to the role (or roles) expected of you as a woman or man in your culture? Discuss.

Topic: My role as a woman in my culture
    —Some of what I do fulfills the expectations of women in my culture (wife and mother).
    —Some of what I do has been an effort to redefine myself as an individual.

Then write the first draft of your paragraph or essay. (See Appendixes D and E for more on how to write paragraphs and essays.)

Revising and Editing Your Writing

REVISING YOUR WRITING

Use the Revision Checklist in Appendix F (p. 271) to evaluate the first draft of your (or your classmate's) writing in terms of content and organization. After deciding how your paragraph or essay can be improved, write a second draft incorporating the changes. On the checklist identify the areas in which you had difficulty so you can doublecheck these areas in later writings.

EDITING YOUR WRITING

After you are satisfied with content and organization, use the Editing Checklist in Appendix G (p. 272) to reevaluate your (or your classmate's) writing. On the checklist identify the areas in which you had difficulty so you can doublecheck these areas in later writings.

6

Liza and Family

CAROLA HANSSON AND KARIN LIDEN

In "Liza and Family," an interview published in *Moscow Women: Thirteen Interviews* (1983), Swedish journalists Carola Hansson and Karin Liden convey through Liza's own words a vivid description of her life as a single parent living and working in Moscow, in the former Soviet Union.

Getting Ready to Read

THINKING ABOUT THE TITLE

How do you define a *family*? How do the members of a family relate to each other?

KEY VOCABULARY/CONCEPTS

Discuss with your classmates what you know about some of the following words and concepts.

husband	marriage	divorce
daily routine	day-care center	affect
boarding school	surname	alimony
free time	birthrate	conceive
wages	afford	moral guidance
health	safety	good mother
good father	wife	children
childhood	spiritual/ethical values	teach
qualities	upbringing	housework
contraceptives	abortion	punishment

Before reading the selection, ask yourself and/or discuss with your class-mates the following questions.

1. Do you think it is important to have a family? Why or why not?
2. Is it important to have children? Why or why not?
3. What are the advantages and disadvantages of having children?
4. What advantages and disadvantages face families with two parents? What about families with one parent?

Tell us something about yourself.   1

I'm twenty-eight. I have a degree in literature and work for a publishing   2
house. I have a son, Emil. I had a husband, who was an artist, but now he's
gone. We got married in 1970 and divorced in 1975, I think.

I own my apartment, which my father bought for me, since it's so diffi-   3
cult to get an apartment here; for someone my age it's totally impossible. I
lived here with my husband, and now I live here alone.

What is your daily routine like? Can you tell us what you did yesterday, for   4
instance?

I got up at seven o'clock and went to work. Mostly I have to travel during   5
rush hours; the streetcar was so crowded that I was almost knocked down . . .
horrible.

Oh no! Yesterday was Monday! I woke at six, pulled my child out of   6
bed, packed a bag full of stuff for the whole week, and then he and I took
off for the subway. The two of us were practically knocked down. A woman
was sitting and reading and wouldn't give up her seat, even though my
son was squashed against the doors. He almost fell on her, and I tightened
my grip to keep him from falling and getting hurt. I told him, "Emil, a
child could die in front of that woman while she sat there reading.
Don't you ever be like that." It took us fifty minutes to get to the day-care
center.

I took him inside and undressed him and then I had to rush off to work.   7
He cried, "Mama, I don't want to stay here. I want to go home." I said,
"Emil, sweetheart, please stay in the day-care center now. I'll come and get
you soon. I'll pick you up on Friday." And yesterday was Monday. It was terrible, but I had to hurry off to work.

I left him crying. The teachers took him by the arm and brought him over to the group because I couldn't stay to comfort him. I picked up my things and put my shawl over my head. Outside it was still rush hour. And I was going to the opposite end of Moscow. It was another hour's trip, and I was already late for work. When I dashed out of the subway I was planning to transfer to a bus, and I felt as if I were about to have a minor heart attack. But the bus was just pulling away, so I had to run instead, knowing I'd be in trouble because I was late. I was trying to work out a scheme. If only there were an open window at my office so that I could throw my stuff in and crawl in after it! That way no one would know I was late. . . . 8

So Emil's at the day-care center all week. Is he there at night as well? 9

Yes, it's called weekly boarding school. I could pick him up on Wednes-days, but it doesn't seem to work out. If I fetch him after work we don't get home until eight. He goes to bed at nine, and then I have to get up at six to get him back to the day-care center. The rush again, the mobs. That isn't good for him. He might catch influenza since he wears his little fur coat in the subway, although it's terribly hot and he's soaked with perspiration when we get into the street to walk to the center. As a result he has a cold almost the whole winter. 10

Does he like the boarding school? 11

It's O.K. By Friday when I pick him up he's happy. He's been playing with his friends and it's hard to tear him away. He's gotten used to it. But on Monday it's the same story all over again. 12

Doesn't his father spend time with him? 13

No, he rarely sees his father. The situation is complicated. When the baby was born I gave him my surname. I decided that since I had had to carry the whole burden and I suffered the most, I wanted to give him my name. His father was very upset that the boy didn't have his name. They almost never see each other, although Emil is the image of his father. He never gets any-thing from him, but I do get alimony, 35 rubles a month.* 14

*One ruble was then equivalent to around $1.36 at the official rate of exchange.

How do you spend your free time? 15

Saturdays and Sundays are mostly devoted to my child. When he sleeps I 16
have some time to read, but a lot of my energy goes into him. Free time?
Yes, on weekdays after work. Of course I'm tired, but at least I can do as I
please. Sometimes when I have a few moments I try to write; I couldn't
imagine not writing. I'll probably write all my life—how regularly I don't
know, since I don't have the time. But when I have a free evening I write po-
etry.

Can you envisage a life without children? 17

Definitely not. If a couple already in their forties haven't heard the sound 18
of children's voices in their home, life is meaningless, period. Of course, it's
obvious that the woman suffers the most. Formerly, among the peasants, divorce was granted on the grounds [of not being able to have children], and
I think that was right. One should have children, no matter how difficult
the situation. Also, because of the low birthrate, Russia is wasting away . . .
although I myself don't intend to give birth to a second, third, fourth.

Would you like to have more children? 19

Yes, but I don't have a husband. If I did, I'd have a second and a third. I 20
would want a girl because they're so much closer to their mother.

How would you find the time? 21

I would leave the children in one of the weekly boarding schools. What 22
else can you do? Tsvetayeva* had three children, but she kept on writing.

You just said that the birthrate was low in the Soviet Union. What could be 23
done to raise it?

To raise the birthrate one has to raise wages. They're so low now that 24
women can't afford the luxury of two or three children.

*A Russian poet.

What is a good mother?

25

Naturally, a good mother has to take care of her baby, take it out for walks
and make sure it develops physically. But she should also give the child
moral guidance—a feeling that life has a spiritual dimension. A mother
who is concerned only with the child's health and safety is not a good
mother. Of course she has to be a social being as well—she has to suffer the
sorrows of her people. Then her child will turn out well. I'm quite con-
vinced of that.

And how would you define a good father?

A good father? I know only one example of a good father, and that's
mine. In the Soviet Union the father usually loves the wife above the children, but a good father ought to put his children first. When I was a baby
my father always used to carry me in his arms at night. He didn't worry
about his time, although he wrote a lot—carrying me on his arm. A father
should spend as much time with his child as possible, and not only treat it
as a child, but as an adult. Perhaps my husband would have made a good father, but after six months he was conscripted. He was twenty-seven, and it
was his last call of duty. He was gone for a year, and I was allotted 15 rubles
per month. When he returned, the child was a year and a half old already,
and he was like a stranger to the child. Things just kept on getting worse
and worse between us until we divorced.

I was much closer to my father than my mother, but I feel that for a son
a father is absolutely necessary. I can't imagine my own childhood without
my father, and I don't know what I would have done without him. I have a
feeling that he gave me everything.

Do you consider yourself a good mother?

30

No, I'm a disgusting mother! I bring up my son on the run. I get tired of
trying to keep him amused and give him a pencil so that he can keep himself busy drawing.

However, I do try to teach him the love of work. That's the most important thing one can teach a child—aside from spiritual and ethical values, of
course. But I don't see these qualities in my son, and therefore I consider
myself a bad mother. I should have taught him better.

Do you think one ought to give boys and girls a different upbringing? 33

No. I believe that girls ought to be taught to cook, clean, and do house- 34
work, but so should boys. People ought to be free and independent, but not
arrogant. There's really not much difference between a boy and a girl, except that boys have to develop more physically, and that of course is the father's job.

Do you have contraceptives in the Soviet Union? 35

We have the I.U.D., although it isn't used very much. Women who want 36
one have to stand in line a long time. We try not to use the pill because of
the possible danger to a future fetus. Some also use aspirin, but that's also
considered to be dangerous.

But above all we have many abortions. They're horrible, absolutely horri- 37
ble. But what's the answer? Our contraceptives aren't any good. There are
condoms, but they're so repulsive and bad that we would rather go through
an abortion. . . . The first Christians copulated only in order to procreate. In
my opinion, abortions are punishments for our sins.

Have you ever had an abortion? 38

Yes, many—seven. It's hard both physically and psychologically. Now 39
that it's done with drugs there's no pain, but it's hard on the psyche.

How are women affected? 40

There are painful repercussions. There's no way of thinking about 41
anything else when you're pregnant and you have to wait two months
for an abortion. Then the aftermath is difficult. It affects not only your sex
life, but also life in general. Sometimes I fear that I may be pregnant again;
then I can't think about anything else, can't write, can't read, can't do anything.

People say that when a woman gives birth to a child she gets younger, 42
and when she has an abortion she gets twice as old. So I have become seven
times as old! . . . The only concern doctors seem to have is to make abortions relatively painless. Previously no drugs were given. But the dread of
pregnancy still remains stronger than anything else.

How did you react when you discovered that you were pregnant the first time? 43

I was hysterical. It was totally unexpected, since I didn't believe. . . . I 44
couldn't imagine that children were conceived that quickly. No one had told
me anything. I got together with my husband, and I got pregnant immediately. It was so strange and unexpected that I had an abortion, though naturally I should have had that first baby. I went through with the second
pregnancy and mostly felt fine, but I developed toxemia. The delivery was
very difficult. They don't use drugs, gas, anything. None of the women
around me wanted them either. I begged for a cesarean, howled like an animal, couldn't stand the pain any longer. I screamed so much that they finally
had to give me something to induce labor, and I had terrible contractions
and kept on screaming until there was blood in my mouth.

A friend had a baby two months later and told me that an old lady who 45
had taken a three months' course told her how to prepare for each contrac-
tion. She gave no drugs, but only explained in what position my friend
should lie. They also give massage, but that doesn't help. One feels like an
animal.

My baby was born in a special clinic, but still. . . . During the delivery I 46
was badly torn, but they didn't even sew me up. Recently I went to a gyne-
cologist who asked me whether I had given birth in the country—but in
fact I gave birth at a special clinic in the capital.

Did you feel that the pains you suffered affected your relationship to the child? 47

No, I felt it was quite normal. I knew that it would hurt. I was so happy 48
to see him that I forgot it all. □

Thinking about the Reading

TRUE/FALSE QUESTIONS

In the space provided, write T if the sentence is true and F if the sentence
is false, based on your reading of the preceding selection.

_____ 1. Liza is a divorced, single parent who works and has a son who goes
to a day-care center.
_____ 2. Liza's son Emil spends every other weekend with his father and receives monthly support from him.
_____ 3. The birthrate in the Soviet Union is low because wages are low.

_____ 4. Contraceptives are safe and easily available in the Soviet Union.
_____ 5. Abortions are also safe and easily available in the Soviet Union.

COMPREHENSION QUESTIONS

In answering the following comprehension questions, *paraphrase* the selection—that is, restate it in your own words without copying phrases of more than three or four words from the reading. (See Appendix A for more on how to answer comprehension questions.) Here is an example:

Sample question:
Why is Emil in a weekly boarding school, at night as well as during the day?

Sample answer (words and phrases from the reading are italicized):
Liza leaves Emil at the *weekly boarding school* from Monday to Friday because taking him home, even just on Wednesdays, was too stressful and tiring for both of them due to the commute, and they did not have much more time to spend together.

Here are the questions:

1. How do Liza and Emil each feel about his staying at the boarding school?
2. Why doesn't Emil see his father much?
3. How does Liza evaluate herself as a mother?
4. Why is abortion common in the Soviet Union?

OUTLINE

Complete the following outline of the reading by listing the topics it discusses in the space provided.

Paragraph(s) 1–3: Introduction to Liza's life
   4–8: _____
   9–12: Emil's weekly boarding school
  13–14: _____
  15–16: Liza's limited free time
  17–24: _____
  25–26: Definition of a good mother
  27–29: _____
  30–32: Liza's image of herself as a mother
  33–34: _____
  35–37: Contraceptives

38–42: _____

43–48: Pregnancy and delivery

SUMMARY

Use the preceding outline to write a summary of the reading. In the first sentence of your summary, mention the title, the authors, and the main topic of the selection. Paraphrase the writers' points in your own words. (See Appendix B for more on how to write a summary.)

Making Connections

REACTING TO THE READING

Write about your personal reaction to the reading. Some possible topics include your agreement or disagreement with a specific issue; a relevant personal experience; an idea that is new to you; a related idea from another source (such as a book, a movie, or a television program); or why you like or dislike the selection.

FINDING RELATED SOURCES

1. Find a picture related to one of the following topics: family life, single parenting, or another topic discussed in the selection. In writing, describe the picture and relate your thoughts and feelings about it. Discuss your picture and writing with your classmates.
2. Find a passage in a book, magazine, or newspaper that is related to the selection. In writing, summarize the passage and describe how it relates to the reading. Discuss the passage and your writing with your classmates.

Getting Ready to Write

PREWRITING ACTIVITIES

Using the topic *family life* or another topic from the reading, spend 10 minutes on *one* of the following prewriting activities: freewriting, clustering, listing, or cubing. (See Appendix C.) Then discuss your prewriting with your classmates.

DISCUSSION AND COMPOSITION QUESTIONS

Choose one or more of the following questions to discuss with your classmates in preparation for writing.

On Peacemaking Issues

1. What issues raised in the reading are related to the goal of achieving world peace?
2. Is "family life" related to world peace? Discuss.
3. Is "moral guidance" related to world peace? Discuss.
4. Do you believe that most people learn spiritual and ethical values from their families? Discuss.
5. If people do learn spiritual and ethical values from their families, why does unethical behavior still exist in the world? What could be done to instill stronger spiritual and ethical values in a specific place that you can think of?
6. Describe a particular type of family life that exists in a specific place or culture and explain why it exists there.
7. What particular family situation are you most concerned about? Could you (on your own or with others) do anything to improve this situation? If so, what? If not, why?

On Related Issues

8. Describe the family planning services (such as contraceptives, prenatal health care, childbirth procedures, and abortion) that exist in one particular country.
9. Do you believe that women have a right to determine whether or not and when to have children? Discuss.
10. Discuss a movie or book that examines family life. What happens in the movie or book? What is its message?
11. Tell about an example of divorce that you know of or have read about. What caused the divorce? Could it have been avoided? Why or why not?
12. Explain why you think Liza is or is not a good mother.
13. Is it important for people to become parents? Why or why not?
14. If someone chooses not to become a parent, how else might he or she contribute to spiritual and ethical values in the world?
15. Describe someone you know who is a good parent.
16. Do you live according to the spiritual and ethical values taught by your family? Discuss.

Choose one of the preceding Composition Questions as your writing topic. Begin to plan your paragraph or essay by identifying the topic and listing your thoughts about that topic.

Example: If someone chooses not to become a parent, how else might he or she contribute to spiritual and ethical values in the world?

Topic: The contributions of single people without children to spiritual and ethical values

—An individual's contributions are not limited by one's ability to procreate.

—Historically, individuals have contributed in diverse ways to their local and global communities.

Then write the first draft of your paragraph or essay. (See Appendixes D and E for more on how to write paragraphs and essays.)

Revising and Editing Your Writing

REVISING YOUR WRITING

Use the Revision Checklist in Appendix F (p. 271) to evaluate the first draft of your (or your classmate's) writing in terms of content and organization. After deciding how your paragraph or essay can be improved, write a second draft incorporating the changes. On the checklist identify the areas in which you had difficulty so you can doublecheck these areas in later writings.

EDITING YOUR WRITING

After you are satisfied with content and organization, use the Editing Checklist in Appendix G (p. 272) to reevaluate your (or your classmate's) writing. On the checklist identify the areas in which you had difficulty so you can doublecheck these areas in later writings.

7

American Men Don't Cry

ASHLEY MONTAGU

As a professor of anthropology, Ashley Montagu has written many books on diverse aspects of humankind. Among these is *The American Way of Life* (1952), from which the following selection is taken. In it the writer discusses the human activity of crying both in general and specifically in terms of American men.

Getting Ready to Read

THINKING ABOUT THE TITLE

Why do people cry? Do you cry? In some cultures crying is accepted as more natural than in others, and for some people more than for others.

KEY VOCABULARY/CONCEPTS

Discuss with your classmates what you know about some of the following words and concepts.

unmasculine	sissy	weakness
female/male	childishness	dependence
crybaby	adult	permissible
sex	natural	emotional
mark	credo	biological time clock
capacity	trained	inferior creature

repress	desire	function
human organism	disequilibrated	homeostasis
interference	mechanism	damaging
maintenance of health	human species	defect

PREREADING QUESTIONS

Before reading the selection, ask yourself and/or discuss with your class-mates the following questions.

1. Do you consider it acceptable for men to cry?
2. What are your reasons for considering it acceptable or unacceptable?
3. What advantages or disadvantages are there for men who are able to cry?
4. What advantages or disadvantages are there for anyone who cries?

American men don't cry because it is considered unmasculine to do so. Only sissies cry. Crying is a "weakness" characteristic of the female, and no American male wants to be identified with anything in the least weak or feminine. Crying, in our culture, is identified with childishness, with weakness and dependence. No one likes a crybaby, and we disapprove of crying even in children, discouraging it in them as early as possible. In a land so devoted to the pursuit of happiness as ours, crying really is rather un-American. Adults must learn not to cry in situations in which it is permissible for a child to cry. Women being the "weaker" and "dependent" sex, it is only natural that they should cry in certain emotional situations. In women, crying is excusable. But in men, crying is a mark of weakness. So goes the American credo with regard to crying.

"A little man," we impress on our male children, "never cries. Only sissies and crybabies do." And so we condition males in America not to cry whenever they feel like doing so. It is not that American males are unable to cry because of some biological time clock within them which causes them to run down in that capacity as they grow older, but that they are trained not to cry. No "little man" wants to be like that "inferior creature," the female. And the worst thing you can call him is a sissy or a crybaby. And so the "little man" represses his desire to cry and goes on doing so until he is unable to cry even when he wants to. Thus do we produce a trained inca-pacity in the American male to cry. And this is bad. Why is it bad? Because crying is a natural function of the human organism which is designed to re-store the emotionally disequilibrated person to a state of equilibrium. The return of the disequilibrated organ systems of the body to steady states or dynamic stability is known as homeostasis. Crying serves a homeostatic function for the organism as a whole. Any interference with homeostatic mechanisms is likely to be damaging to the organism. And there is good reason to believe that the American male's trained incapacity to cry is seriously damaging to him.

It is unnecessary to cry whenever one wants to cry, but one should be able to cry when one ought to cry—when one needs to cry. For to cry under certain emotionally disequilibrating conditions is necessary for the maintenance of health.

To be human is to weep. The human species is the only one in the whole of animated nature that sheds tears. The trained inability of any human being to weep is a lessening of his capacity to be human—a defect which usually goes deeper than the mere inability to cry. And this, among other things, is what American parents—with the best intentions in the world— have achieved for the American male. It is very sad. If we feel like it, let us all have a good cry—and clear our minds of those cobwebs of confusion which have for so long prevented us from understanding the ineluctable necessity of crying. □

3

4

Thinking about the Reading

TRUE/FALSE QUESTIONS

In the space provided, write T if the sentence is true or F if the sentence is false, based on your reading of the preceding selection.

_____ 1. American men cry whenever they need to.
_____ 2. In American culture, crying is identified with women and children.
_____ 3. Some people are naturally unable to cry.
_____ 4. The inability to cry is damaging to the human organism.
_____ 5. Of all species, only human beings cry.

COMPREHENSION QUESTIONS

In answering the following comprehension questions, *paraphrase* the selection—that is, restate it in your own words without copying phrases of more than three or four words from the reading. (See Appendix A for more on how to answer comprehension questions.) Here is an example:

Sample question:
Why don't most American men cry?

Sample answer (words and phrases from the reading are italicized):
American men are *trained not to cry* from a young age so as not to be stereotyped as *feminine or weak*.

Here are the questions:

1. In American culture, who is permitted to cry in certain circumstances?
2. How are boys conditioned not to cry?
3. Why is it bad to be unable to cry?
4. What effects does the incapacity to cry have on people?

OUTLINE

Complete the following outline of Montagu's selection by listing the topics he discusses in the space provided.

Paragraph(s) 1: Why American men don't cry
     2: _____
  2–3: Why it is bad not to cry
     4: _____

SUMMARY

Use the preceding outline to write a summary of the reading. In the first sentence of your summary, mention the title, the author, and the main topic of the selection. Paraphrase the writer's points in your own words. (See Appendix B for more on how to write a summary.)

Making Connections

REACTING TO THE READING

Write about your personal reaction to the reading. Some possible topics include your agreement or disagreement with a specific issue; a relevant personal experience; an idea that is new to you; a related idea from another source (such as a book, movie, or television program); or why you like or dislike the selection.

FINDING RELATED SOURCES

1. Interview someone you know about crying or another topic discussed in the selection. Here are some sample questions:

   Do you ever cry? Why or why not?

   Is it helpful for people to be able to cry? Why or why not?

   Take notes during the interview. Then, using your notes, write a summary of the interview that includes your reaction as well. Discuss the interview and your summary with your classmates.

2. Find a passage in a book, magazine, or newspaper that is related to the selection. In writing, summarize the passage and describe how it relates to the reading. Discuss the passage and your writing with your classmates.

Getting Ready to Write

PREWRITING ACTIVITIES

Using the topic crying or another topic from the reading, spend 10 minutes on one of the following prewriting activities: freewriting, clustering, listing, or cubing. (See Appendix C.) Then discuss your prewriting with your classmates.

DISCUSSION AND COMPOSITION QUESTIONS

Choose one or more of the following questions to discuss with your classmates in preparation for writing.

On Peacemaking Issues

1. What issues raised in the reading are related to the goal of achieving world peace?
2. Is "crying" or "emotional equilibrium" related to world peace? Discuss one of these two issues.
3. Do you believe that most people (in your own country or the country you are living in) are trained to hide or disregard their feelings? If people hide or disregard their feelings, how does this affect the world we live in? Discuss.
4. Describe how and why a particular emotion (such as sadness, anger, or sexual attraction) is handled or viewed in a specific place or culture.

What, if anything, might be done to change the way this emotion is viewed or handled?

5. Are you concerned about attitudes (in your culture or another culture) toward a particular emotion? Could you (on your own or with others) do anything to improve this situation? If so, what? If not, why?

ON RELATED ISSUES

6. Describe the way in which a certain emotion is, in your opinion, mishandled in a specific culture.
7. Do you think the inability to cry makes a person less human? Discuss.
8. Describe a movie or book that portrays a character who is unable to communicate (or has difficulty communicating) his or her feelings to others. What happens in the movie or book? What is its message?
9. Tell about someone you saw or read about who was "emotionally disequilibrated." Was the person helped? How, or why not?
10. Montagu argues that American men don't cry. In "Where I Come from Is Like This," Allen says she was "supposed to be strong and balanced to be a proper girl" (see Chapter 5). What were you taught?
11. Is it important for people to overcome such cultural constraints as "men don't cry"? Why or why not?
12. For people seeking to overcome such cultural constraints, how might they do so?
13. Tell about someone you know who has rejected sexual stereotypes and is happy with his or her life.
14. Do you feel limited by sexual or cultural stereotypes? Discuss.

PLANNING TO WRITE

Choose one of the preceding Composition Questions as your writing topic. Begin to plan your paragraph or essay by identifying the topic and listing your thoughts on that topic.

Example: Is it important for people to overcome such cultural constraints as "men don't cry"? Why or why not?

Topic: Overcoming cultural constraints
—Cultural constraints are not necessarily bad or good, and we may even be unaware of following them.

—If we become aware of cultural constraints, we can choose those we feel are helpful to us and try to minimize the effects of those that are not.

Then write the first draft of your paragraph or essay. (See Appendixes D and E for more on how to write paragraphs and essays.)

Revising and Editing Your Writing

REVISING YOUR WRITING

Use the Revision Checklist in Appendix F (p. 271) to evaluate the first draft of your (or your classmate's) writing in terms of content and organization. After deciding how your paragraph or essay can be improved, write a second draft incorporating the changes. On the checklist identify the areas in which you had difficulty so you can doublecheck these areas in later writings.

EDITING YOUR WRITING

After you are satisfied with content and organization, use the Editing Checklist in Appendix G (p. 272) to reevaluate your (or your classmate's) writing. On the checklist identify the areas in which you had difficulty so you can doublecheck these areas in later writings.

8

Machismo in Washington

I. F. STONE

I. F. Stone was a well-known journalist and a contributing editor of the *New York Review of Books*. He was respected for the kind of thoughtful and knowledgeable writing seen in the following selection, which was written in 1972 during American military involvement in Vietnam. In the reading, Stone examines the U.S. government's policy in the Vietnam War in terms of "machismo."

Getting Ready to Read

THINKING ABOUT THE TITLE

Are you familiar with the Spanish word *machismo*? The term relates to one's sense of manhood. Look up its definition in an English dictionary. As you read the selection, note the connections between the dictionary definition of *machismo* and Stone's use of the term.

KEY VOCABULARY/CONCEPTS

Discuss with your classmates what you know about some of the following words and phrases.

Vietnam	rival gangs	peace efforts
fight	aggression	test of will
Nixon	Senate	justification

surrender	Moscow	intimidated
machismo	small boy mentality	Johnson-McNamara years
the Pentagon	adversary	"chicken"
confrontation	nuclear age	Hiroshima
world peace	backing down	world order
Peking (Beijing)	virility	superpowers
NATO	United Nations	showdown
statecraft		

PREREADING QUESTIONS

Before reading the selection, ask yourself and/or discuss with your class-mates the following questions.

1. What is your idea of how a "man" is supposed to behave? Why?
2. What are the advantages and disadvantages of being a "man"?
3. What might be the connections between one's sense of manhood and government policy?
4. What might be the connections between one's sense of manhood and political negotiations among nations?

I see by the New York papers that the Bronx, like Vietnam, is plagued by civil war. I feel for Congressman Biaggi, who has been trying to bring its rival gangs together. There was something more than faintly familiar in the *New York Times* account on April 22[, 1972] of his peace efforts. One gang leader, Ted Gonzalez of the Seven Immortals, avowed that his gang's intentions were utterly peaceful, unlike its rival the Black Spades. "The Spades just want to fight while we want to make peace," he told Biaggi. "But I tell you, if fight we must, then we're prepared for a rumble too. No one's going to tread on our turf." This manly readiness to stand up against aggression, to face up to the test of will at whatever cost—this sounds like those who rallied to support Nixon's bombing of Haiphong in the Senate a few days earlier.

If we fail to stand up to the aggressor in Vietnam, Thurmond of South Carolina told the Senate during the bombing debate on April 19, [1972,] "our nation will be regarded with justification as a paper tiger." "The invasion of Vietnam," Dole of Kansas said, "is a test of our national will." "Should we accept Hanoi's terms now and surrender," Tower of Texas de-

clared, "the President would have to crawl on his belly to Moscow in May."
"The President," averred Allott of Colorado, "will not be intimidated. . . ."
And Goldwater promised that the actions taken by Nixon "will overcome
the weak-kneed, jelly-backed attitude of Members of this body and citizens
of this country who think you can end a war overnight by snapping your
fingers. . . ." These Senators and the Bronx's Seven Immortals have
machismo in common.

A related maxim of statesmanly behavior was reported by Terence Smith   3
in the *New York Times* April 23. The day after the bombing of Hanoi and
Haiphong the President ran into an old friend as he was leaving a luncheon
on Capitol Hill. When the friend asked about the bombings, Mr. Nixon
punched him affectionately on the shoulder and said, "When they jump on
you, you have to let them have it."

The small boy mentality is also visible in military pronouncements. Orr   4
Kelly, the Washington *Star*'s Pentagon reporter, was given a "background
briefing" on the tactics being pursued in the new bombings of the North.
"US Following 'Classic' Script in Escalation," said the headline over his story
of April 23. The military in the Johnson-McNamara years claimed that the
bombings of the North failed because the escalation was too gradual. The
theory now being applied by the Pentagon, Mr. Kelly was told, "calls for
rapidly increasing pressure on the enemy until he gives up." The theory is
certainly classic in its simplicity. The rationale, Mr. Kelly's Pentagon infor-
mant explained, in an unconsciously revealing simile, "is much like the tactics of two boys fighting": *If one boy gets the other in an arm lock, he can probably get
his adversary to say "uncle" if he increases the pressure in sharp, painful jolts and gives every indication of willingness to break the other boy's arm.*

There are subtleties involved, as in any systems analysis. "Between each   5
painful move," so Mr. Kelly was briefed, "he must pause long enough to
give the other boy a chance to think things over and give up." But if the
pressure is applied "slowly and with obvious reluctance," as under Johnson
and McNamara, "the boy on the ground has a chance to get used to the
pain." This is the mistake the Joint Chiefs of Staff under Nixon are determined to avoid. Why read Clausewitz or consult Herman Kahn, why drop
more coins in the computers, when the military can draw upon so rich a
store of puerilities?

The first rule of this small boy statecraft is that the leader of a gang, like   6
the leader of a tribe, horde, or nation, dare not appear "chicken." This
axiom is as old as the cave man, but it remains a guiding principle of inter-

national confrontation a quarter-century after the nuclear age began at Hiroshima. It still charts our course as, in the waters of the Tonkin Gulf, we may be drifting toward the world's second nuclear "crunch," if wiser second thoughts do not prevail.

In the first, world peace was saved because Khrushchev backed down. **7** Khrushchev soon after lost his job. Kennedy, had he lived, would have found it hard to keep his at the next election if he had made the sacrifice for peace and "blinked," leaving Soviet missiles aimed at us from Cuba. Now again, as then, the desire not to appear a pitiful, helpless giant, a patsy in office, is predominant. *The risks to the leader's political future outweigh the risks to his country and the world.* Crunch may become catastrophe because the man in power would rather risk a nuclear showdown than lose the next election or his majority in the Politbureau. This is not rational planetary order. But it would be too easy to blame this on the "politicians." Their calculus of political expediency rests on the existence within each nation's boundaries of a sizable population of small boy mentalities and primitives who still see war as a test of their virility.

The leaders of the superpowers look toward their coming meeting in **8** Moscow in mutual suspicion and fear. Mr. Nixon, as Senator Gravel told the Senate in the bombing debate, believes "what is happening" in Vietnam "is part of a diabolical plan by Mr. Brezhnev to pressure him into going to Moscow in a much more humble fashion than he would be prone to." On the other hand, Gravel continued, "it has been said, and accurately so, that the situation that exists in Moscow today is not unlike the situation that existed prior to the political demise of Nikita Khrushchev." The present Kremlin leadership may be feeling the hot breath of the hard liners down its neck, too.

When Ted Gonzalez of the Bronx gang, the Seven Immortals, told Con- **9** gressman Biaggi, "If fight we must. . . . No one's going to tread on our turf," Biaggi—an ex-policeman, swamped with complaints from all over the Bronx about chronic gang warfare—retorted angrily, "You shouldn't rumble—get that out of your heads. It's not your turf. It's the community's. And you aren't laws unto yourselves." But who is to say to Washington and Moscow that the planet is not their turf—"You aren't laws unto yourselves"? When, indeed, they are.

Had the Cuban missile crisis erupted into nuclear war, Western Europe **10** would have been doomed, too. But Kennedy did not consult our allies in NATO, much less the United Nations. Acheson was sent, after the decision was made, to inform de Gaulle, not to ask his consent to the showdown. Should the Vietnamese confrontation erupt into nuclear war, Japan, the Philippines, Taiwan, and South Korea, our allies in the Far East, would all suffer gravely, perhaps irremediably, even if only from radioactive fallout. But Nixon is not consulting them either.

No doubt Moscow and Peking are terrified of a nuclear confrontation.   11 Nixon's strategy of spreading terror by unpredictability recalls Hitler. I do not compare the President to the Fuehrer, but in this respect their tactics are similar. Hitler won one Munich-style concession after another by them, but at a cost Germany and the world remember all too well.

In the Tonkin Gulf we are again entering treacherous waters. The other   12 day an American guided missile frigate, the Worden, was badly damaged by what appeared at first to be enemy planes. It turned out later that the ship was hit by two air-to-ground missiles from American planes assigned to bomb Haiphong. What if an American ship, what if a carrier, should be sunk with heavy loss of American lives? What if the headlines proclaim it an enemy attack? And we do not find out until too late, or perhaps ever, that our own bombs did the dirty work?

If we move toward blockade, if we mine the harbors, if Moscow sends   13 protective vessels and minesweepers, if the havoc done to Haiphong and Hanoi becomes unendurable even to the most appeasement-minded in Moscow and Peking . . . ? The chances of the situation getting out of hand, through accident or loss of nerve or design, will multiply swiftly, the flash point at which neither side can back down may pass much too quickly for anything as archaic as the Congressional right to declare war.

Secretary Rogers told the Senate Foreign Relations Committee that rein-   14 troducing U.S. combat troops and using nuclear weapons were the only op- tions excluded in escalating the war against North Vietnam. How easily these limits could be swept aside by some unexpected catastrophe! It is time again to "Remember the *Maine*," whose mysterious and still unsolved sink- ing precipitated the Spanish-American war.

The simple fact is that the world as now organized lives on the edge of   15 destruction. Everyone knows it but everyone tries to forget about it. Most of the planet can be incinerated within less than a day should a crunch get out of hand. This didn't happen over Cuba, but it may happen over Vietnam. If it doesn't happen over Vietnam, it may happen over the Middle East. If it doesn't happen there, there will be other flash points—Bangladesh was the first flicker of the lightening over the Indian Ocean, the newest theater of confrontation. With each crunch, the probability—by sheer arithmetic—of its getting out of control will increase. The safety of mankind depends on somehow finding a way to a new world order in which no nation is so "sovereign" that it can press the button that may mean planetary extinction.

And what if Nixon "succeeds"? What if he escalates the bombing of the North without precipitating a third World War? What a price to prove that he and America are not "chicken." How many must die in the smaller countries, how many millions elsewhere must be placed in jeopardy because a superpower suffers from an inferiority complex? □

16

Thinking about the Reading

TRUE/FALSE QUESTIONS

In the space provided, write T if the sentence is true and F if the sentence is false, based on your reading of the preceding selection.

_____ 1. Stone uses the example of the rival gangs in the Bronx to make the point that their attitude is similar to that of the American members of Congress who supported the bombing of Vietnam.

_____ 2. The "small boy mentality" means that one is afraid and seeks the protection of parents (the protectors).

_____ 3. According to the Pentagon, the bombing of Vietnam under President Johnson was successful because pressure was applied gradually to the enemy.

_____ 4. In small boy statecraft, nothing is more important than ensuring the leader's political future.

_____ 5. The only way to protect the world today is to find a way to keep any one nation from being able to destroy all the others.

COMPREHENSION QUESTIONS

In answering the following comprehension questions, *paraphrase* the selection—that is, restate it in your own words without copying phrases of more than three or four words from the reading. (See Appendix A for more on how to answer comprehension questions.) Here is an example:

Sample question:
If the Seven Immortals truly wanted peace, what would make them fight?

Sample answer (words and phrases from the reading are italicized):

Although the Seven Immortals claimed they wanted *peace*, they said they would *fight* if they had to protect their *turf* from a *rival* gang.

Here are the questions:

1. What reasons were given for the bombing of Vietnam?
2. Now that we live in a nuclear age, what makes small boy statecraft particularly dangerous?
3. Who does Stone consider responsible for allowing the "politicians" to practice machismo?
4. According to Stone, even if Nixon "succeeded" in bombing Vietnam, why would this type of statesmanship be dangerous?

OUTLINE

Complete the following outline of Stone's selection by listing the topics he discusses in the space provided.

Paragraph(s) 1: Comparison of Seven Immortals to supporters of bombing in Vietnam

    2–3: _____

    4–5: Small boy tactics applied to war

      6: _____

      7: Individual political risks outweigh danger to the world

      8: _____

      9: Whose turf and whose laws?

    10: _____

    11: Effects of Nixon's strategy

  12–14: _____

    15: Potential for destruction of the world

    16: _____

SUMMARY

Use the preceding outline to write a summary of the reading. In the first sentence of your summary, mention the title, the author, and the main topic of the selection. Paraphrase the writer's points in your own words. (See Appendix B for more on how to write a summary.)

Making Connections

Write about your personal reaction to the reading. Some possible topics include your agreement or disagreement with a specific issue; relevant personal experience; an idea that is new to you; a related idea from another source (such as a book, a movie, or a television program); or why you like or dislike the selection.

FINDING RELATED SOURCES

1. Find a picture related to one of the following topics: machismo, war, or another topic discussed in the selection. In writing, describe the picture and relate your thoughts and feelings about it. Discuss your picture and writing with your classmates.
2. Find a passage in a book, magazine, or newspaper that is related to the reading. In writing, summarize the passage and describe how it relates to the selection. Discuss the passage and your writing with your classmates.

Getting Ready to Write

PREWRITING ACTIVITIES

Using the topic machismo or war, or another topic from the reading, spend 10 minutes on one of the following prewriting activities: freewriting, clustering, listing, or cubing. (See Appendix C.) Then discuss your prewriting with your classmates.

DISCUSSION AND COMPOSITION QUESTIONS

Choose one or more of the following questions to discuss with your classmates in preparation for writing.

On Peacemaking Issues

1. What issues raised in the reading are related to the goal of achieving world peace?
2. Is "small boy statecraft" related to world peace? Discuss.

3. Is a sense of living "on the edge of destruction" related to world peace? Discuss.

4. Do you believe most people feel they are living "on the edge of destruction"? If so, why isn't there more pressure to find peaceful means of resolving differences? Discuss.

5. Describe an example of "small boy statecraft" that exists in a particular place or culture. Explain why it exists there.

6. What machismo-related situation are you most concerned about? Could you (on your own or with others) do anything to improve the situation? If so, what? If not, why?

7. Describe a situation involving two or more nations that illustrates "war as a test of virility."

On Related Issues

8. Discuss the connections between the Stone reading and Montagu's "American Men Don't Cry" (Chapter 7).

9. Describe a movie or book that has a political message. What happens in the movie or book? What is its political message?

10. Tell about an example of machismo that you saw or read about. Was the macho person "successful"? Why or why not?

11. Is machismo limited to one culture or one nation? Discuss.

12. Compare and contrast Stone's essay with Neil Boothby's "Children and War" (Chapter 12).

13. If, according to Congressman Biaggi, the world is the "turf of the community," why do some nations believe they can act as "laws unto themselves"?

14. Tell about someone you know who lives and behaves in a non-macho, communal way.

15. Do you live in a non-macho, communal way? Discuss.

PLANNING TO WRITE

Choose one of the preceding Composition Questions as your writing topic. Begin to plan your paragraph or essay by identifying the topic and listing your thoughts on that topic.

Example: What issues raised in the reading are related to the goal of achieving world peace?

Topic: Machismo and world peace

    —Small boy statecraft affects world peace.

    —A new world order is needed.

Then write the first draft of your paragraph or essay. (See Appendixes D and E for more on how to write paragraphs and essays.)

Revising and Editing Your Writing

REVISING YOUR WRITING

Use the Revision Checklist in Appendix F (p. 271) to evaluate the first draft of your (or your classmate's) writing in terms of content and organization. After deciding how your paragraph or essay can be improved, write a second draft incorporating the changes. On the checklist identify the areas in which you had difficulty so you can doublecheck these areas in later writings.

EDITING YOUR WRITING

After you are satisfied with content and organization, use the Editing Checklist in Appendix G (p. 272) to reevaluate your (or your classmate's) writing. On the checklist identify the areas in which you had difficulty so you can doublecheck these areas in later writings.

PART II: RESEARCH TOPICS

Choose one of the following topics on men and women for research. Refer to Appendix H for specific assignments. In addition, you may find it helpful to consult the list of Suggested Further Reading (at the end of this book) for sources related to your topic.

Native American tribes

traditional gender/sex roles

biological clock

beliefs/myths/rituals

dialects

linguistics

images of women/men

Vietnam

civil war

femininity/masculinity

values/ethics

abortion

psychology

family life

childbirth

marriage

divorce

day care

working parents

parenthood

childhood

contraceptives/family planning

prenatal health care

cross-cultural communication

relations between men and women

homeostasis

the human species

feelings/emotions

cultural constraints

stereotypes

status

aggression

Richard Nixon

Lyndon B. Johnson

U.S. Senate

machismo

statesmanship

citizenship

the Pentagon

Hiroshima

NATO

the nuclear age

social norms

THE READINGS in Part III discuss some of the ways in which we relate to children, interact as families, and socialize the young through educational institutions. An important step toward improving our world will be the directions we choose for our children, the ways they learn in our homes and in school.

In "Grandparents Have Copped Out," Margaret Mead discusses the roles previously played by the elderly in American society and why "a new style of aging" should be developed. Sonia Nieto's case study of a Vietnamese immigrant in "From *Affirming Diversity*" presents, through a student's own words, a cross-cultural perspective on education and the strengths gained from culture and family. School success and family relationships are also addressed by Richard Rodriguez in "An Education in Language." Finally, Neil Boothby urges us in "Children and War" to be responsible for the rights of children.

9

Grandparents Have Copped Out

MARGARET MEAD

Margaret Mead was a distinguished anthropologist who worked in a variety of fields related to culture and family structure. In the following selection, written in 1971, she discusses her ideas about the past and present roles of the elderly in society, inviting us to consider new ways for grandparents to contribute to society in the future.

Getting Ready to Read

THINKING ABOUT THE TITLE

The expression *to cop out* suggests an evasion of responsibility. Mead discusses the lives of the elderly in American society and what grandparents could offer to the young. What do you think grandparents should do during their later years?

KEY VOCABULARY/CONCEPTS

Discuss with your classmates what you know about some of the following words and concepts.

aging	autonomy	grandmother
style	ethnic group	mother
the old country	practical	raising children
an ideal	harm	a burden

independence	unselfishness	three- or four-generation families
small family unit	old people's hotels	cut off
a price paid	isolated	function
generation gap	perspective	youth
contribution	taking the lead	

PREREADING QUESTIONS

Before reading the selection, ask youself and/or your classmates the following questions.

1. What is your relationship with your grandparents?
2. What is your relationship with your parents?
3. What are the advantages and disadvantages of aging?
4. What are the advantages and disadvantages of independence?

I would like particularly to talk about the need to develop a new style of aging in our own society. I would like to suggest that maybe we could do a little more for the older American than we are doing in the present. Everyone who is aging has a chance to develop this new style. Everyone who is working with old people can contribute to this new style. 1

Young people in this country have been accused of not caring for their parents the way they would have in the old country, in Puerto Rico, in the Old South, or in Italy. And this is true, but it is also true that old people in this country have been influenced by an American ideal of independence and autonomy. The most important thing in the world is to be independent. So we live alone, perhaps on the verge of starvation, in time without friends, but we are independent. This standard American style has been forced on every ethnic group in the country, although there are many groups in this country for whom the ideal is not practical. It is a poor ideal and pursuing it does a great deal of harm. 2

This ideal of independence also contains a tremendous amount of unselfishness. In talking to today's young mothers, I have asked them what kind of grandmothers they think they are going to be. I hear devoted, loving mothers say that when they are through raising their children, they have no intention of becoming grandmothers. They are astonished to hear that in most of the world throughout most of its history, families have been three- 3 or four-generation families, living under the same roof. We have over-emphasized the small family unit—father, mother, small children. We think it is wonderful if Grandma and Grandpa, if [they're] still alive, can live alone.

We have reached the point where we think the only thing we can do for our children is to stay out of their hair and the only thing we can do for our daughter-in-law is to see as little of her as possible. Old people's hotels, even the best run, are filled with older people who believe the only thing they can do for their children is to look cheerful when they come to visit. So in the end, older people have to devote all their energies to "not being a burden."

We are beginning to see what a tremendous price we've paid for our emphasis on independence and autonomy. We have isolated old people and we've cut off the children, the young people, from their grandparents. One of the reasons we have as bad a generation gap today as we do is that grandparents have copped out. Young people are being deprived of the thing they need most—perspective, to know why their parents behave so peculiarly and why their grandparents say the things they do.

In peasant communities where things didn't change and where people died in the beds they were born in, grandparents taught the young what the end of life was going to be. So you looked at your mother, if you were a girl, and learned what it was like to be a bride, a young mother. Then you looked at your grandmother and you knew what it was like to be old. Children learned what it was to age and die while they were small. They were prepared for the end of life at the beginning.

It is interesting to realize that early in human society we developed a method of keeping old women alive. The human being is the only animal to have a menopause. So women do stop having babies, and if they haven't died by the time they stop, women can become quite strong and can live quite a long time. For countless centuries, old women have been around who knew things that no one else knew . . . that ten, twenty, thirty years ago there was a hurricane or a famine, and they knew what people did. And this emphasizes one of the functions of older people in a society. However, today this is a function whose usefulness is disappearing. We can be dead certain that when our grandchildren reach our age, they will not be living as we live today.

Today grandparents, old people in general, have something quite different to contribute. Their generation has seen the most change in the world, and the young today need to learn that there has been change. They need to know about their past before they can understand the present and plot the future.

Young people also need reassurance that change does not mean the end of the world, merely an end to the world as they first saw it. Older people remember that we have had periods of disorder in this country before. Some of them can remember the Time of Troubles in Ireland. Some of them remember the riots after World War I and those after World War II and they remember that we got them in hand. Because the ties between generations have been broken, young people have lost this perspective. 9

Normally we talk about the heartless young people who don't have room for their parents in their lives, much less in their apartments. But old people today have tremendous advantages, and these advantages make them much less dependent. 10

We all look so young to each other. Sometimes we kid ourselves that we look young to the young, which is nonsense. But we have our hair cut and styled in the most modern fashion, dye it in the most modern colors. It is wonderful how young your old friends look. Old people have never been cheered up in this way before. 11

My grandmother may have been treated with a certain respect, but she was formally dressed in a way that her grandmother had been, in a way that made her feel old. Today we dress old people in a way that makes them feel young. 12

On the subways, which I've been riding for fifty years, two things have happened: people have stopped giving up their seats to the old, and old people have stopped accepting seats when they are offered. "I'll stand, thank you." 13

What we need to do is to find a style of aging that will keep and foster this independence, but will encourage old people to be thinking of what they can do for someone else. If we are going to change the style, change the relationship between young and old, older people have to take the lead by finding ways to relate either to their own grandchildren or to someone else's. 14

As long as we say that youth has no need for age, young people in this country aren't interested in old people, in seeing them or listening to them, there will be an enormous number of things in our society that are not being done, but which could be done by old people. □ 15

Thinking about the Reading

TRUE/FALSE QUESTIONS

In the space provided, write T if the sentence is true and F if the sentence is false, based on your reading of the preceding selection.

_____ 1. Young Americans treat their parents in ways similar to how young people in other countries treat their parents.

_____ 2. Historically, more people in the world have lived in multigenerational families than in small family units.

_____ 3. The most important thing the elderly can offer the young is a sense of independence and autonomy.

_____ 4. Today's elderly have seen a lot of change and can share their perspective with the young.

_____ 5. The elderly today dress very differently than elderly people did in the past.

COMPREHENSION QUESTIONS

In answering the following comprehension questions, *paraphrase* the selection—that is, restate it in your own words without copying phrases of more than three or four words from the reading. (See Appendix A for more on how to answer comprehension questions.) Here is an example:

Sample question:
Why does Mead describe the American emphasis on independence and autonomy as "a poor ideal"?

Sample answer (words and phrases from the reading are italicized):
Mead describes the *American* emphasis on *independence and autonomy* as "*a poor ideal*" because it often means people end up *living alone, without friends,* even near *starvation,* so as to be *independent* and not a "*burden*" to anyone.
Here are the questions:

1. What do older Americans presently do for the younger generation?
2. How has the emphasis on independence and autonomy affected both young and old in this country?
3. How does menopause affect both women and society, according to Mead?
4. What does Mead think elderly people of today have to contribute?

OUTLINE

Complete the following outline of Mead's essay by listing the topics she discusses in the space provided.

Paragraph(s) 1: Need for "a new style of aging"
     2: _____
     3: Family units
     4: _____
    5–6: Generational perspective
     7: _____
    8–9: Important contributions of the elderly
  10–13: _____
  14–15: Finding "a new style of aging"

SUMMARY

Use the preceding outline to write a summary of the reading. In the first sentence of your summary, mention the title, the author, and the main topic of the selection. Paraphrase the writer's points in your own words. (See Appendix B for more on how to write a summary.)

Making Connections

REACTING TO THE READING

Write about your personal reaction to the reading. Some possible topics include your agreement or disagreement with a specific issue; a relevant personal experience; an idea that is new to you; a related idea from another source (such as a book, a movie, or a television program); or why you like or dislike the selection.

FINDING RELATED SOURCES

1. Find a picture related to one of the following topics: aging, independence, or another topic discussed in the selection. In writing, describe the picture and relate your thoughts and feelings about it. Discuss your picture and writing with your classmates.
2. Locate a passage in a book, magazine, or newspaper that is related to the reading. In writing, summarize the passage and describe how it relates

to the selection. Discuss the passage and your writing with your class-mates.

Getting Ready to Write

Using the topic *aging* or *generation gap*, or another topic from the reading, spend 10 minutes on *one* of the following prewriting activities: freewriting, clustering, listing, or cubing. (See Appendix C.) Then discuss your prewriting with your classmates.

DISCUSSION AND COMPOSITION QUESTIONS

Choose one or more of the following questions to discuss with your class-mates in preparation for writing.

On Peacemaking Issues

1. What issues raised in the reading are related to the goal of achieving world peace? (For example, are aging or independence and autonomy related to world peace?) Discuss.
2. Do you believe a generation gap exists? Discuss the relations between old and young in a particular place, such as the country you came from or the one you are living in now.
3. What particular situation involving the elderly are you most concerned about? Could you (on your own or with others) do anything to change that situation? If so, what? If not, why?
4. What could be done to work toward the "new style of aging" Mead de-scribes?

On Related Issues

5. Do you believe that we learn what it is to be a woman/man from our mother/father? What it is to be old from our grandparents? Discuss.
6. Describe a movie or book that taught you something about aging. What happens in the movie or book? What is its message?
7. Tell about an independent elderly person you know or have read about. Is the person happy? Why or why not?
8. How do you think you will age?
9. Is it important for people to feel young? Why or why not?

10. If elderly people do not find ways to relate to young people, what will happen?
11. Tell about an elderly person who is happy with her or his life and discuss what the reasons might be.
12. What kind of grandparent will you be? Discuss.

PLANNING TO WRITE

Choose one of the preceding Composition Questions as your writing topic. Begin to plan your paragraph or essay by identifying the topic and listing your thoughts on that topic.

Example: Are independence and autonomy related to world peace? Discuss.

Topic: Independence and autonomy are related to world peace.
—Independence and autonomy are important for human development.
—Recognition of human interdependence is important for world peace.

Then write the first draft of your paragraph or essay. (See Appendixes D and E for more on how to write paragraphs and essays.)

Revising and Editing Your Writing

REVISING YOUR WRITING

Use the Revision Checklist in Appendix F (p. 271) to evaluate the first draft of your (or your classmate's) writing in terms of content and organization. After deciding how your paragraph or essay can be improved, write a second draft incorporating the changes. On the checklist identify the areas in which you had difficulty so you can doublecheck these areas in later writings.

EDITING YOUR WRITING

After you are satisfied with content and organization, use the Editing Checklist in Appendix G (p. 272) to reevaluate your or your classmate's writing. On the checklist identify the areas in which you had difficulty so you can doublecheck these areas in later writings.

10

From Affirming Diversity

SONIA NIETO

Sonia Nieto is an educator working to implement cultural diversity in the higher education curriculum. The following selection is a case study taken from her book *Affirming Diversity* (1992), which examines the sociopolitical context of multicultural education. In this excerpt, Hoang Vinh, a Vietnamese immigrant and high school student, discusses his ideas about education, family, and culture. Through Vinh's own words, Nieto shows us how various factors—personal, social, political, cultural, and educational—can influence the success or failure of students.

Getting Ready to Read

THINKING ABOUT THE TITLE

People define education differently. They also have different ideas about the importance of family and culture. How do you define education? What strengths do you draw from your family? From your culture?

KEY VOCABULARY/CONCEPTS

Discuss with your classmates what you know about some of the following words and concepts.

Vietnam	custom	psychology
good person	educated	good job
school system	teach	punish
grades	college	exam

master's degree	doctorate	help oneself and others
concern	culture	study
language	truth	sensitive

PREREADING QUESTIONS

Before reading the selection, ask yourself and/or discuss with your class-mates the following questions.

1. Are you an "educated" person? What are your reasons for describing yourself in this way?
2. What do you plan to do with your education? Why?
3. What advantages and disadvantages are there to close family relations?
4. What advantages and disadvantages are there to cultural values?

On Becoming "Educated People"

In Vietnam, we go to school because we want to become educated people. But in the United States, most people, they say, "Oh, we go to school because we want to get a good job." But my idea, I don't think so. I say, if we go to school, we want a good job also, but we want to become a good person.

[In Vietnam] we go to school, we have to remember *every single word*. . . . We don't have textbooks, so my teacher write on the blackboard. So we have to copy and go home. . . . So, they say, "You have to remember all the things, like all the words. . . ." But in the United States, they don't need for you remember all the words. They just need you to understand. . . . But two different school systems. They have different things. I think in my Vietnamese school, they are good. But I also think the United States school system is good. They're not the same. . . . They are good, but good in different ways.

When I go to school [in Vietnam], sometimes I don't know how to do something so I ask my teacher. She can spend *all the time* to help me, anything I want. So, they are very nice. . . . My teacher, she was very nice. When I asked her everything, she would answer me, teach me something. That's why I remember. . . . But some of my teachers, they always punished me.

[Grades] are not important to me. Important to me is education. . . . I [am] not concerned about them [test scores] very much. I just need enough for me to go to college. . . . Sometimes, I never care about [grades]. I just know I do my exam very good. But I don't need to know I got A or B. I have to learn more and more.

Sometimes, I got C but I learned very much, I learned a lot, and I feel 5 very sorry, "Why I got only C?" But sometimes, if I got B, that's enough, I don't need A.

Some people, they got a good education. They go to school, they got 6 master's, they got doctorate, but they're just helping themselves. So that's not good. . . . If I got a good education, I get a good job, not helping only myself. I like to help other people. . . . I want to help other people who don't have money, who don't have a house. . . . The first thing is money. If people live without money, they cannot do nothing. So even if I want to help other people, I have to get a good job. I have the money, so that way I can help them.

In class, sometimes we [students] speak Vietnamese because we don't 7 know the words in English. . . . Our English is not good, so that's why we have to speak Vietnamese.

In school, if we get good and better and better, we have to work in 8 groups. Like if we want to discuss something, we have to work in groups, like four people. And we discuss some projects, like that. And different people have different ideas, so after that we choose some best idea. I like work in groups.

Sometimes, the English teachers, they don't understand about us. Be- 9 cause something we not do good, like my English is not good. And she say, "Oh, your English is great!" But that's the way the American culture is. But my culture is not like that. . . . If my English is not good, she has to say, "Your English is not good. So you have to go home and study." And she tell[s] me what to study and how to study to get better. But some Americans, you know, they don't understand about myself. So they just say, "Oh! You're doing a good job! You're doing great! Everything is great!" Teachers talk like that, but my culture is different. . . . They say, "You have to do better. . . ." So, sometimes when I do something not good, and my teachers say, "Oh, you did great!" I don't like it. . . . I want the truth better.

Some teachers, they never concerned to the students. So, they just do 10 something that they have to do. But they don't really do something to help the people, the students. Some teachers, they just go inside and go to the blackboard. . . . They don't care. So that I don't like. . . .

I have a good teacher, Ms. Brown. She's very sensitive. She understands   11
the students, year to year, year after year. . . . She understands a lot. So
when I had her class, we discussed some things very interesting about
America. And sometimes she tells us about something very interesting
about another culture. But Ms. Mitchell, she just knows how to teach for
the children, like ten years old or younger. So some people don't like her.
Like me, I don't like her. I like to discuss something. Not just how to write
"A"; "You have to write like this." So I don't like that. . . . She wants
me to write perfectly. So that is not a good way because we learn another
language. Because when we learn another language, we learn to discuss,
we learn to understand the word's *meaning*, not about how to *write* the
word.

I want to go to college, of course. Right now, I don't know what will   12
happen for the future. . . . If I think of my future, I have to learn more about
psychology. If I have a family, I want a perfect family, not really perfect, but I
want a very good family. So that's why I study psychology. . . . When I grow
up, I get married, I have children, so I have to let them go to school, I have
good education to teach them. So, Vietnamese want their children to grow
up and be polite and go to school, just like I am right now. . . . I just want
they will be a good person.

I don't care much about money. So, I just want to have a normal job that   13
I can take care of myself and my family. So that's enough. I don't want to
climb up compared to other people, because, you know, different people
have different ideas about how to live. So I don't think money is important
to me. I just need enough money for my life.

Strength from Culture and Family

Sometimes I think about [marrying] a Vietnamese girl, because my son   14
or my daughter, in the future, they will speak Vietnamese. So, if I have an
American girlfriend, my children cannot speak Vietnamese. Because I saw
other families who have an American wife or an American husband, their
children cannot speak Vietnamese. It is very hard to learn a language. . . .
In the United States, they have TV, they have radio, every kind of thing, we
have to do English. So, that why I don't think my children can learn
Vietnamese.

When I sleep, I like to think a little bit about my country. And I feel very   15
good. I always think about my fathers [parents] . . . my family . . . what gifts

they get me before, how they were with me when I was young. . . . Those are very good things to remember and to try to repeat again.

I've been here for three years, but the first two years I didn't learn anything. I got sick, mental. I got mental. Because when I came to the United States, I missed my fathers [parents], my family, and my friends, and my Vietnam.

So, everytime I go to sleep, I cannot sleep. I don't want to eat anything. So I become sick.

I am a very sad person. Sometimes, I just want to be alone to think about myself. I feel sorry about what I do wrong with someone. Whatever I do wrong in the past, I just think and I feel sorry for myself.

I never have a good time. I go to the mall, but I don't feel good. . . . I just sit there, I don't know what to do.

Before I got mental, okay, I feel very good about myself, like I am smart, I learn a lot of things. . . . But after I got mental, I don't get enjoyment. . . . I'm not smart anymore.

After I got mental, I don't enjoy anything. Before that, I enjoy lots. Like I listen to music, I go to school and talk to my friends. . . . But now I don't feel I enjoy anything. Just talk with my friends, that's enough, that's my enjoyment.

My culture is my country. We love my country; we love our people; we love the way Vietnamese, like they talk very nice and they are very polite to all the people.

For Vietnamese, [culture] is very important. . . . I think my country is a great country. The people is very courageous. They never scared to do anything. . . . If we want to get something, we have to get it. Vietnamese culture is like that. . . . We work hard, and we get something we want.

If I have children, I have teach them from [when] they grow up to when they get older. So, when they get older, I don't have to teach them, but they listen to me. Because that's education, not only myself, but all Vietnamese, from a long time ago to now. That's the custom. So that's why I like my customs and my culture.

Every culture . . . they have good things and they have bad things. And my culture is the same. But sometimes they're different because they come from different countries. . . . America is so different. . . .

[My teachers] understand something, just not all Vietnamese culture. Like they just understand something outside. . . . But they cannot understand something inside our hearts.

[Teachers should] understand the students. Like Ms. Mitchell, she just say, 27
"Oh, you have to do it this way, you have to do that way." But some people,
they came from different countries. They have different ideas, so they might
think about school in different ways. So maybe she has to know why they
think in that way. . . . Because different cultures, they have different mean-
ings about education. So she has to learn about that culture.

I think they just think that they understand our culture. . . . But it is very 28
hard to tell them, because that's our feelings.

When I came to United States, I heard English, so I say, "Oh, very funny 29
sound." Very strange to me. But I think they feel the same like when we
speak Vietnamese. So they hear and they say, "What a strange language."
Some people like to listen. But some people don't like to listen. So, if I talk
with Americans, I never talk Vietnamese.

Some teachers don't understand about the language. So sometimes, my 30
language, they say it sounds funny. And sometimes, all the languages sound
funny. Sometimes, she [teacher] doesn't let us speak Vietnamese, or some
people speak Cambodian. Sometimes, she already knows some Spanish, so
she lets Spanish speak. But because she doesn't know about Vietnamese language, so she doesn't let Vietnamese speak. . . .

[Teachers] have to know about our culture. And they have to help the 31
people learn whatever they want. From the second language, it is very difficult for me and for other people.

I want to learn something good from my culture and something good 32
from American culture. And I want to take both cultures and select something good . . . you know. . . . If we live in the United States, we have to
learn something about new people.

[To keep reading and writing Vietnamese] is very important. . . . So, I 33
like to learn English, but I like to learn my language too. Because different
languages, they have different things, special. [My younger sisters] are very
good. They don't need my help. They already know. They write to my parents and they keep reading Vietnamese books. . . . Sometimes they forget to
pronounce the words, but I help them. . . .

At home, we eat Vietnamese food. . . . The important thing is rice. Every- 34
body eats rice, and vegetables, and meat. They make different kinds of food.
. . . The way I grew up, I had to learn, I had to know it. By looking at other
people—when my mother cooked, and I just see it, and so I know it.

Right now, I like to listen to my music and I like to listen to American 35
music. . . . And I like to listen to other music from other countries.

We tell them [parents] about what we do at school and what we do at home and how nice the people around us, and what we will do better in the future to make them happy. Something not good, we don't write. . . . 36

They miss us and they want ourselves to live together. . . . They teach me how to live without them. □ 37

Thinking about the Reading

TRUE/FALSE QUESTIONS

In the space provided, write T if the sentence is true and F if the sentence is false, based on your reading of the preceding selection.

_____ 1. The school systems in Vietnam and the United States are the same.

_____ 2. Hoang Vinh believes that it is not good if one has an education and does not help others too.

_____ 3. According to Hoang Vinh, we learn another language in order to understand more, not just to write it.

_____ 4. Hoang Vinh was fortunate because he had no problems adjusting to his new life in America.

_____ 5. People from different countries may have different ideas about school.

COMPREHENSION QUESTIONS

In answering the following comprehension questions, *paraphrase* the selection—that is, restate it in your own words without copying phrases of more than three or four words from the reading. (See Appendix A for more on how to answer comprehension questions.) Here is an example:

Sample question:
How does Hoang Vinh describe the differences between the Vietnamese and American school systems?

Sample answer (words and phrases from the reading are italicized):
According to Hoang Vinh, people in Vietnam go to school *to become "educated,"* but people in the United States go to school *to get a good job.* Also, in Vietnamese schools, students memorize a lot, whereas in American schools students are supposed to *understand.*

Here are the questions.

1. What do teachers do that Vinh feels is helpful?
2. Why does Vinh think of marrying a Vietnamese woman?
3. What was Vinh's condition when he "got mental"?
4. How does Vinh feel about his language and culture?

OUTLINE

Complete the following outline of the Nieto selection by listing the topics discussed in the space provided.

Paragraph(s) 1: Definition of *educated*

    2–3: _____

    4–5: Grades

       6: _____

    7–11: What helps students to learn

  12–13: _____

  14–15: Thoughts about culture and family

  16–21: _____

  22–25: Feelings about Vietnamese culture

  26–27: _____

  28–30: Feelings about use of first language

  31–35: _____

  36–37: Correspondence with parents

SUMMARY

Use the preceding outline to write a summary of the reading. In the first sentence of your summary, mention the title, the author, and the main topic of the selection. Paraphrase the writer's points in your own words. (See Appendix B for more on how to write a summary.)

Making Connections

REACTING TO THE READING

Write about your personal reaction to the reading. Some possible topics include your agreement or disagreement with a specific issue; a relevant personal experience; an idea that is new to you; a related idea from another source (such as a book, a movie, or a television program); or why you like or dislike the selection.

FINDING RELATED SOURCES

1. Find a picture related to one of the following topics: culture and learning style, school systems, or another topic discussed in the selection. In writing, describe the picture and relate your thoughts and feelings about it. Discuss your picture and writing with your classmates.
2. Find a passage in a book, magazine, or newspaper that is related to the reading. In writing, summarize the passage and describe how it relates to the selection. Discuss the passage and your writing with your classmates.

Getting Ready to Write

PREWRITING ACTIVITIES

Using the topic *culture and learning*, or another topic from the reading, spend 10 minutes on *one* of the following prewriting activities: freewriting, clustering, listing, or cubing. (See Appendix C.) Then discuss your prewriting with your classmates.

DISCUSSION AND COMPOSITION QUESTIONS

Choose one or more of the following questions to discuss with your classmates in preparation for writing.

On Peacemaking Issues

1. What issues raised in the reading are related to the goal of achieving world peace through intercultural harmony?
2. Is culture related to world peace? Discuss.
3. Is learning related to world peace? Discuss.
4. Do many people understand how culture and learning influence each other? Discuss.
5. Describe a situation of cross-cultural conflict in a particular place and explain why it exists there.
6. What could help resolve a particular cross-cultural conflict? For example, might education play a role? Why or why not?
7. Tell about an example of cross-cultural conflict that you saw or read about. Was it resolved? Why or why not?

8. What particular educational situation are you most concerned about? Could you (on your own or with others) do anything to improve the situation? If so, what? If not, why?

9. Describe an educational situation in which the dominant culture is different from the culture of the students.

10. Does culture affect how you learn? Have you made cultural adjustments? Discuss.

11. Tell about a movie or book that presents an educational issue. What happens in the movie or book? What is its message?

12. Is education the most important factor in your future? Why or why not?

13. Why is it important for people to understand other cultures? If people do not understand other cultures, how will it affect their lives?

14. Tell about someone who has resolved cultural conflicts and is happy with her or his life.

PLANNING TO WRITE

Choose one of the preceding Composition Questions as your writing topic. Begin to plan your paragraph or essay by identifying the topic and listing your thoughts on that topic.

Example: Why is it important for people to understand other cultures?

Topic: The importance of cross-cultural understanding

—If we understand other cultures, we have more opportunities for learning.

—If we do not understand other cultures, we have less of a chance of achieving world peace.

Then write the first draft of your paragraph or essay. (See Appendixes D and E for more on how to write paragraphs and essays.)

Revising and Editing Your Writing

REVISING YOUR WRITING

Use the Revision Checklist in Appendix F (p. 271) to evaluate the first draft of your (or your classmate's) writing in terms of content and organization. After deciding how your paragraph or essay can be improved, write a second

draft incorporating the changes. On the checklist identify the areas in which you had difficulty so you can doublecheck these areas in later writings.

EDITING YOUR WRITING

After you are satisfied with content and organization, use the Editing Checklist in Appendix G (p. 272) to reevaluate your (or your classmate's) writing. On the checklist identify the areas in which you had difficulty so you can doublecheck these areas in later writings.

II

An Education
in Language

RICHARD RODRIGUEZ

Born in the United States to immigrant parents, Richard Rodriguez did not learn English until he went to school. He has written about his experience with learning the "public language" of education and the effects of his efforts in *Hunger of Memory* (1982). In the following selection, taken from *State of the Language* (1990), Rodriguez, a native speaker of Spanish, discusses how learning English and succeeding in school affected him and his family.

Getting Ready to Read

THINKING ABOUT THE TITLE

Do you remember learning your first language? How did that experience differ from your efforts to learn a second language?

KEY VOCABULARY/CONCEPTS

Discuss with your classmates what you know about some of the following words and concepts.

education	dilemma	public/classroom language
family language	anglicize	socially disadvantaged
gringo	progress	tutoring

public identity	loss	academic success
achievement	anger	guilt
Americanization	silence	authority figure
self-consciousness	intimacy	job advancement
condescending	confidence	separation
anti-poverty agency	secret	scholarship
submit	shame	bilingual

PREREADING QUESTIONS

Before reading the selection, ask yourself and/or discuss with your classmates the following questions.

1. How do you feel about the way you use your first language? Why?
2. How do you feel about the way you use your second language? Why?
3. In what situations do you use your first language?
4. In what situations do you use your second language?
5. Why do you use one language more or less frequently than the other in
   certain situations?

Some educationists have recently told me that I received a very bad education. They are proponents of bilingual schooling, that remarkable innova-
tion—the latest scheme—to improve education. They think it is a shame, a
disgrace, that my earliest teachers never encouraged me to speak Spanish,
"my family language," when I entered the classroom.

Those educators who tell me such things, however, do not understand
the kind of dilemma I faced when I started my schooling. A socially disadvantaged child, I desperately needed to be taught that I had the obligation—
the right—to speak *public* language. (Until I was nearly seven years old, I
had been almost always surrounded by the sounds of my family's Spanish,
which kept me safely at home and made me a stranger in public.) In school,
I was initially terrified by the language of *gringos.* Silent, waiting for the bell
to go home, dazed, diffident, I couldn't believe that English concerned me.
The teacher in the (Catholic) school I attended kept calling out my name,
anglicizing it as *Rich-heard Road-ree-guess,* telling me with her sounds that I had
a public identity. But I couldn't believe her. I wouldn't respond.

Classroom words were used in ways very different from family words;
they were directed to a general audience. (The nun remarked in a friendly,

but oddly theatrical voice, "Speak up, Richard. And tell it to the entire class, not just to me.") Classroom words, moreover, meant just what they said. (*Grammar* school.) The teacher quizzed: Why do we use that word in this sentence? Could I think of a better word to use there? Would the sentence change its meaning if the words were differently arranged? And wasn't there a much better way of saying the same thing?

I couldn't say. 4

Eventually my teachers connected my silence with the difficult progress 5 my older brother and sister were making. All three of us were directed to daily tutoring sessions. I was the "slow learner" who needed a year and a half of special attention. I also needed my teachers to keep my attention from straying in class by calling out, "Richard!" And most of all I needed to hear my parents speak English at home—as my teachers had urged them to do.

The scene was inevitable: one Saturday morning, when I entered a room 6 where my mother and father were talking, I did not realize that they were speaking Spanish until the moment they saw me they abruptly started speaking English. The *gringo* sounds they uttered (had previously spoken only to strangers) startled me, pushed me away. In that moment of trivial misunderstanding and profound insight I felt my throat twisted by a grief I didn't sound as I left the room. But I had no place to escape to with Spanish. (My brothers were speaking English in another part of the house.) Again and again in the weeks following, increasingly angry, I would hear my parents uniting to urge, "Speak to us now, *en inglés.*" Only then did it happen, my teachers' achievement, my greatest academic success: I raised my hand in the classroom and volunteered an answer and did not think it remarkable that the entire class understood. That day I moved very far from the disadvantaged child I had been only weeks before.

But this great public success was measured at home by a feeling of loss. 7 We remained a loving family—enormously different. No longer were we as close as we had earlier been. (No longer so desperate for the consolation of intimacy.) My brothers and I didn't rush home after school. Even our parents grew easier in public, following the Americanization of their children. My mother started referring to neighbors by name. My father continued to speak about *gringos*, but the word was no longer charged with bitterness and suspicion. Hearing it sometimes, I wasn't even sure if my father was saying the Spanish word, *gringo*, or saying, gringo, in English.

Our house was no longer noisy. And for that I blamed my mother and father, since they had encouraged our classroom success. I flaunted my second-grade knowledge as a kind of punishment. ("Two negatives make a positive!") But this anger was spent after several months, replaced by a feeling of guilt as school became more and more important to me. Increasingly successful in class, I would come home a troubled son, aware that education was making me different from my parents. Sadly I would listen as my mother or father tried unsuccessfully (laughing self-consciously) to help my brothers with homework assignments. 8

My teachers became the new figures of authority in my life. I began imitating their accents. I trusted their every direction. Each book they told me to read, I read and then waited for them to tell me which books I enjoyed. Their most casual opinions I adopted. I stayed after school "to help"—to get their attention. It was their encouragement that mattered to me. Memory caressed each word of their praise so that compliments teachers paid me in grammar school classes come quickly to mind even today. 9

Withheld from my parents was any mention of what happened at school. In late afternoon, in the midst of preparing our dinner, my mother would come up behind me while I read. Her head just above mine, her breath scented with food, she'd ask, "What are you reading?" Or: "Tell me about all your new courses." I would just barely respond. "Just the usual things, ma." (Silence, Silence! Instead of the intimate sounds which had once flowed between us, there was this silence.) After dinner, I would rush off to a bedroom with papers and books. As often as possible, I resisted parental pleas to "save lights" by staying in the kitchen to work. I kept so much, so often to myself. Nights when relatives visited and the front room was warmed by familiar Spanish sounds, I slipped out of the house. 10

I was a fourth-grade student when my mother asked me one day for a "nice" book to read. ("Something not too hard which you think I might like.") Carefully, I chose Willa Cather's My Antonia.* When, several days later, I happened to see it next to her bed, unread except for the first several pages, I felt a surge of sorrow, a need for my mother's embrace. That feeling passed by the time I had taken the novel back to my room. 11

*A novel written in 1918 about the life of an immigrant from Bohemia who lives on the western frontier of the United States and whose strength of character sees her through many hardships.

"Your parents must be so proud of you. . . ." People began to say that to   12
me about the time I was in sixth grade. I'd smile shyly, never betraying my
sense of the irony.

"Why didn't you tell me about the award?" my mother scolded—al-   13
though her face was softened by pride. At the grammar school ceremony,
several days later, I heard my father speak to a teacher and felt ashamed of
his accent. Then guilty for the shame. My teacher's words were edged sharp
and clean. I admired her until I sensed that she was condescending to them.
I grew resentful. Protective, I tried to move my parents away. "You both
must be so proud of him," she said. They quickly responded. (They were
proud.) "We are proud of all our children." Then this afterthought: "They
sure didn't get their brains from us." They laughed.

Always I knew my parents wanted for my brothers and me the chances   14
they had never had. It saddened my mother to learn of relatives who forced
their children to start working right after high school. To her children she
would say, "Get all the education you can." In schooling she recognized the
key to job advancement. As a girl, new to America, she had been awarded
a high school diploma by teachers too careless or busy to notice that she
hardly spoke English. On her own, she determined to learn how to type.
That skill got her clean office jobs in "letter shops" and nurtured her opti-
mism about the possibility of advancement. (Each morning, when her sisters put on uniforms, she chose a bright-colored dress.) The years of young
womanhood passed and her typing speed increased. Also, she became an
excellent speller of words she mispronounced. ("And I've never been to college," she would say, smiling when her children asked her to spell a word
they didn't want to look up in a dictionary.)

After her youngest child began high school, my mother once more got   15
an office job. She worked for the (California) state government in civil service positions, numbered and secured by examinations. The old ambition of
her youth was still bright then. Regularly she consulted bulletin boards for
news of openings, further advancements. Until one day she saw mentioned
something about an "anti-poverty agency." A typing job—part of the governor's staff. ("A knowledge of Spanish required.") Without hesitation she applied, and grew nervous only when the job was suddenly hers.

"Everyone comes to work all dressed up," she reported at night. And   16
didn't need to say more than that her co-workers would not let her answer
the phones. She was, after all, only a typist, though a very fast typist. And an
excellent speller. One day there was a letter to be sent to a Washington cabi-

net officer. On the dictating tape there was reference to urban guerillas. My mother typed (the wrong word, correctly): "gorillas." The mistake horrified the anti-poverty bureaucrats. They returned her to her previous job. She would go no further. So she willed her ambition to her children.

"Get all the education you can," she would repeatedly say. "With education you can do anything." When I was a freshman in high school, I admitted to her one day that I planned to become a teacher. And that pleased her. Though I never explained that it was not the occupation of teaching I yearned for as much as something more elusive and indefinite: I wanted to know what my teachers knew; to possess their authority and their confidence. 17

The separation which slowly unraveled (so long) between my parents and me was not the much-discussed "generation gap" caused by the tension of youth and experience. Age figured in our separation, but in a very odd way. Year after year, advancing in my studies, I would notice that my parents had not changed as much as I. They oddly measured my progress. Often I realized that my command of English was improving, for example, because at home I would hear myself simplify my diction and syntax when addressing my parents. 18

Too deeply troubled, I did not join my brothers when, as high school students, they toyed with our parents' opinions, devastating them frequently with superior logic and factual information. My mother and father would usually submit with sudden silence, although there were times when my mother complained that our "big ideas" were going to our heads. More acute was her complaint that the family wasn't as close as some of our relatives. It was toward me that she most often would glance when she mimicked the "yes" and "no" answers she got in response to her questions. (My father never asked.) Why was everyone "so secret," she wondered. (I never said.) 19

When the time came to go to college, I was the first in the family who asked to leave home. My departure only made physically apparent the separation that had occurred long before. But it was too stark a reminder. In the months preceding my departure, I heard the question my mother never asked except indirectly. In the hot kitchen, tired at the end of the workday, she demanded to know, "Why aren't the colleges around here good enough for you? They were for your brother and sister." Another time, in the car, never turning to face me, she wondered, "Why do you need to go so far 20 away?" Late one night, ironing, she said with disgust, "Why do you have to put us through this big expense? You know your scholarship will never cover it all." But when September came, there was a rush to get everything ready. In a bedroom that last night, I packed the brown valise. My mother sat nearby sewing my initials onto the clothes I would take. And she said nothing more about my leaving. ☐

Thinking about the Reading

TRUE/FALSE QUESTIONS

In the space provided, write T if the sentence is true and F if the sentence is false, based on your reading of the preceding selection.

_____ 1. Rodriguez was one of the first students to experience bilingual education.

_____ 2. Rodriguez's "family language" and classroom language were different.

_____ 3. Academic success gave Rodriguez a sense of loss at home.

_____ 4. He succeeded because his parents helped him each day with his schoolwork.

_____ 5. Although he went away to college, Rodriguez remained close to his parents.

COMPREHENSION QUESTIONS

In answering the following comprehension questions, paraphrase the selection—that is, restate it in your own words without copying phrases of more than three or four words from the reading. (See Appendix A for more on how to answer comprehension questions.) Here is an example:

Sample question:
Why do certain educators who support bilingual schooling think that Rodriguez had a bad education?

Sample answer (words and phrases from the reading are italicized):
Some educators who support *bilingual education* believe Rodriguez had *a bad education* because he was discouraged from maintaining his first language.

Here are the questions:

1. In what ways was Rodriguez "a socially disadvantaged child"?
2. How did his parents' use of English at home affect Rodriguez?
3. What stopped his mother from further advancement at work?
4. How did his parents react to his going away to college?

OUTLINE

Complete the following outline of the Rodriguez selection by listing the topics he discusses in the space provided.

Paragraph(s) 1–2: Young Rodriguez's need to learn the "public language"

   3: _____

4–5: His family's difficulty with English

   6: _____

7–8: Sense of loss at home

   9: _____

10–11: Withdrawal from parents

12–13: _____

   14: Importance of education to parents

15–16: _____

   17: Rodriguez's desire to be a teacher

18–19: _____

   20: Rodriguez's departure for college

SUMMARY

Use the preceding outline to write a summary of the reading. In the first sentence of your summary, mention the title, the author, and the main topic of the selection. Paraphrase the writer's points in your own words. (See Appendix B for more on how to write a summary.)

Making Connections

REACTING TO THE READING

Write about your personal reaction to the reading. Some possible topics include your agreement or disagreement with a specific issue; a relevant experience; an idea that is new to you; a related idea from another source (such as a book, a movie, or a television program); or why you like or dislike the selection.

1. Interview someone you know about language education or another topic discussed in the selection. Here are some sample questions:

   Do you know more than one language? Why or why not?

   Is it important to learn other languages? Explain.

   Take notes during the interview. Then, using your notes, write a summary of the interview that includes your reaction as well. Discuss the interview and your summary with your classmates.

2. Find a passage in a book, magazine, or newspaper that is related to the reading. In writing, summarize the passage and describe how it relates to the selection. Discuss the passage and your writing with your classmates.

Getting Ready to Write

PREWRITING ACTIVITIES

Using the topic *language education* or *academic success*, or another topic from the reading, spend 10 minutes on *one* of the following prewriting activities: freewriting, clustering, listing, or cubing. (See Appendix C.) Then discuss your prewriting with your classmates.

DISCUSSION AND COMPOSITION QUESTIONS

Choose one or more of the following questions to discuss with your classmates in preparation for writing.

On Peacemaking Issues

1. What issues raised in the reading are related to the goal of achieving world peace?
2. Is language education related to world peace? Discuss.
3. How is being socially disadvantaged related to world peace? Discuss.
4. Is language education related to social advantages and disadvantages? Discuss.
5. If learning other languages is useful, why might some people have mixed or negative feelings about learning other languages? For example, you might compare and contrast the views expressed by Rodriguez in this selection with those of the Vietnamese student Hoang Vinh in "From *Affirming Diversity*" by Nieto (Chapter 10).

6. Describe a difficult language-learning situation and explain why it is difficult. What could be done to encourage language learning in this situation? Will the situation be improved in the future? Why or why not?

7. What particular language-learning situation are you most concerned about? Could you (on your own or with others) do anything to improve the situation? If so, what? If not, why?

On Related Issues

8. Describe a situation in which you or another student had difficulties learning a second language.

9. Based on your own experience, has learning another language changed you as a person? Discuss.

10. Describe a movie or book that examines a language-learning experience. What happens in the movie or book? What is its message?

11. Tell about an example of language learning that you saw or read about. Was the learner successful? Why or why not?

12. In your opinion, is learning another language useful? Why or why not? If people do not use any language well, how might this affect their lives?

13. Tell about someone who is both bilingual (or multilingual) and successful.

14. Do you consider yourself a competent language user? Discuss. (You might compare your own experience with Rodriguez's in this chapter or Hoang Vinh's in Chapter 10.)

PLANNING TO WRITE

Choose one of the preceding Composition Questions as your writing topic. Begin to plan your paragraph or essay by identifying the topic and listing your thoughts on that topic.

Example: Do you consider yourself a competent language user? Discuss.

Topic: Competent language use
       —Confidence in my abilities in my first language
       —Abilities and limitations in my other languages

Then write the draft of your paragraph or essay. (See Appendixes D and E for more on how to write paragraphs and essays.)

Revising and Editing Your Writing

REVISING YOUR WRITING

Use the Revision Checklist in Appendix F (p. 271) to evaluate the first draft of your (or your classmate's) writing in terms of content and organization. After deciding how your paragraph or essay can be improved, write a second draft incorporating the changes. On the checklist identify the areas in which you had difficulty so you can doublecheck these areas in later writings.

EDITING YOUR WRITING

After you are satisfied with content and organization, use the Editing Checklist in Appendix G (p. 272) to reevaluate your (or your classmate's) writing. On the checklist identify the areas in which you had difficulty so you can doublecheck these areas in later writings.

Children and War

NEIL BOOTHBY

Neil Boothby is a psychologist who has worked with war refugees in Asia, Africa, and Central America. In the following selection from *Generations—A Universal Family Album* (1987), which evolved from an exhibit at the Smithsonian Institution's International Gallery, the writer discusses children's involvement in modern warfare and our obligation to protect them from it.

Getting Ready to Read

THINKING ABOUT THE TITLE

Do you know of any children who have been directly involved in or affected by a war? In what ways were their lives affected?

KEY VOCABULARY/CONCEPTS

Discuss with your classmates what you know about some of the following words and concepts.

victim	conflict	battlefield
casualty	witness	morale
civil war	intervene	recruit
outside forces	survivor	indiscriminate
exterminate	select target	retaliation
methodical	popular support	indoctrination
terrorism	national pride	call to duty

religious fervor	rite of passage	execution
relief worker	quiet diplomacy	moral sensibility/ purpose
basic rights	civilian	perpetrator

PREREADING QUESTIONS

Before reading the selection, ask yourself and/or discuss with your classmates the following questions.

1. Should children be involved in war activities?
2. What are your reasons for believing that children should or should not be
   involved in war?
3. If children should be protected from war activities, what could be done to
   protect them?
4. If children are affected by war, what should happen to those who are responsible for involving them?

The drawing is stark and simple, devoid of any details that give a sense of   1
time or place. A nine-year-old Maya Indian, at my urging, has drawn a picture of his homeland. But nowhere in the image are the verdant mountains
or the adobe homes of his former village, in Guatemala's highland province
of Huehuetenango. Only three black figures are evident on an otherwise
blank sheet of paper. Tumbled onto the right half of the page are a head and
an arm, both having been severed by a bayonet-wielding figure on the left.
The small, dark-eyed boy told me he was so close to the murder that he
heard the gurgles as the victim's throat was cut. As he related this grisly
detail, his face flushed and he began to perspire. Then, in a whisper, he
recalled: "Both of them were boys not much older than me."

At least 50,000 Maya Indians died in Guatemala between 1981 and   2
1984, and probably many more. No one knows exactly how many or what
percentage of the victims were children. But it is known that children com-
prised over 60 percent of the populations in villages like Coya, Suntelaj,
Finca San Francisco, Santa Teresa, Estancia de la Virgen—where all, or nearly
all, the residents were killed.

In one sense, Guatemala is only in part unique. Indeed, the almost un-   3
imaginable experience of the young boy, in which the victim, the perpetrator, and the witness of violence were all children, tells us much about
war in our age.

Wartime deaths of civilians in general, and of children in particular, have been rising sharply throughout this century. Only about 5 percent of World War I's casualties were civilians. During the Second World War, that figure rose to 50 percent. By the Vietnam War, the civilian death toll reached the 80 percent mark, only to be eclipsed by current-day conflicts, such as in Lebanon, in which 90 percent of the casualties are mothers and children. Today, more children than ever are bombed in their schools, burned alive in their homes, and shot while fleeing down urban alleyways or mountain paths.

Much of this steep increase in civilian casualties is because wars are no longer fought on battlefields between two opposing armies. In what are now largely internal conflicts or civil wars (even though outside forces often intervene), insurgents camouflage themselves within larger populations, and in many cases forcibly recruit children into their cause. Counterinsurgents respond by destroying entire regions of the countryside in an effort to undermine a people's economic base and morale, and to expose and exterminate enemy forces. Rather than attempting to distinguish civilian from combatant, whole villages are massacred and survivors relocated to zones controlled by the military.

But not all of these children are killed as a result of indiscriminate attacks on villages or towns. Or because, at least for older boys, they might someday become insurgents. Children of both sexes and all ages are being methodically maimed or murdered. In Guatemala, parents from seven villages in Huehuetenango told me how children were killed while adults were left unharmed. In Afghanistan, children have lost hands, eyes, and even their lives by picking up booby-trapped miniature airplanes, stuffed animals, or other tempting toys. In El Salvador, Nicaragua, Ethiopia, and elsewhere, children have become the select target of violence. This is how one 24-year-old Guatamalan mother described the military's retaliation against a village suspected of aiding the guerrillas:

> [This] time the soldiers said we had to be punished. They pushed five boys forward, made them lie face-down on the ground, and shot them in the back. A baby girl was then pulled from her mother's arms and her skull crushed against the side of a house. The last death occurred when a soldier cut open the stomach of a pregnant woman, saying that even our unborn will not be spared.

Why are children, the future of any community, if not the world itself, being singled out in today's wars? Paradoxically, it is precisely because they are so precious to us. To destroy what is of highest value to someone is clearly an "effective" form of terrorism; to kill and injure children is to rob a family or an entire group of its future. What better way to undermine popular support for a cause than to attack what we love and value most?

And today, more than ever, children themselves are bearing weapons in armed conflicts. Often, the young recruits undergo heavy indoctrination mixing religious fervor with national pride to intensify the call to duty; schools and media reinforce the message. In Iran, thousands of 10- and 11-year-olds were sent to their deaths carrying keys they were told would ensure their entrance into paradise. Handicapped children were used as human mine detectors to explode mines in the path of advancing tanks. 9

The lack of food and protection has turned many a child into a soldier. "I have a gun, food, and a place to sleep," one nine-year-old Ugandan recently told a relief worker. "That's more than I had in my village. If I'd stayed there I'd probably be dead by now." 10

Children also have been expected to commit violent murders against civilians as a kind of rite of passage into the combat forces. During "la violencia" in Colombia, boys were sometimes forced to kill children their own age to gain entry into paramilitary groups, often their sole protection from the same fate. Most carried out the executions only after they were severely beaten. Indeed, many of these child executioners were reluctant at first but—under the watchful eye of adult overseers—their initial feelings of fear and guilt were transformed into the kind of rage that obliterates all moral sensibility. As one Khmer Rouge leader told me: "It usually takes a little time but the younger ones become the most efficient soldiers of all." 11

Why have we failed so miserably to protect these children? Not because we lack legislation, it seems, but because we lack the will and the means to implement it. While most countries have signed the Geneva Conventions, few have abided by them when directly involved in war themselves, or when selling arms and providing military aid to other embattled nations. On the other hand, less than 30 countries have formally agreed to uphold the 1977 Geneva Protocols, which set forth the strongest prohibitions against the use of children in armed conflicts. Moreover, a number of these signatories have since recruited and trained underaged children as armed combatants. 12

And despite all the past tragedies, there is still no viable structure, no Amnesty International for Children so to speak, to safeguard their basic rights. In war and refugee situations, the International Committee of the 13

Red Cross and the United Nations High Commissioner for Refugees have mandates to do so. As United Nations bodies, however, both must function through quiet diplomacy with national governments, whose cooperation is seen as essential, especially when operating in countries that have not ratified the conventions and protocols. Critics suggest that this sometimes leads to silent bargains in which protection issues are neither aggressively pursued nor publicly disclosed. Nongovernmental relief organizations, which often provide assistance directly to children endangered by war and uprooting, also have been caught in this bind. Since they are only "guests" of the governments in most of the countries in which they work, they find that their programs are sometimes shut down and their personnel threatened or expelled when they protest too loudly.

But no one can expect any of these organizations to shoulder the burden alone. Any attempt to realize a moral purpose demands the constant attention of a much broader audience: us. As people and parents, as members of professional and religious groups, and as citizens of nations and the world, the obligation to ensure that children's rights are recognized and protected is ultimately our own. "Why don't more people know who the guns are pointed at?" is the way one Guatemalan mother once put it to me, a question many of our world's children need answered. □

14

Thinking about the Reading

TRUE/FALSE QUESTIONS

In the space provided, write T if the sentence is true and F if the sentence is false, based on your reading of the preceding selection.

_____ 1. Wartime deaths of civilians have remained basically the same throughout history.

_____ 2. Children have become targets of violence because it is an effective form of terrorism.

_____ 3. Children kill others for food, protection, and as a result of indoctrination.

_____ 4. Children remain unprotected because we lack the will and the means to implement existing legislation.

_____ 5. Organizations such as the International Red Cross and the United Nations are the best means available to protect children from modern warfare.

COMPREHENSION QUESTIONS

In answering the following comprehension questions, *paraphrase* the selection—that is, restate it in your own words without copying phrases of more than three or four words from the reading. (See Appendix A for more on how to answer comprehension questions.) Here is an example:

Sample question:
What do the Guatemalan child's drawing and experience suggest about modern warfare?

Sample answer (words and phrases from the reading are italicized):
The Guatemalan child's *drawing* and *experience* show us that modern warfare increasingly involves children of all ages as *victims, perpetrators,* and *witnesses.*
Here are the questions:

1. Why have children become increasingly more involved in war?
2. How are children forced into participating in war?
3. According to Boothby, why haven't we succeeded in protecting children from war?
4. What political or diplomatic means might we use to protect children from war?

OUTLINE

Complete the following outline of the Boothby reading by listing the topics he discusses in the space provided.

Paragraph(s) 1–3: Guatemalan child's story as example of modern war

    4: _____

    5: Changing nature of war

  6–7: _____

    8: Children as pawns in war

    9: _____

10–11: Turning children into soldiers

   12: _____

   13: Inadequate safeguarding of children's rights

   14: _____

SUMMARY

Use the preceding outline to write a summary of the reading. In the first sentence of your summary, mention the title, the author, and the main topic of the selection. Paraphrase the writer's points in your own words. (See Appendix B for more on how to write a summary.)

Making Connections

REACTING TO THE READING

Write about your personal reaction to the reading. Some possible topics include your agreement or disagreement with a specific issue; a relevant personal experience; an idea that is new to you; a related idea from another source (such as a book, a movie, or a television program); or why you like or dislike the selection.

FINDING RELATED SOURCES

1. Find a picture related to one of the following topics: children in war, terrorism, or another topic discussed in the selection. In writing, describe the picture and relate your thoughts and feelings about it. Discuss your picture and writing with your classmates.
2. Find a passage in a book, magazine, or newspaper that is related to the reading. In writing, summarize the passage and describe how it relates to the selection. Discuss the passage and your writing with your classmates.

Getting Ready to Write

PREWRITING ACTIVITIES

Using the topic *children in war* or *terrorism*, or another topic from the reading, spend 10 minutes on *one* of the following prewriting activities: freewriting, clustering, listing, or cubing. (See Appendix C.) Then discuss your prewriting with your classmates.

DISCUSSION AND COMPOSITION QUESTIONS

Choose one or more of the following questions to discuss with your classmates in preparation for writing.

On Peacemaking Issues

1. What issues raised in the reading are related to the goal of achieving world peace?
2. How is the protection of children related to world peace?
3. Is moral purpose related to world peace? Do most people have a sense of moral purpose? Discuss.
4. If it is important to protect children, why do so many children continue to die in wars?
5. Describe a particular situation that you know of in which many civilians were hurt or killed as a result of a military conflict.
6. Explain why in a particular situation civilians' lives are at risk. What could be done to help eliminate the threat to civilian life? Will the situation improve in the future? Why or why not?
7. What particular situation involving a risk to civilians are you most concerned about? Could you (on your own or with others) do anything to improve the situation? If so, what? If not, why?

On Related Issues

8. Describe the circumstances (if any) under which you could understand or accept an outcome involving civilian casualties.
9. How has the increase in civilian casualties of war affected the world today? Discuss.
10. Describe a movie or book about war. What happens in the movie or book? What is its message?
11. Tell about an example of wartime injustice that you saw or read about. Was the guilty person (or persons) punished? Why or why not?
12. What might be the effects on a child who has witnessed, has been a victim of, or has been a perpetrator of a violent conflict? Discuss.
13. Describe how one particular country has failed to protect its children from violence.
14. Tell about one or more ways that we might better protect the welfare of children in the future.
15. Why aren't countries that violate the existing rules prohibiting the use of children in armed conflicts punished for their actions?

16. How might we increase the number of "people [who] know who the guns are pointed at" (paragraph 14)? Discuss.

PLANNING TO WRITE

Choose one of the preceding Composition Questions as your writing topic. Begin to plan your paragraph or essay by identifying the topic and listing your thoughts on that topic.

Example: If it is important to protect children from war, why do so many children continue to die in wars?

Topic: Why children remain unprotected from war
—Some people remain ignorant of what is happening to children in other parts of the world.
—Some people do not care about issues that do not affect them directly.

Then write the first draft of your paragraph or essay. (See Appendixes D and E for more on how to write paragraphs and essays.)

Revising and Editing Your Writing

REVISING YOUR WRITING

Use the Revision Checklist in Appendix F (p. 271) to evaluate the first draft of your (or your classmate's) writing in terms of content and organization. After deciding how your paragraph or essay can be improved, write a second draft incorporating the changes. On the checklist identify the areas in which you had difficulty so you can doublecheck these areas in later writings.

EDITING YOUR ESSAY

After you are satisfied with content and organization, use the Editing Checklist in Appendix G (p. 272) to reevaluate your (or your classmate's) writing. On the checklist identify the areas in which you had difficulty so you can doublecheck these areas in later writings.

PART III: RESEARCH TOPICS

Choose one of the following topics on children, family, and education for research. Refer to Appendix H for specific assignments. In addition, you may find it helpful to consult the list of Suggested Further Reading (at the end of this book) for sources related to your topic.

reading

literacy

school

academic failure/success

teaching

learning styles

education

teaching methodologies

aging

autonomy/independence

menopause

generation gap

cultural differences

International Red Cross

United Nations

bilingual education

language learning

affirmative action

assimilation

language education

the socially disadvantaged

immigrants/refugees

violence/war

children and war

civilian casualties

terrorism

guerrilla warfare

relief organizations

Amnesty International

AN IMPORTANT STEP in building a more peaceful world involves redefining the scope of human relationships to include not only our families, friends, and neighbors but also people from other cultures. Cross-cultural relationships can increase our understanding of and improve our communication with those who are less familiar to us. The readings in Part IV offer us ways of looking at ourselves and others from a new perspective, one that can help us to develop more constructive approaches for living together. The writers stress the importance of cross-cultural understanding and mutual respect to improved relations among the peoples of the world.

In "The Arab World," Edward T. Hall gives insight into how basic differences in perspective can affect cross-cultural communication. Arthur L. Campa provides a historical context for cultural differences in "Anglo versus Chicano: Why?" to encourage our understanding that such diversity need not be irreconcilable. At a more personal level, Jeanne Wakatsuki Houston tells us of the rewards of "Living in Two Cultures." Finally, Martin Luther King, Jr., in "The Ways of Meeting Oppression," offers a rationale against acquiescence and physical violence as means of resolving conflict.

13

The Arab World

EDWARD T. HALL

In the following selection from *The Hidden Dimension* (1966), Edward T. Hall, an anthropologist, examines the concept of "space" in Middle Eastern and Western cultures to show us its potential for cross-cultural misunderstandings.

Getting Ready to Read

THINKING ABOUT THE TITLE

What do you know about "the Arab world"? Do you consider yourself a part of it? How is the concept of "space" perceived differently by Arabs and Westerners?

KEY VOCABULARY/CONCEPTS

Discuss with your classmates what you know about some of the following words and concepts.

Westerners	Arabs	in public
culture	assumptions	touching
rule	privacy	inviolate/violate
sphere/zone	mannerisms	gestures
pattern	feelings	rights
manner	defer	permission
protection	self	adaptation
set distances	the "silent treatment"	senses
olfaction	interpersonal relations	shame
boundary	emotions	cultural frames

Before reading the selection, ask yourself and/or discuss with your class-mates the following questions.

1. What do you know about Arab customs?
2. In what ways might your own customs be similar to or different from Arab customs?
3. In what ways might your own customs be similar to or different from Western customs?
4. How might people benefit from a better understanding of the Arab world and its customs?

In spite of over two thousand years of contact, Westerners and Arabs still do not understand each other. Proxemic research reveals some insights into this difficulty. Americans in the Middle East are immediately struck by two conflicting sensations. In public they are compressed and overwhelmed by smells, crowding, and high noise levels; in Arab homes Americans are apt to rattle around, feeling exposed and often somewhat inadequate because of too much space! (The Arab houses and apartments of the middle and upper classes which Americans stationed abroad commonly occupy are much larger than the dwellings such Americans usually inhabit.) Both the high sensory stimulation which is experienced in public places and the basic in-security which comes from being in a dwelling that is too large provide Americans with an introduction to the sensory world of the Arab.

Behavior in Public

Pushing and shoving in public places is characteristic of Middle Eastern culture. Yet it is not entirely what Americans think it is (being pushy and rude) but stems from a different set of assumptions concerning not only the relations between people but how one experiences the body as well. Para-doxically, Arabs consider northern Europeans and Americans pushy, too. This was very puzzling to me when I started investigating these two views. How could Americans who stand aside and avoid touching be considered pushy? I used to ask Arabs to explain this paradox. None of my subjects was able to tell me specifically what particulars of American behavior were re-sponsible, yet they all agreed that the impression was widespread among

Arabs. After repeated unsuccessful attempts to gain insight into the cognitive world of the Arab on this particular point, I filed it away as a question that only time would answer. When the answer came, it was because of a seemingly inconsequential annoyance.

While waiting for a friend in a Washington, D.C., hotel lobby and wanting to be both visible and alone, I had seated myself in a solitary chair outside the normal stream of traffic. In such a setting most Americans follow a rule, which is all the more binding because we seldom think about it, that can be stated as follows: as soon as a person stops or is seated in a public place, there balloons around him a small sphere of privacy which is considered inviolate. The size of the sphere varies with the degree of crowding, the age, sex, and the importance of the person, as well as the general surroundings. Anyone who enters this zone and stays there is intruding. In fact, a stranger who intrudes, even for a specific purpose, acknowledges the fact that he has intruded by beginning his request with "Pardon me, but can you tell me . . . ?"

To continue, as I waited in the deserted lobby, a stranger walked up to where I was sitting and stood close enough so that not only could I easily touch him but I could even hear him breathing. In addition, the dark mass of his body filled the peripheral field of vision on my left side. If the lobby had been crowded with people, I would have understood his behavior, but in an empty lobby his presence made me exceedingly uncomfortable. Feeling annoyed by this intrusion, I moved my body in such a way as to communicate annoyance. Strangely enough, instead of moving away, my actions seemed only to encourage him, because he moved even closer. In spite of the temptation to escape the annoyance, I put aside thoughts of abandoning my post, thinking, "To hell with it. Why should I move? I was here first and I'm not going to let this fellow drive me out even if he is a boor." Fortunately, a group of people soon arrived whom my tormentor immediately joined. Their mannerisms explained his behavior, for I knew from both speech and gestures that they were Arabs. I had not been able to make this crucial identification by looking at my subject when he was alone because he wasn't talking and he was wearing American clothes.

In describing the scene later to an Arab colleague, two contrasting patterns emerged. My concept and my feelings about my own circle of privacy in a "public" place immediately struck my Arab friend as strange and puzzling. He said, "After all, it's a public place, isn't it?" Pursuing this line of

3

4

5

inquiry, I found that in Arab thought I had no rights whatsoever by virtue of occupying a given spot; neither my place nor my body was inviolate! For the Arab, there is no such thing as an intrusion in public. Public means public. With this insight, a great range of Arab behavior that had been puzzling, annoying, and sometimes even frightening began to make sense. I learned, for example, that if *A* is standing on a street corner and *B* wants his spot, *B* is within his rights if he does what he can to make *A* uncomfortable enough to move. In Beirut only the hardy sit in the last row in a movie theater, because there are usually standees who want seats and who push and shove and make such a nuisance that most people give up and leave. Seen in this light, the Arab who "intruded" on my space in the hotel lobby had apparently selected it for the very reason I had: it was a good place to watch two doors and the elevator. My show of annoyance, instead of driving him away, had only encouraged him. He thought he was about to get me to move.

Another silent source of friction between Americans and Arabs is in an   **6** area that Americans treat very informally—the manners and rights of the road. In general, in the United States we tend to defer to the vehicle that is bigger, more powerful, faster, and heavily laden. While a pedestrian walking along a road may feel annoyed he will not think it unusual to step aside for a fast-moving automobile. He knows that because he is moving he does not have the right to the space around him that he has when he is standing still (as I was in the hotel lobby). It appears that the reverse is true with the Arabs who apparently *take on rights to space as they move*. For someone else to move into a space an Arab is also moving into is a violation of his rights. It is infuriating to an Arab to have someone else cut in front of him on the highway. It is the American's cavalier treatment of moving space that makes the Arab call him aggressive and pushy.

Concepts of Privacy

The experience described above and many others suggested to me that   **7** Arabs might actually have a wholly contrasting set of assumptions concerning the body and the rights associated with it. Certainly the Arab tendency to shove and push each other in public and to feel and pinch women in public conveyances would not be tolerated by Westerners. It appeared to me that they must not have any concept of a private zone outside the body. This proved to be precisely the case.

In the Western world, the person is synonymous with an individual inside a skin. And in northern Europe generally, the skin and even the clothes may be inviolate. You need permission to touch either if you are a stranger. This rule applies in some parts of France, where the mere touching of another person during an argument used to be legally defined as an assault. For the Arab the location of the person in relation to the body is quite different. The person exists somewhere down inside the body. The ego is not completely hidden, however, because it can be reached very easily with an insult. It is protected from touch but not from words. The dissociation of the body and the ego may explain why the public amputation of a thief's hand is tolerated as standard punishment in Saudi Arabia. It also sheds light on why an Arab employer living in a modern apartment can provide his servant with a room that is a boxlike cubicle approximately 5 by 10 by 4 feet in size that is not only hung from the ceiling to conserve floor space but has an opening so that the servant can be spied on.

As one might suspect, deep orientations toward the self such as the one just described are also reflected in the language. This was brought to my attention one afternoon when an Arab colleague who is the author of an Arab-English dictionary arrived in my office and threw himself into a chair in a state of obvious exhaustion. When I asked him what had been going on, he said, "I have spent the entire afternoon trying to find the Arab equivalent of the English word 'rape.' There is no such word in Arabic. All my sources, both written and spoken, can come up with no more than an approximation, such as 'He took her against her will.' There is nothing in Arabic approaching your meaning as it is expressed in that one word."

Differing concepts of the placement of the ego in relation to the body are not easily grasped. Once an idea like this is accepted, however, it is possible to understand many other facets of Arab life that would otherwise be difficult to explain. One of these is the high population density of Arab cities like Cairo, Beirut, and Damascus. . . . While it is probable that Arabs are suffering from population pressures, it is also just as possible that continued pressure from the desert has resulted in a cultural adaptation to high density which takes the form described above. Tucking the ego down inside the body shell not only would permit higher population densities but would explain why it is that Arab communications are stepped up as much as they are when compared to northern European communication patterns. Not

8

9

10

only is the sheer noise level much higher, but the piercing look of the eyes, the touch of the hands, and the mutual bathing in the warm moist breath during conversation represent stepped-up sensory inputs to a level which many Europeans find unbearably intense.

The Arab dream is for lots of space in the home, which unfortunately many Arabs cannot afford. Yet when he has space, it is very different from what one finds in most American homes. Arab spaces inside their upper middle-class homes are tremendous by our standards. They avoid partitions because Arabs *do not like to be alone*. The form of the home is such as to hold the family together inside a protective shell, because Arabs are deeply involved with each other. Their personalities are intermingled and take nourishment from each other like the roots and the soil. If one is not with people and actively involved in some way, one is deprived of life. An old Arab saying reflects this value: "Paradise without people should not be entered because it is Hell." Therefore, Arabs in the United States often feel socially and sensorially deprived and long to be back where there is human warmth and contact.

Since there is no physical privacy as we know it in the Arab family, not even a word for privacy, one could expect that the Arabs might use some other means to be alone. Their way to be alone is to stop talking. Like the English, an Arab who shuts himself off in this way is not indicating that anything is wrong or that he is withdrawing, only that he wants to be alone with his own thoughts or does not want to be intruded upon. One subject said that her father would come and go for days at a time without saying a word, and no one in the family thought anything of it. Yet for this very reason, an Arab exchange student visiting a Kansas farm failed to pick up the cue that his American hosts were mad at him when they gave him the "silent treatment." He only discovered something was wrong when they took him to town and tried forcibly to put him on a bus to Washington, D.C., the headquarters of the exchange program responsible for his presence in the U.S.

Arab Personal Distances

Like everyone else in the world, Arabs are unable to formulate specific rules for their informal behavior patterns. In fact, they often deny that there are any rules, and they are made anxious by suggestions that such is the case. Therefore, in order to determine how the Arabs set distances, I investigated the use of each sense separately. Gradually, definite and distinctive behavioral patterns began to emerge.

Olfaction occupies a prominent place in the Arab life. Not only is it one of the distance-setting mechanisms, but it is a vital part of a complex system of behavior. Arabs consistently breathe on people when they talk. However, this habit is more than a matter of different manners. To the Arab good smells are pleasing and a way of being involved with each other. To smell one's friend is not only nice but desirable, for to deny him your breath is to act ashamed. Americans, on the other hand, trained as they are not to breathe in people's faces, automatically communicate shame as they are trying to be polite. Who would expect that when our highest diplomats are putting on their best manners they are also communicating shame? Yet this is what occurs constantly, because diplomacy is not only "eyeball to eyeball" but breath to breath.

By stressing olfaction, Arabs do not try to eliminate all the body's odors, only to enhance them and use them in building human relationships. Nor are they self-conscious about telling others when they don't like the way they smell. A man leaving his house in the morning may be told by his uncle, "Habib, your stomach is sour and your breath doesn't smell too good. Better not talk too close to people today." Smell is even considered in the choice of a mate. When couples are being matched for marriage, the man's go-between will sometimes ask to smell the girl, who may be turned down if she doesn't "smell nice." Arabs recognize that smell and disposition may be linked.

In a word, the olfactory boundary performs two roles in Arab life. It enfolds those who want to relate and separates those who don't. The Arab finds it essential to stay inside the olfactory zone as a means of keeping tabs on changes in emotion. What is more, he may feel crowded as soon as he smells something unpleasant. While not much is known about "olfactory crowding," this may prove to be as significant as any other variable in the crowding complex because it is tied directly to the body chemistry and hence to the state of health and emotions. . . . It is not surprising, therefore, that the olfactory boundary constitutes for the Arabs an informal distance-setting mechanism in contrast to the visual mechanism of the Westerner. . . .

In summary, proxemic patterns differ. By examining them it is possible to reveal hidden cultural frames that determine the structure of a given people's perceptual world. Perceiving the world differently leads to differential definitions of what constitutes crowded living, different interpersonal relations, and a different approach to both local and international politics. □

Thinking about the Reading

TRUE/FALSE QUESTIONS

In the space provided, write T if the sentence is true and F if the sentence is false, based on your reading of the preceding selection.

_____ 1. Proxemic research has improved relations between Arabs and Westerners so that they now understand each other well.

_____ 2. An American seated on a bus or train is protected by an invisible zone of privacy.

_____ 3. Because of high population density in its cities, the Arab world values the opportunity to be alone in one's home.

_____ 4. To an American, not speaking may be an indication that something is wrong.

_____ 5. The Arab use of smell is similar to the American use of sight.

COMPREHENSION QUESTIONS

In answering the following comprehension questions, *paraphrase* the selection—that is, restate it in your own words without copying phrases of more than three or four words from the reading. (See Appendix A for more on how to answer comprehension questions.) Here is an example:

Sample question:
Why would an American, approaching a stranger in a public place, begin the exchange with the comment "Pardon me" or "Excuse me"?

Sample answer (words and phrases from the reading are italicized):
In American culture, a stranger approaching someone else in public often begins by saying "Excuse me" or *"Pardon me"* because of an unspoken rule: in public a person is surrounded by a zone of *privacy* and anyone approaching that person may be *intruding*.
Here are the questions:

1. How do Americans and Arabs differ in their assumptions about the use of space as they move?
2. How do Arabs find privacy if not through physical means?
3. When an American avoids breathing into another's face, what does this behavior communicate to an Arab?
4. How might different perceptions of the world affect the relationships among people?

OUTLINE

Complete the following outline of the Hall reading by listing the topics he discusses in the space provided.

Paragraph(s) 1: Proxemic research on Arab-Westerner relations

2: _____

3: American zone of privacy in public places

4: _____

5: Arab perception of public space as "public"

6: _____

7: Arab assumptions about the body in "space"

8: _____

9: Arab sense of self is reflected in the language

10: _____

11: Arab use of space at home

12: _____

13: Distance-setting mechanisms in Arab culture

14: _____

15: Arab link between sense of smell and interpersonal relations

16: _____

17: Cultural differences in proxemic patterns create different perceptions of the world

SUMMARY

Use the preceding outline to write a summary of the reading. In the first sentence of your summary, mention the title, the author, and the main topic of the selection. Paraphrase the writer's points in your own words. (See Appendix B for more on how to write a summary.)

Making Connections

Write about your personal reaction to the reading. Some possible topics include your agreement or disagreement with a specific issue; a relevant personal experience; an idea that is new to you; a related idea from another source (such as a book, a movie, or a television program); or why you like or dislike the selection.

FINDING RELATED SOURCES

1. Interview someone you know about cultural perceptions or another topic discussed in the reading. Here are some sample questions:

   How do you communicate to others your desire to be alone?

   When in conversation with others, do you prefer to maintain close eye contact? Why or why not?

   If, while speaking, your communication partner stands close enough to breathe on you, would you feel uncomfortable? Why or why not?

   Take notes during the interview. Then, using your notes, write a summary of the interview that includes your reaction as well. Discuss the interview and your summary with your classmates.

2. Find a passage in a book, magazine, or newspaper that is related to the selection. In writing, summarize the passage and describe how it relates to the reading. Discuss the passage and your writing with your classmates.

Getting Ready to Write

PREWRITING ACTIVITIES

Using the topic *cultural perceptions* or *sensory world*, or another topic from the reading, spend 10 minutes on *one* of the following prewriting activities: freewriting, clustering, listing, or cubing. (See Appendix C.) Then discuss your prewriting with your classmates.

DISCUSSION AND COMPOSITION QUESTIONS

Choose one or more of the following questions to discuss with your classmates in preparation for writing.

On Peacemaking Issues

1. What issues raised in the reading are related to the goal of achieving world peace?

2. How might attitudes about public and private behavior be related to world peace? Discuss.

3. How are cultural assumptions related to world peace? Do people make assumptions about others who are culturally different? Discuss.

4. Given the greater amount of information about cultural assumptions today, why do cultural misunderstandings still exist?

5. Explain why a particular attitude about public or private behavior exists in a particular place or culture. How might people from other cultures gain a better understanding of that attitude?

6. What single cultural perception are you most concerned about? Could you (on your own or with others) do anything to clarify it? If so, what? If not, why?

On Related Issues

7. Describe a cultural perception (such as of public space, of privacy, of the body, or of the senses) from your own culture.

8. How do cultural assumptions influence communication among people of different backgrounds? Discuss.

9. Describe a movie or book with a cross-cultural theme. What happens in the movie or book? What is its message?

10. Tell about an example of cultural misunderstanding that you experienced, witnessed, or read about. Was the misunderstanding resolved? Why or why not?

11. Do you agree with Hall that proxemic patterns affect political relations between nations? Why or why not?

12. Is it important for people to understand the perceptual differences among cultures? Why or why not?

13. What have you learned about cultural differences in perception from the Hall reading? How might you compare or contrast this selection with another in the book (for example, Houston's "Living in Two Cultures" in Chapter 15 or Campa's "Anglo versus Chicano: Why?" in Chapter 14)?

14. Tell about someone who has experienced the type of perceptual differences due to culture explained by Hall.

15. How might you become more aware of your own cultural assumptions and/or perceptions through contact with someone from another culture? Discuss.

PLANNING TO WRITE

Choose one of the preceding Composition Questions as your writing topic. Begin to plan your paragraph or essay by identifying the topic and listing your thoughts on that topic.

Example: How might you become more aware of your own cultural assumptions and/or perceptions through contact with someone from another culture? Discuss.

Topic: Cross-cultural contact brings greater awareness of one's own cultural assumptions

—American informality and directness
—"Crossing the boundary" of acceptability of someone who is not from my culture

Then write the first draft of your paragraph or essay. (See Appendixes D and E for more on how to write paragraphs and essays.)

Revising and Editing Your Writing

REVISING YOUR WRITING

Use the Revision Checklist in Appendix F (p. 271) to evaluate the first draft of your (or your classmate's) writing in terms of content and organization. After deciding how your paragraph or essay can be improved, write a second draft incorporating the changes. On the checklist identify the areas in which you had difficulty so you can doublecheck these areas in later writings.

EDITING YOUR WRITING

After you are satisfied with content and organization, use the Editing Checklist in Appendix G (p. 272) to reevaluate your (or your classmate's) writing. On the checklist identify the areas in which you had difficulty so you can doublecheck these areas in later writings.

Anglo versus Chicano: Why?

ARTHUR L. CAMPA

Arthur L. Campa was chair of the Department of Modern Languages at the University of Denver and the director of the Center of Latin American Studies from 1946 to 1978. In the following selection, which first appeared in *Western Review* (1972), he examines cross-cultural differences and conflict in relation to what he identifies, respectively, as the Hispanic American and Anglo-American cultures.

Getting Ready to Read

THINKING ABOUT THE TITLE

In the first half of the title, Campa cites the Spanish terms for Americans of Hispanic and English descent and places them in an adversarial relationship. Why do you think he does that? In the second half of the title, he asks, "Why?" How would you explain the conflict between these two groups?

KEY VOCABULARY/CONCEPTS

Discuss with your classmates what you know about some of the following words and concepts.

cultural differences	Hispanic	Anglo
values	conflict	conceptual
historical	insular	peninsular

regionalism	individualism	colonizing
social order	relativistic	characteristic
collectivity	standardization	fixed rule
self-determination	objectivity	absolutist
moral considerations	pragmatic	being/doing
personalism	accomplishment	materialism
compliment/insult	compromise	mutual respect

PREREADING QUESTIONS

Before reading the selection, ask yourself and/or discuss with your classmates the following questions.

1. What do you know about the history of Spanish and English colonists in the Americas?
2. What other two groups of people have shared the same geographic area over a long period of time?
3. What might characterize the relations between two groups of people who share the same geographic area?
4. How might sharing the same geographic area influence each group?

The cultural differences between Hispanic and Anglo-American people have been dwelt upon by so many writers that we should all be well informed about the values of both. But audiences are usually of the same persuasion as the speakers, and those who consult published works are for the most part specialists looking for affirmation of what they believe. So, let us consider the same subject, exploring briefly some of the basic cultural differences that cause conflict in the Southwest, where Hispanic and Anglo-American cultures meet.

Cultural differences are implicit in the conceptual content of the languages of these two civilizations, and their value systems stem from a long series of historical circumstances. Therefore, it may be well to consider some of the English and Spanish cultural configurations before these Europeans set foot on American soil. English culture was basically insular, geographically and ideologically; was more integrated on the whole, except for some strong theological differences; and was particularly zealous of its racial purity. Spanish culture was peninsular, a geographical circumstance that made it a catchall of Mediterranean, central European and north African peoples. The composite nature of the population produced a marked regionalism that prevented close integration, except for religion, and led to a strong sense of individualism. These differences were reflected in the colonizing enterprise of the two cultures. The English isolated themselves from the Indians physically and culturally; the Spanish, who had strong notions about *pureza de sangre* [purity of blood] among the nobility, were not collectively averse to adding one more strain to their racial cocktail. Cortés led the way by siring the first *mestizo* in North America, and the rest of the conquistadores followed suit. The ultimate products of these two orientations meet today in the Southwest.

Anglo-American culture was absolutist at the onset; that is, all the dominant values were considered identical for all regardless of time and place. Such values as justice, charity, and honesty were considered the superior social order for all men and were later embodied in the American Constitution. The Spaniard brought with him a relativistic viewpoint and saw fewer moral implications in man's actions. Values were looked upon as the result of social and economic conditions.   3

The motives that brought Spaniards and Englishmen to America also differed. The former came on an enterprise of discovery, searching for a new route to India initially, and later for new lands to conquer, the fountain of youth, minerals, the Seven Cities of Cíbola and, in the case of the missionaries, new souls to win for the Kingdom of Heaven. The English came to escape religious persecution, and once having found a haven, they settled down to cultivate the soil and establish their homes. Since the Spaniards were not seeking refuge or running away from anything, they continued their explorations and circled the globe twenty-five years after the discovery of the New World.   4

The peripatetic tendency of the Spaniard may be accounted for in part by the fact that he was the product of an equestrian culture. Men on foot do not venture far into the unknown. It was almost a century after the landing on Plymouth Rock that Governor Alexander Spotswood of Virginia crossed the Blue Ridge Mountains, and it was not until the nineteenth century that the Anglo-Americans began to move west of the Mississippi.   5

The Spaniard's equestrian role meant that he was not close to the soil, as was the Anglo-American pioneer, who tilled the land and built the greatest agricultural industry in history. The Spaniard cultivated the land only when he had Indians available to do it for him. The uses to which the horse was put also varied. The Spanish horse was essentially a mount, while the more   6 robust English horse was used in cultivating the soil. It is therefore not surprising that the viewpoints of these two cultures should differ when we consider that the pioneer is looking at the world at the level of his eyes while the *caballero* [horseman] is looking beyond and down at the rest of the world.

One of the most commonly quoted, and often misinterpreted, characteristics of Hispanic peoples is the deeply ingrained individualism in all walks of life. Hispanic individualism is a revolt against the incursion of collectivity, strongly asserted when it is felt that the ego is being fenced in. This attitude leads to a deficiency in those social qualities based on collective standards, an attitude that Hispanos do not consider negative because it manifests a measure of resistance to standardization in order to achieve a measure of individual freedom. Naturally, such an attitude has no *reglas fijas* [fixed rules].

Anglo-Americans who achieve a measure of success and security through institutional guidance not only do not mind a few fixed rules but demand them. The lack of a concerted plan of action, whether in business or in politics, appears unreasonable to Anglo-Americans. They have a sense of individualism, but they achieve it through action and self-determination. Spanish individualism is based on feeling, on something that is the result not of rules and collective standards but of a person's momentary, emotional reaction. And it is subject to change when the mood changes. In contrast to Spanish emotional individualism, the Anglo-American strives for objectivity when choosing a course of action or making a decision.

The Southwestern Hispanos voiced strong objections to the lack of courtesy of the Anglo-Americans when they first met them in the early days of the Santa Fe trade. The same accusation is leveled at the *Americanos* today in many quarters of the Hispanic world. Some of this results from their different conceptions of polite behavior. Here too one can say that the Spanish have no *reglas fijas* because for them courtesy is simply an expression of the way one person feels toward another. To some they extend the hand, to some they bow and for the more *intimos* [close friends] there is the well-known *abrazo* [embrace]. The concepts of "good or bad" or "right or wrong" in polite behavior are moral considerations of an absolutist culture.

Another cultural contrast appears in the way both cultures share part of their material substance with others. The pragmatic Anglo-American contributes regularly to such institutions as the Red Cross, the United Fund and a myriad of associations. He also establishes foundations and quite often leaves millions to such institutions. The Hispano prefers to give his contribution directly to the recipient so he can see the person he is helping.

A century of association has inevitably acculturated both Hispanos and Anglo-Americans to some extent, but there still persist a number of culture traits that neither group has relinquished altogether. Nothing is more disquieting to an Anglo-American who believes that time is money than the time perspective of Hispanos. They usually refer to this attitude as the "*mañana* [tomorrow] psychology." Actually, it is more of a "today psychology," because Hispanos cultivate the present to the exclusion of the future; because the latter has not arrived yet, it is not a reality. They are reluctant to relinquish the present, so they hold on to it until it becomes the past. To an Hispano, nine is nine until it is ten, so when he arrives at nine-thirty, he jubilantly exclaims: "*¡Justo!*" [right on time]. This may be why the clock is slowed down to a walk in Spanish while in English it runs. In the United States, our future-oriented civilization plans our lives so far in advance that the present loses its meaning. January magazine issues are out in December; 1973 cars have been out since October; cemetery plots and even funeral arrangements are bought on the installment plan. To a person engrossed in living today the very idea of planning his future sounds like the tolling of the bells.

It is a natural corollary that a person who is present oriented should be compensated by being good at improvising. An Anglo-American is told in advance to prepare for an "impromptu speech," but an Hispano usually can improvise a speech because "*Nosotros lo improvisamos todo*" [we improvise everything].

Another source of cultural conflict arises from the difference between *being* and *doing*. Even when trying to be individualistic, the Anglo-American achieves it by what he does. Today's young generation decided to be themselves, to get away from standardization, so they let their hair grow, wore ragged clothes and even went barefoot in order to be different from the Establishment. As a result they all ended up doing the same things and created another stereotype. The freedom enjoyed by the individuality of *being* makes it unnecessary for Hispanos to strive to be different.

In 1963 a team of psychologists from the University of Guadalajara in Mexico and the University of Michigan compared 74 upper-middle-class students from each university. Individualism and personalism were found to be central values for the Mexican students. This was explained by saying that a Mexican's value as a person lies in his *being* rather than, as is the case of the

11

12

13

14

Anglo-Americans, in concrete accomplishments. Efficiency and accomplishments are derived characteristics that do not affect worthiness in the Mexican, whereas in the American it is equated with success, a value of highest priority in the American culture. Hispanic people disassociate themselves from material things or from actions that may impugn a person's sense of being, but the Anglo-American shows great concern for material things and assumes responsibility for his actions. This is expressed in the language of each culture. In Spanish one says, *"Se me cayó la taza"* [the cup fell away from me] instead of "I dropped the cup."

In English, one speaks of money, cash and all related transactions with frankness because material things of this high order do not trouble Anglo-Americans. In Spanish such materialistic concepts are circumvented by referring to cash as *efectivo* [effective] and when buying or selling something *al contado* [counted out], and when without it by saying *No tengo fondos* [I have no funds]. This disassociation from material things is what produces *sobriedad* [sobriety] in the Spaniard according to Miguel de Unamuno, but in the Southwest the disassociation from materialism leads to *dejadez* [lassitude] and *desprendimiento* [disinterestedness]. A man may lose his life defending his honor but is unconcerned about the lack of material things. *Desprendimiento* causes a man to spend his last cent on a friend, which when added to a lack of concern for the future may mean that tomorrow he will eat beans as a result of today's binge.

15

The implicit differences in words that appear to be identical in meaning are astonishing. Versatile is a compliment in English and an insult in Spanish. An Hispano student who is told to apologize cannot do it, because the word doesn't exist in Spanish. *Apologia* means words in praise of a person. The Anglo-American either apologizes, which is a form of retraction abhorrent in Spanish, or compromises, another concept foreign to Hispanic culture. *Compromiso* means a date, not a compromise. In colonial Mexico City, two hidalgos once entered a narrow street from opposite sides, and when they could not go around, they sat in their coaches for three days until the viceroy ordered them to back out. All this because they could not work out a compromise.

16

It was that way then and to some extent now. Many of today's conflicts in the Southwest have their roots in polarized cultural differences, which need not be irreconcilable when approached with mutual respect and understanding. □

17

Thinking about the Reading

TRUE/FALSE QUESTIONS

In the space provided, write T if the sentence is true and F if the sentence is false, based on your reading of the preceding selection.

_____ 1. Although cultural differences exist between Hispanic Americans and Anglo-Americans, their ways of thinking and their values are very similar.

_____ 2. The reasons for which the Spaniards came to America were different from those of the English.

_____ 3. Hispanic rules of courtesy are less fixed than those of Anglo-Americans.

_____ 4. Spanish and English have similar words (such as *versatile* and *compromise*) that make it easier for speakers of the two languages to understand each other.

_____ 5. Campa believes that conflicts between Anglo-Americans and Hispanic Americans might be resolved if handled with mutual respect and understanding.

COMPREHENSION QUESTIONS

In answering the following comprehension questions, *paraphrase* the selection—that is, restate it in your own words without copying phrases of more than three or four words from the reading. (See Appendix A for more on how to answer comprehension questions.) Here is an example:

Sample question:
What is Campa's purpose in examining cultural differences between Hispanic Americans and Anglo-Americans?

Sample answer (words and phrases from the reading are italicized):
By examining *cultural differences* between Hispanic Americans and Anglo-Americans, Campa intends to show potential sources of *conflict*.

Here are the questions:

1. Why does Campa begin his contrast historically with the culture of each group while it was still in Europe and the group's reasons for coming to America?

2. How was the horse used differently by each group in America?

3. According to Campa, how is individualism expressed by each group?

4. What does the writer mean by "the clock is slowed down to a walk in Spanish while in English it runs"?

OUTLINE

Complete the following outline of Campa's selection by listing the topics he discusses in the space provided.

Paragraph(s) 1: Cultural differences that can cause conflict

        2: _____

        3: Absolutist Anglos; relativist Hispanos

        4: _____

    5–6: Horsemen versus farmers

        7: _____

        8: Fixed rules versus momentary emotion

        9: _____

     10: Sharing material goods

11–12: _____

13–14: Being versus doing

     15: _____

     16: Same words, different meanings

     17: _____

SUMMARY

Use the preceding outline to write a summary of the reading. In the first sentence of your summary, mention the title, the author, and the main topic of the selection. Paraphrase the writer's points in your own words. (See Appendix B for more on how to write a summary.)

Making Connections

REACTING TO THE READING

Write about your personal reaction to the reading. Some possible topics include your agreement or disagreement with a specific issue; a relevant personal experience; an idea that is new to you; a related idea from another source (such as a book, a movie, or a television program); or why you like or dislike the selection.

FINDING RELATED SOURCES

1. Find a picture related to one of the following topics: cultural differences, individualism, or another topic discussed in the reading. In writing, describe the picture and relate your thoughts and feelings about it. Discuss your picture and writing with your classmates.
2. Find a passage in a book, magazine, or newspaper that is related to the reading. In writing, summarize the passage and describe how it relates to the selection. Discuss the passage and your writing with your classmates.

Getting Ready to Write

PREWRITING ACTIVITIES

Using the topic *cultural differences* or *individualism*, or another topic from the reading, spend 10 minutes on *one* of the following prewriting activities: freewriting, clustering, listing, or cubing. (See Appendix C.) Then discuss your prewriting with your classmates.

DISCUSSION AND COMPOSITION QUESTIONS

Choose one or more of the following questions to discuss with your classmates in preparation for writing.

On Peacemaking Issues

1. What issues raised in the reading are related to the goal of achieving world peace?
2. How might cultural differences be related to world peace? Discuss.
3. How might mutual respect and understanding be related to world peace? Discuss.
4. Do most people have a sense of mutual respect and understanding of other cultures? If so, why do cultural conflicts still exist in the world?
5. Describe a conflict that exists between two particular cultures and explain why it exists. What could be done to improve the understanding between these two groups?

6. What one cultural conflict are you most concerned about? Could you (on your own or with others) do anything to improve the situation? If so, what? If not, why?

On Related Issues

7. Describe the ways in which two cultures that coexist within one nation sometimes conflict.
8. Do you believe it is important for people to develop mutual respect and understanding of other cultures? Discuss.
9. Describe a movie or book that deals with cultural conflict. What happens in the movie or book? What is its message?
10. Tell about an example of cultural conflict that you saw or read about. Was the conflict resolved? Why or why not?
11. Why is it important for people to be tolerant of others? Discuss.
12. Compare and contrast your own culture with that of the Anglos or Hispanos described by Campa in this selection or with that of the Arabs examined by Hall in "The Arab World" (Chapter 13).
13. Tell about someone whose life-style demonstrates his or her respect for and understanding of other cultures.
14. Do you behave in ways that show respect and understanding of other cultures? Discuss.

PLANNING TO WRITE

Choose one of the preceding Composition Questions as your writing topic. Begin to plan your paragraph or essay by identifying the topic and listing your thoughts on that topic.

Example: How might mutual respect and understanding be related to world peace? Discuss.

Topic: The relationship of mutual respect and understanding to world peace

   —Whether we understand their culture or not, it is important to treat other people respectfully in order to get along.
   —It is easier to get along with people when we understand what they value and why they act as they do.

Then write the first draft of your paragraph or essay. (See Appendixes D and E for more on how to write paragraphs and essays.)

Revising and Editing Your Writing

REVISING YOUR WRITING

Use the Revision Checklist in Appendix F (p. 271) to evaluate the first draft of your (or your classmate's) writing in terms of content and organization. After deciding how your paragraph or essay can be improved, write a second draft incorporating the changes. On the checklist identify the areas in which you had difficulty so you can doublecheck these areas in later writings.

EDITING YOUR WRITING

After you are satisfied with content and organization, use the Editing Checklist in Appendix G (p. 272) to reevaluate your (or your classmate's) writing. On the checklist identify the areas in which you had difficulty so you can doublecheck these areas in later writings.

15

Living in Two Cultures

JEANNE WAKATSUKI HOUSTON

As an American of Japanese descent, Jeanne Wakatsuki Houston along with her family was relocated to an internment camp in the United States for three and a half years during World War II. She describes this experience, in collaboration with her husband, in *Farewell to Manzanar* (1973), from which the following selection is taken. In this excerpt Houston tells us about her experiences of growing up as a Japanese American and later marrying an American man, and how in the process she became "enriched with the heritage of both" cultures.

Getting Ready to Read

THINKING ABOUT THE TITLE

Have you ever lived within a culture different from your own? Have you ever lived with someone of a culture different from your own?

KEY VOCABULARY/CONCEPTS

Discuss with your classmates what you know about some of the following words and concepts.

awareness	values	Caucasian
peers	Asian-ness	self-image
female	married	duty
sex differences	maleness	authority
resent	reciprocation	protective

identity	cooperate	social barriers
stereotyped model	personality trait	double standard
role	pattern	reaction
cultural norms	compromise	instinct
hybridness	strength	weakness

PREREADING QUESTIONS

Before reading the selection, ask yourself and/or discuss with your classmates the following questions.

1. How does your culture influence your sense of being male/female?
2. How did going to school and out into the world on your own influence the way you thought about yourself?
3. How have the ways and values of another culture influenced the way you think about yourself?
4. What are the advantages and disadvantages of marrying someone from a different culture?

The memories surrounding my awareness of being female fall into two categories: those of the period before World War II, when the family made up my life, and those after the war, when I entered puberty and my world expanded to include the ways and values of my Caucasian peers. I did not think about my Asian-ness and how it influenced my self-image as a female until I married.

In remembering myself as a small child, I find it hard to separate myself from the entity of my family. I was too young to be given "duties" according to my sex, and I was unaware that this was the organizational basis for operating the family. I took it for granted that everyone just did what had to be done to keep things running smoothly. My five older sisters helped my mother with the domestic duties. My four older brothers helped my father in the fishing business. What I vaguely recall about the sensibility surrounding our sex differences was that my sisters and I all liked to please our brothers. More so, we tried to attract positive attention from Papa. A smile or affectionate pat from him was like a gift from heaven. Somehow, we never felt this way about Mama. We took her love for granted. But there was something special about Papa.

I never identified this specialness as being one of the blessings of male- 3
ness. After all, I played with my brother Kiyo, two years older than myself,
and I never felt there was anything special about him. I could even make
him cry. My older brothers were fun-loving, boisterous and very kind to
me, especially when I made them laugh with my imitations of Carmen
Miranda dancing or of Bonnie Baker singing "Oh, Johnny." But Papa was
different. His specialness came not from being male, but from being the
authority.

After the war and the closing of the camps, my world drastically 4
changed. The family had disintegrated; my father was no longer godlike,
despite my mother's attempt to sustain that pre-war image of him. I was
spending most of my time with my new Caucasian friends and learning
new values that clashed with those of my parents. It was also time that I
assumed the duties girls were supposed to do, like cooking, cleaning the
house, washing and ironing clothes. I remember washing and ironing my
brothers' shirts, being careful to press the collars correctly, trying not to dis-
please them. I cannot ever remember my brothers performing domestic
chores while I lived at home. Yet, even though they may not have been
working "out there," as the men were supposed to do, I did not resent it.
It would have embarrassed me to see my brothers doing the dishes. Their
reciprocation came in a different way. They were very protective of me and
made me feel good and important for being a female. If my brother Ray had
extra money, he would sometimes buy me a sexy sweater like my Caucasian
friends wore, which Mama wouldn't buy for me. My brothers taught me to
ride a bicycle and to drive a car, took me to my first dance, and proudly introduced me to their friends.

Although the family had changed, my identity as a female within it did 5
not differ much from my older sisters who grew up before the war. The
males and females supported each other but for different reasons. No longer
was the survival of the family as a group our primary objective; we cooper-
ated to help each other survive "out there" in the complicated world that
had weakened Papa.

We were living in Long Beach then. My brothers encouraged me to run 6
for school office, to try out for majorette and song leader, and to run for
queen of various festivities. They were proud that I was breaking social
barriers still closed to them. It was acceptable for an Oriental male to excel
academically and in sports. But to gain recognition socially in a society that
had been fed the stereotyped model of the Asian male as cook, houseboy or

crazed kamikaze pilot was almost impossible. The more alluring myth of mystery and exotica that surrounds the Oriental female made it easier, though no less inwardly painful, for me.

Whenever I succeeded in the *Hakujin* world, my brothers were supportive, whereas Papa would be disdainful, undermined by my obvious capitulation to the ways of the West. I wanted to be like my Caucasian friends. Not only did I want to look like them, I wanted to act like them. I tried hard to be outgoing and socially aggressive and to act confidently, like my girlfriends. At home I was careful not to show these personality traits to my father. For him it was bad enough that I did not even look very Japanese: I was too big, and I walked too assertively. My breasts were large, and besides that I showed them off with those sweaters the *Hakujin* girls wore! My behavior at home was never calm and serene, but around my father I still tried to be as Japanese as I could. 7

As I passed puberty and grew more interested in boys, I soon became aware that an Oriental female evoked a certain kind of interest from males. I was still too young to understand how or why an Oriental female fascinated Caucasian men, and of course, far too young to see then that it was a form of "not seeing." My brothers would warn me, "Don't trust the *Hakujin* boys. They only want one thing. They'll treat you like a servant and expect you to wait on them hand and foot. They don't know how to be nice to you." My brothers never dated Caucasian girls. In fact, I never really dated Caucasian boys until I went to college. In high school, I used to sneak out to dances and parties where I would meet them. I wouldn't even dare to think what Papa would do if he knew. 8

What my brothers were saying was that I should not act toward Caucasian males as I did toward them. I must not "wait on them" or allow them to think I would, because they wouldn't understand. In other words, to be a Japanese female around Japanese men and act *Hakujin* around Caucasian men. This double identity within a "double standard" resulted not only in confusion for me of my role or roles as female, but also in who or what I was racially. With the admonitions of my brothers lurking deep in my consciousness, I would try to be aggressive, assertive and "come on strong" toward Caucasian men. I mustn't let them think I was submissive, passive and all-giving like Madame Butterfly.* With Asian males I would tone down my 9

*The heroine of an American play and an Italian opera, Madame Butterfly married an American navy lieutenant for love, then committed ritual suicide when he left her to marry an American woman.

natural enthusiasm and settle into patterns instilled in me through the models of my mother and my sisters. I was not comfortable in either role.

Although I was attracted to males who looked like someone in a Coca-Cola ad, I yearned for the expressions of their potency to be like that of Japanese men, like that of my father: unpredictable, dominant, and brilliant—yet sensitive and poetic. I wanted a blond samurai. 10

When I met my blond samurai, during those college years in San Jose, I was surprised to see how readily my mother accepted the idea of our getting married. My father had passed away, but I was still concerned about her reaction. All of my brothers and sisters had married Japanese-American mates. I would be the first to marry a Caucasian. "He's a strong man and will protect you. I'm all for it," she said. Her main concern for me was survival. Knowing that my world was the world of the *Hakujin*, she wanted me to be protected, even if it meant marriage to one of them. It was 1957, and interracial couples were a rare sight to see. She felt that my husband-to-be was strong because he was acting against the norms of his culture, perhaps even against his parents' wishes. From her vantage point, where family and group opinion outweighed the individual's, this willingness to oppose them was truly a show of strength. 11

When we first married I wondered if I should lay out his socks and underwear every morning like my mother used to do for my father. But my brothers' warning would float up from the past: don't be subservient to Caucasian men or they will take advantage. So I compromised and laid them out sporadically, whenever I thought to do it . . . which grew less and less often as the years passed. (Now my husband is lucky if he can even find a clean pair of socks in the house!) His first reaction to this wifely gesture was to be uncomfortably pleased. Then he was puzzled by its sporadic occurrence, which did not seem to coincide as an act of apology or because I wanted something. On the days when I felt I should be a good Japanese wife, I did it. On other days, when I felt American and assertive, I did not. 12

When my mother visited us, as she often did when she was alive, I had to be on good behavior, much to my husband's pleasure and surprise. I would jump up from the table to fill his empty water glass (if she hadn't beat me to it) or butter his roll. If I didn't notice that his plate needed refilling, she would kick me under the table and reprimand me with a disapproving look. Needless to say, we never had mother-in-law problems. He would often ask, with hope in his voice, "When is your mother coming to visit?" 13

My mother had dutifully served my father throughout their marriage, but 14
I never felt she resented it. I served my brothers and father and did not resent it. I was made to feel not only important for performing duties of my
role, but absolutely integral for the functioning of the family. I realized a
very basic difference in attitude between Japanese and American cultures
toward serving another. In my family, to serve another could be uplifting, a
gracious gesture that elevated oneself. For many white Americans, it seems
that serving another is degrading, an indication of dependency or weakness
in character, or a low place in the social ladder. To be ardently considerate is
to be "self-effacing" or apologetic.

My father used to say, "Serving humanity is the greatest virtue. Giving 15
service of yourself is more worthy than selling the service or goods of
another." He would prefer that we be maids in someone's home, serving
someone well, than be salesgirls where our function would be to exchange
someone else's goods, handling money. Perhaps it was his way of rationaliz-
ing and giving pride to the occupations open to us as Orientals. Nevertheless, his words have stayed with me, giving me spiritual sustenance at times
when I perceived that my willingness to give was misconstrued as a need to
be liked or an act of manipulation to get something.

My husband and I often joke that the reason we have stayed married for 16
so long is that we continually mystify each other with responses and attitudes that are plainly due to our different backgrounds. For years I frus-
trated him with unpredictable silences and accusing looks. I felt a great
reluctance to tell him what I wanted or what needed to be done in the
home. I was inwardly furious that I was being put into the position of having to tell him what to do. I felt my femaleness, in the Japanese sense, was
being degraded. I did not want to be the authority. That would be humiliat-
ing for him and for me. He, on the other hand, considering the home to be
under my dominion, in the American sense, did not dare to impose on me
what he thought I wanted. He wanted me to tell him or make a list, like his
parents did in his home.

Entertaining socially was also confusing. Up to recent times, I still hesi- 17
tated to sit at the head of our rectangular dining table when my husband
sat at the other end. It seemed right to be seated next to him, helping him
to serve the food. Sometimes I did it anyway, but only with our close
friends who didn't misread my physical placement as psychological sub-
servience.

At dinner parties I always served the men first, until I noticed the women glaring at me. I became self-conscious about it and would try to remember to serve the women first. Sometimes I would forget and automatically turn to a man. I would catch myself abruptly, dropping a bowl of soup all over him. Then I would have to serve him first anyway, as a gesture of apology. My unconscious Japanese instinct still managed to get what it wanted. 18

Now I just entertain according to how I feel that day. If my Japanese sensibility is stronger, I act accordingly and feel comfortable. If I feel like going all-American, I can do that, too, and feel comfortable. I have come to accept the cultural hybridness of my personality, to recognize it as a strength and not a weakness. Because I am culturally neither pure Japanese nor pure American does not mean I am less of a person. It means I have been enriched with the heritage of both. 19

How my present attitudes will affect my children in later years remains to be seen. My world is radically different from my mother's world, and all indications point to an even wider difference between our world and our children's. Whereas my family's and part of my struggle was racially based, I do not foresee a similar struggle for our children. Their biracialism is, indeed, a factor in their identity and self-image, but I feel their struggle will be more to sustain human dignity in a world rapidly dehumanizing itself with mechanization and technology. My hope is they have inherited a strong will to survive, that essential trait ethnic minorities in this country have so sharply honed. ☐ 20

Thinking about the Reading

TRUE/FALSE QUESTIONS

In the space provided, write T if the sentence is true and F if the sentence is false, based on your reading of the preceding selection.

_____ 1. Sex differences were the organizational basis for operating the family when Houston was growing up.

_____ 2. After World War II, many social barriers for Oriental males and females disappeared.

_____ 3. Because she was a product of both cultures, as a teenager Houston found it easy to be herself, whether with Japanese or Americans.

_____ 4. Houston's mother felt that Houston's American husband-to-be was a strong person who would protect her daughter in *Hakujin* society.

_____ 5. Houston sees the two cultures that have formed her personality as a benefit, not a loss.

COMPREHENSION QUESTIONS

In answering the following comprehension questions, *paraphrase* the selection—that is, restate it in your own words without copying phrases of more than three or four words from the reading. (See Appendix A for more on how to answer comprehension questions.) Here is an example:

Sample question:
How did Houston view her role as a female within her traditional Japanese family?

Sample answer (words and phrases from the reading are italicized):
Within her family, Houston's *self-image as a female* was influenced by being Asian. Initially she was *too young* to do chores that girls did, but she wanted to *please her brothers* and father. Eventually she took on the same chores as her sisters, but *did not resent* that her brothers didn't do these too. They made her *feel good* about being a girl.

Here are the questions:

1. How did Houston change as a consequence of contact with the *Hakujin* world?
2. Why did her brothers warn her against Caucasian men?
3. How do Japanese and American attitudes differ in relation to serving guests?
4. Why did Houston find her role as wife confusing at times?

OUTLINE

Complete the following outline of Houston's selection by listing the topics she discusses in the space provided.

Paragraph(s) 1: Early memories of being an Asian female

2: _____

3: Papa as authority

4–5: _____

6: Breaking social barriers

7: _____

8: Brothers' warnings about American men

9: _____

10: Wanted both cultures in a spouse

11: _____

12: Confusion about role as wife

13: _____

14: Cultural differences with regard to serving others

15: _____

16: Cultural differences in marriage

17–18: _____

19: Acceptance of cultural hybridness

20: _____

SUMMARY

Use the preceding outline to write a summary of the reading. In the first sentence of your summary, mention the title, the author, and the main topic of the selection. Paraphrase the writer's points in your own words. (See Appendix B for more on how to write a summary.)

Making Connections

REACTING TO THE READING

Write about your personal reaction to the reading. Some possible topics include your agreement or disagreement with a specific issue; a relevant experience; an idea that is new to you; a related idea from another source (such as a book, a movie, or a television program); or why you like or dislike the selection.

FINDING RELATED SOURCES

1. Interview someone about cultural hybridness, a personal experience in another culture, or another topic discussed in the reading. Here are some sample questions:

   Have the ways and values of another culture influenced the way you think of yourself? Why or why not?

How has your culture influenced your sense of being a male/female?
Take notes during the interview. Then, using your notes, write a summary of the interview that includes your reaction as well. Discuss the interview and your summary with your classmates.

2. Find a passage in a book, magazine, or newspaper that is related to the reading. In writing, summarize the passage and describe how it relates to the selection. Discuss the passage and your writing with your classmates.

Getting Ready to Write

PREWRITING ACTIVITIES

Using the topic *cultural hybridness* or *double standards*, or another topic from the reading, spend 10 minutes on one of the following prewriting activities: freewriting, clustering, listing, or cubing. (See Appendix C.) Then discuss your prewriting with your classmates.

DISCUSSION AND COMPOSITION QUESTIONS

Choose one or more of the following questions to discuss with your classmates in preparation for writing.

On Peacemaking Issues

1. What issues raised in the reading are related to the goal of achieving world peace?
2. How is what Houston terms "cultural hybridness" related to world peace? Discuss.
3. How are social barriers related to world peace? Discuss.
4. Are most people tolerant of other cultures or races? If so, why does ethnic or racial intolerance still exist? Discuss.
5. Describe a kind of cultural hybridness that exists in a particular place and explain why it exists there. What could be done to improve the situation?
6. What particular situation involving an intolerance of others are you most concerned about? Could you (on your own or with others) do anything to improve the situation? If so, what? If not, why?

On Related Issues

7. Describe a situation in which one racial or ethnic group was treated with a lack of tolerance or subjected to social barriers by another group within the same nation.

8. Do young people, when they begin school or become independent, learn new values that clash with those of their parents? Discuss.

9. Describe a movie or book that deals with ethnic and/or racial relations. What happens in the movie or book? What is its message?

10. Tell about an example of cultural or racial intolerance that you saw or read about. Why was the intolerance accepted or rejected by others?

11. In your opinion, is what Houston calls "cultural hybridness" a strength or weakness? Explain.

12. Are people today more tolerant of interracial couples than in the past? Why or why not?

13. In terms of entertaining guests, which cultural norms are you more comfortable with, those of the Japanese or those of the Americans? Explain.

14. Tell about someone who is a "cultural hybrid," who accepts the riches of both heritages.

15. How has your way of life been influenced by more than one culture? Discuss.

PLANNING TO WRITE

Choose one of the preceding Composition Questions as your writing topic. Begin to plan your paragraph or essay by identifying the topic and listing your thoughts on that topic.

Example: How is what Houston terms "cultural hybridness" related to world peace? Discuss.

Topic: The relationship of cultural hybridness to world peace

—People raised in multicultural environments better understand the value of culture and are more apt to tolerate and accept cultural diversity.

—Because such people feel a connection to more than one cultural group, their sense of interrelatedness with others increases.

Then write the first draft of your paragraph or essay. (See Appendixes D and E for more on how to write paragraphs and essays.)

Revising and Editing Your Writing

REVISING YOUR WRITING

Use the Revision Checklist in Appendix F (p. 271) to evaluate the first draft of your (or your classmate's) writing in terms of content and organization. After deciding how your paragraph or essay can be improved, write a second draft incorporating the changes. On the checklist identify the areas in which you had difficulty so you can doublecheck these areas in later writings.

EDITING YOUR WRITING

After you are satisfied with content and organization, use the Editing Checklist in Appendix G (p. 272) to reevaluate your (or your classmate's) writing. On the checklist identify the areas in which you had difficulty so you can doublecheck these areas in later writings.

16

The Ways of Meeting Oppression

MARTIN LUTHER KING, JR.

A leading spokesman for the U.S. civil rights movement of the 1950s and 1960s, Martin Luther King, Jr., organized and inspired many people before he was assassinated in 1968. The following selection, taken from his book *Stride toward Freedom* (1958), looks at three ways in which oppressed people have historically reacted to their oppressors.

Getting Ready to Read

THINKING ABOUT THE TITLE

What does it mean to be oppressed? How might oppression be a consequence of cross-cultural conflict?

KEY VOCABULARY/CONCEPTS

Discuss with your classmates what you know about some of the following words and concepts.

oppression	acquiescence	freedom
Moses	slavery	emancipation
Negro	cooperate	moral obligation
conscience	segregation	safety
physical violence	hatred	solve
social problem	understanding	community

brotherhood	nonviolent resistance	reconcile
submit	race relations	struggle
rights	contribution	example
courage	good will	equality

PREREADING QUESTIONS

Before reading the selection, ask yourself and/or discuss with your class-mates the following questions.

1. What group of people, at present or historically, could you describe as "oppressed"? Who are (or were) their oppressors?
2. Why can you describe this group of people as oppressed?
3. How did they react (or not react) to their oppression?
4. What were the effects of oppression on them?

Oppressed people deal with their oppression in three characteristic ways. One way is acquiescence: the oppressed resign themselves to their doom. They tacitly adjust themselves to oppression, and thereby become condi-tioned to it. In every movement toward freedom some of the oppressed pre-fer to remain oppressed. Almost 2,800 years ago Moses set out to lead the children of Israel from the slavery of Egypt to the freedom of the promised land. He soon discovered that slaves do not always welcome their deliverers. They become accustomed to being slaves. They would rather bear those ills they have, as Shakespeare pointed out, than flee to others that they know not of. They prefer the "fleshpots of Egypt" to the ordeals of emancipation.

There is such a thing as the freedom of exhaustion. Some people are so worn down by the yoke of oppression that they give up. A few years ago in the slum areas of Atlanta, a Negro* guitarist used to sing almost daily: "Been down so long that down don't bother me." This is the type of nega-tive freedom and resignation that often engulfs the life of the oppressed.

But this is not the way out. To accept passively an unjust system is to cooperate with that system; thereby the oppressed become as evil as the oppressor. Noncooperation with evil is as much a moral obligation as is cooperation with good. The oppressed must never allow the conscience of the oppressor to slumber. Religion reminds every man that he is his

*In the United States, more contemporary terms are *African American* and *black*.

brother's keeper. To accept injustice or segregation passively is to say to the oppressor that his actions are morally right. It is a way of allowing his conscience to fall asleep. At this moment the oppressed fails to be his brother's keeper. So acquiescence—while often the easier way—is not the moral way. It is the way of the coward. The Negro cannot win the respect of his oppressor by acquiescing; he merely increases the oppressor's arrogance and contempt. Acquiescence is interpreted as proof of the Negro's inferiority. The Negro cannot win the respect of the white people of the South or the peoples of the world if he is willing to sell the future of his children for his personal and immediate comfort and safety.

A second way that oppressed people sometimes deal with oppression is to resort to physical violence and corroding hatred. Violence often brings about momentary results. Nations have frequently won their independence in battle. But in spite of temporary victories, violence never brings permanent peace. It solves no social problem; it merely creates new and more complicated ones.   4

Violence as a way of achieving racial justice is both impractical and immoral. It is impractical because it is a descending spiral ending in destruction for all. The old law of an eye for an eye leaves everybody blind. It is immoral because it seeks to humiliate the opponent rather than win his understanding; it seeks to annihilate rather than to convert. Violence is immoral because it thrives on hatred rather than love. It destroys community and makes brotherhood impossible. It leaves society in monologue rather than dialogue. Violence ends by defeating itself. It creates bitterness in the survivors and brutality in the destroyers. A voice echoes through time saying to every potential Peter, "Put up your sword."* History is cluttered with the wreckage of nations that failed to follow this command.   5

If the American Negro and other victims of oppression succumb to the temptation of using violence in the struggle for freedom, future generations will be the recipients of a desolate night of bitterness, and our chief legacy to them will be an endless reign of meaningless chaos. Violence is not the way.   6

The third way open to oppressed people in their quest for freedom is the way of nonviolent resistance. Like the synthesis in Hegelian philosophy, the principle of nonviolent resistance seeks to reconcile the truths of two oppo-   7

---

*The apostle Peter had drawn his sword to defend Christ from arrest. The voice was that of Christ, who surrendered himself for trial and crucifixion (John 18:11).

sites—the acquiescence and violence—while avoiding the extremes and immoralities of both. The nonviolent resister agrees with the person who acquiesces that one should not be physically aggressive toward his opponent; but he balances the equation by agreeing with the person of violence that evil must be resisted. He avoids the nonresistance of the former and the violent resistance of the latter. With nonviolent resistance, no individual or group need submit to any wrong, nor need anyone resort to violence in order to right a wrong.

It seems to me that this is the method that must guide the actions of the Negro in the present crisis in race relations. Through nonviolent resistance the Negro will be able to rise to the noble height of opposing the unjust system while loving the perpetrators of the system. The Negro must work passionately and unrelentingly for full stature as a citizen, but he must not use inferior methods to gain it. He must never come to terms with falsehood, malice, hate, or destruction. 8

Nonviolent resistance makes it possible for the Negro to remain in the South and struggle for his rights. The Negro's problem will not be solved by running away. He cannot listen to the glib suggestion of those who would urge him to migrate en masse to other sections of the country. By grasping his great opportunity in the South he can make a lasting contribution to the moral strength of the nation and set a sublime example of courage for generations yet unborn. 9

By nonviolent resistance, the Negro can also enlist all men of good will in his struggle for equality. The problem is not a purely racial one, with Negroes set against whites. In the end, it is not a struggle between people at all, but a tension between justice and injustice. Nonviolent resistance is not aimed against oppressors, but against oppression. Under its banner consciences, not racial groups, are enlisted. □ 10

Thinking about the Reading

TRUE/FALSE QUESTIONS

In the space provided, write T if the sentence is true and F if the sentence is false, based on your reading of the preceding selection.

_____ 1. One consequence of acquiescence to oppression is that people accept and become accustomed to living this way.

_____ 2. People choose to use physical violence because it is the most effective way to overcome oppression.

_____ 3. One reason that nonviolent resistance is superior to the other two responses to oppression is because it is easier.

_____ 4. The American Negro could use nonviolent resistance to escape oppression by leaving the South and going elsewhere.

_____ 5. Nonviolent resistance benefits the country as a whole by providing an example of courage and moral strength.

COMPREHENSION QUESTIONS

In answering the following comprehension questions, *paraphrase* the selection—that is, restate it in your own words without copying phrases of more than three or four words from the reading. (See Appendix A for more on how to answer comprehension questions.) Here is an example:

Sample question:
Why might people prefer to resign themselves to oppression?

Sample answer (words and phrases from the reading are italicized):
Sometimes people *resign themselves* to *oppression* because they become used to it and are more afraid of the unknown.

Here are the questions:

1. Why is acquiescence unacceptable to King?
2. If violence sometimes brings results, why is it still considered ineffective?
3. What is the purpose of nonviolent resistance?
4. What does King mean by "Nonviolent resistance is not aimed against oppressors, but against oppression"?

OUTLINE

Complete the following outline of King's selection by listing the topics he discusses in the space provided.

Paragraph(s) 1: Why the oppressed may choose acquiescence

   2: _____

   3: To acquiesce is immoral

   4: _____

   5: Violence is impractical and immoral

   6: _____

   7: Nonviolent resistance tries to reconcile opposites

8: _____

9: Benefits of nonviolent resistance

10: _____

SUMMARY

Use the preceding outline to write a summary of the reading. In the first sentence of your summary, mention the title, the author, and the main topic of the selection. Paraphrase the writer's points in your own words. (See Appendix B for more on how to write a summary.)

Making Connections

REACTING TO THE READING

Write about your personal reaction to the reading. Some possible topics include your agreement or disagreement with a specific issue; a relevant personal experience; an idea that is new to you; a related idea from another source (such as a book, a movie, or a television program); or why you like or dislike the selection.

FINDING RELATED SOURCES

1. Find a picture related to one of the following topics: oppression, freedom, civil rights, or another topic discussed in the reading. In writing, describe the picture and relate your thoughts and feelings about it. Discuss the picture and your writing with your classmates.
2. Find a passage in a book, magazine, or newspaper that is related to the reading. In writing, summarize the passage and describe how it relates to the selection. Discuss the passage and your writing with your classmates.

Getting Ready to Write

PREWRITING ACTIVITIES

Using the topic *oppression* or *acquiescence*, or another topic from the reading, spend 10 minutes on *one* of the following prewriting activities: freewriting, clustering, listing, or cubing. (See Appendix C.) Then discuss your prewriting with your classmates.

DISCUSSION AND COMPOSITION QUESTIONS

Choose one or more of the following questions to discuss with your classmates in preparation for writing.

On Peacemaking Issues

1. What issues raised in the reading are related to the goal of achieving world peace?
2. How is nonviolent resistance related to world peace? Discuss.
3. How is oppression related to world peace? Discuss.
4. Do most people agree that "noncooperation with evil" is a moral obligation? Discuss.
5. If most people believe that "every man is his brother's keeper," why does oppression still exist in the world?
6. Describe a kind of oppression that exists in a specific place, and explain why it exists there. What could be done to change this situation?
7. What one situation involving oppression are you most concerned about? Could you (on your own or with others) do anything to improve the situation? If so, what? If not, why?

On Related Issues

8. People react to oppression in different ways, including acceptance, escape, violent resistance, and nonviolent resistance. Describe two of these reactions in reference to an oppressive situation that you know of through your reading, experience, or observation.
9. What are the advantages and disadvantages of nonviolent resistance? Discuss.
10. Describe a movie or book that deals with a political or moral issue. What happens in the movie or book? What is its message?
11. Tell about an example of nonviolent resistance that you saw or read about. Was the nonviolent person successful? Why or why not?
12. Explain why you agree or disagree with King's assertion that to "accept passively an unjust system is to cooperate with that system."
13. Do you think more people will practice nonviolent resistance in oppressive situations in the future? Why or why not?
14. Some religions and philosophies encourage nonviolent resistance more than others. How does your religion or personal philosophy view nonviolent resistance?

15. Tell about someone you respect because of the way he or she responded to oppression.
16. How might you practice nonviolent resistance? Discuss.

PLANNING TO WRITE

Choose one of the preceding Composition Questions as your writing topic. Begin to plan your paragraph or essay by identifying the topic and listing your thoughts on that topic.

Example: How might you practice nonviolent resistance? Discuss.

Topic: My potential for nonviolent resistance

—I believe that nonviolent resistance is morally superior to violence but difficult to practice.
—Fear and hatred are difficult reactions to overcome.

Then write the first draft of your paragraph or essay. (See Appendixes D and E for more on how to write paragraphs and essays.)

Revising and Editing Your Writing

REVISING YOUR WRITING

Use the Revision Checklist in Appendix F (p. 271) to evaluate the first draft of your (or your classmate's) writing in terms of content and organization. After deciding how your paragraph or essay can be improved, write a second draft incorporating the changes. On the checklist identify the areas in which you had difficulty so you can doublecheck these areas in later writings.

EDITING YOUR WRITING

After you are satisfied with content and organization, use the Editing Checklist in Appendix G (p. 272) to reevaluate your (or your classmate's) writing. On the checklist identify the areas in which you had difficulty so you can doublecheck these areas in later writings.

PART IV: RESEARCH TOPICS

Choose one of the following topics on cross-cultural encounters for research. Refer to Appendix H for specific assignments. In addition, you may find it helpful to consult the list of Suggested Further Reading (at the end of this book) for sources related to your topic.

affection

celebrations

daily habits/customs

greetings/manners

dating/courtship

individualism/collectivity

family relationships

legal/social rights

spiritualism

philosophy

hybridness

proxemics

the Middle East

behavior

public space

privacy

the body

intolerance

mannerisms/gestures

the senses

ego

interpersonal relations

cultural perceptions/assumptions

Moses

slums

hatred

cultural differences/norms

Hispanic

the American Southwest

civilizations

friendship

social order(s)

colonizing

self-determination

personality traits

internment camps during World War II

anthropology

Caucasians/Asians

sex differences

social barriers

double standards

ethnic minorities

interracial/biracial

equality

heritage

instinct

attitudes

oppression

freedom movements

slavery/emancipation

conscience

peace

segregation

religion

brotherhood/community

nonviolent resistance

Negroes/African Americans

social problems

race relations

ONE OF THE ESSENTIAL ingredients in building a better world is the will or determination to accomplish the task. The readings in Part V focus on developing in ourselves and in others spiritual values as motivators for change.

In "From *Who Needs God?*" Rabbi Harold Kushner discusses the positive influence of a belief in God on our lives. Aung San Suu Kyi, a Burmese activist for human rights, examines the spiritual basis of her activism in "From *Freedom from Fear*." J. Krishnamurti, a religious leader from India, describes, in "The Simplicity of Love," a kind of love with the potential to transform the world. Finally, in "Environmentalism of the Spirit," Al Gore explores the relationship between religion and the environment to show us how it is tied to basic human survival.

17

From *Who Needs God?*

HAROLD KUSHNER

Rabbi Harold Kushner has written a number of books, such as *When Bad Things Happen to Good People* (1983), in which he draws from his knowledge as a religious scholar to answer questions that are on the minds of many people today. In the following selection from *Who Needs God?* (1989), Kushner explains how a belief in God can bring meaning to life.

Getting Ready to Read

THINKING ABOUT THE TITLE

Many people today do not believe in God. How would you answer the question "Who needs God?"

KEY VOCABULARY/CONCEPTS

Discuss with your classmates what you know about some of the following words and concepts.

rabbi	good/evil	adultery
the Holocaust	moral behavior	public opinion
the Nazis	atheist	injustice
Hitler	ethical values	punishment
Jews	moral standards	legal code
Judaism	angel/devil	heaven/hell
the human conscience	murder	judgment
monotheism	rape	theology

PREREADING QUESTIONS

Before reading the selection, ask yourself and/or discuss with your classmates the following questions.

1. Do you believe in God?
2. What are your reasons for believing or not believing in God (or for not
being sure whether you believe or not)?
3. What are the advantages and disadvantages of believing in God?
4. What are the advantages and disadvantages of not believing in God?

A rabbi is a teacher. I teach in many ways, formally and informally, by pre-
cept and by examples. Some years ago, I taught a class in modern Jewish
history for teenagers in my congregation. We spent a lot of time on the
Holocaust, the destruction of six million Jewish men, women, and children
at the hands of the Nazis, because they were Jews. As we read example after
example of sadism, butchery, and cruelty, I could see the cumulative outrage
in the souls of my students reaching the boiling point. They were so angry
at what had been done to helpless victims long before they were born, in
some cases in countries where they might well have lived if their grandparents had not left Europe for America.

When we were done studying the history of those years, I asked them,
"Why was Hitler wrong?"

They were confused by my question. "What do you mean, why was
Hitler wrong?" one student asked incredulously. "Do you mean he may have
been right, that the Jews were an inferior race and should be murdered?"

Another cried, "Why was he wrong? You can't just take people and kill
them because you don't like them!"

"Remember," I pointed out to them, "the Nazis were careful to pass laws
sanctioning everything they did. It was all within the law. Was it still
wrong?"

"Well, of course it was," the first student replied. "You can't pass laws
permitting the gassing of little children just because they're Jewish."

"Are you trying to tell me that some things are wrong even if a majority
of the people think they are right? Are you telling me that there is such a
thing as right and wrong built into the human conscience and it's not just a
matter of how you feel about it?"

Again they looked confused, and one finally answered, "Well, yeah, I
guess so. I never thought about it that way before."

Paragraph numbers: 1, 2, 3, 4, 5, 6, 7, 8

The affirmation of monotheism—that there is only one God—is a moral   9
statement, not a mathematical deduction. If there is only one God and He
demands moral behavior, then there can be such a thing as good and evil. . . .
When there are many gods, as in pagan legends, the question is not: What is
God? The question is: Which God shall I serve? Which one has the power to
protect and reward me? Think, for example, of the conflicts in Homer's *Iliad*,
where the gods take sides. What pleases one displeases another. A person of-
fends one of the gods but is under the protection of another, stronger one.
The question is not what is right but who has the might.

The assertion that there is only one God is the assertion that issues of   10
moral behavior are not matters of personal taste. We cannot decide by majority vote that it is all right to steal and lie, any more than we can decide
that winters should be mild, or cookies more nourishing than vegetables.
Bertrand Russell, perhaps the most articulate spokesman for enlightened
atheism in our generation, captured the dilemma with which I confronted
my Holocaust students in these words: "I cannot . . . refute the arguments
for the subjectivity of ethical values, but I find myself incapable of believing
that all that is wrong with wanton cruelty is that I don't like it." In other
words, it may be hard to persuade someone philosophically that there is a
God who sets moral standards for us. We may be more comfortable with the
idea "I will do what I believe is good, and I will leave you free to do what
you believe is good." But we instinctively feel there is something lacking in
our philosophy when it can be reduced to "Personally, I choose not to torture little children or persecute people because of their race or religion, but
if it doesn't bother you to do it, go ahead."

As I see it, there are two possibilities. Either you affirm the existence of a   11
God who stands for morality and makes moral demands of us, who built a
law of truthfulness into His world even as He built a law of gravity (so that
if we violate either one, we suffer the consequences). Or else you give
everyone the right to decide what is good and what is evil by his or her own
lights, balancing the voice of one's conscience against the voice of temptation and need, like some cartoon character with an angel whispering in one
ear and a devil whispering in the other.

Some moral philosophers believe in two kinds of wrongdoing. There are   12
things which are wrong because people have declared them wrong, like
driving over the speed limit or on the wrong side of the road, and there are
things which are wrong in and of themselves, like murder or rape. What
makes them wrong? Not public opinion (it might be possible to get 51 per-

cent of the population to vote in favor of permitting adultery or letting the poor steal from wealthy corporations); they are just wrong whether people like it or not.

Which brings me to my problem with Clint Eastwood. I have seen only one of his very successful "Dirty Harry" movies, but I remember it clearly. I have never responded to a movie the way I did to that one, with as strong a sense of divergence between my mind and my gut. Throughout the movie, my head kept saying, "Why am I watching this? This is cheap, manipulative trash." But at the gut level, my emotional reaction was "Yeah, go get them. Get out the Magnum gun and blast them away. Don't let those punks get away with it." Intellectually, I found it shallow. Emotionally, I found it compelling and satisfying.

The point is not that the millions of people who go to Clint Eastwood movies are less intellectual and more emotional than I am. The point is that there is something instinctive in me, and I suspect in every one of us, that reacts with a surge of anger to injustice, to the prospect of criminals "getting away with it." It is not an intellectual position, a carefully thought out conclusion about what kind of society I want to live in. It is a gut reaction, a sense of "That's not right!" . . .

Edmund Cahn, former professor of law at New York University, suggests that there is such a thing as a "sense of injustice." We may not be able to define justice, he writes, but we all recognize injustice when we see it, and we all respond to injustice in the same way, the way I responded to the villain in the Clint Eastwood movie, with a feeling of outrage and a sense of "That's not fair." Even little children are capable of saying "That's not fair" (and not only about what happens to them, but also about unfair treatment of friends or even strangers).

This sense of injustice is more than a matter of maintaining a safe society. It is not saying it is wrong to steal because it would be maddening to live in a society where other people could take your belongings. It is not saying we should not murder because if it were all right to murder, then the people with the most guns would control the world, and they might not be the best people to do that. It says murder and theft are wrong. Even if you could persuade yourself that the world would be better off if certain people were killed, or if the poor could take what they need from the rich because they need it more, it would still be wrong. Codes of law before the time of Moses were phrased "If a man kills another, this will be his punishment. . . . If a man steals, this is the punishment." The Ten Commandments were the first

13

14

15

16

code to go beyond "If . . . then . . ." and say "You shall not murder! You shall not steal!" not because it is punishable, not because it is illegal, but because it is wrong.

Where does our sense of injustice come from? I would maintain that it comes from God, by which I mean that it is not man-made, not a matter of human consensus, but is built into the world we live in, as part of what makes it a world capable of morality. . . .   17

Unitarian minister G. Peter Fleck recalls seeing a drama on television in which a man dies and finds himself standing on line, addressed by a bored usher who tells him he can choose either door, the one on the right leading to heaven, the one on the left leading to hell.   18

"You mean I can choose either one?" the man asks. "There is no judgment, no taking account of how I lived?"   19

"That's right," the usher says. "Now move along, people are dying and lining up behind you. Choose one and keep the line moving."   20

"But I want to confess, I want to come clean, I want to be judged."   21

"We don't have time for that. Just choose a door and move along."   22

The man chooses to walk through the door on the left, leading to hell.   23

Fleck's conclusion is that "in the end, we want to be held accountable . . . we want to be judged and ultimately to be forgiven."   24

My grandfather was a house painter in Lithuania, eking out a modest living. But in addition to his public life as a house painter, he had a secret identity. He was one of God's agents on earth, maintaining literacy in a sea of ignorance, and kindness in a world of cruelty. His days, his every act became important because he believed it mattered to God what he ate, how he earned and spent money, how he respected his wife and treated his children. That sense of having to live up to God's standard redeemed my grandfather's life from anonymity and insignificance, and it can do the same for each of us. . . .   25

As the Bible says, "For the land you are about to possess is not like the land of Egypt, out of which you came, where you sowed your seed and watered it by foot like a vegetable garden. The land you are going to possess is . . . a land the Lord your God cares for. The eyes of the Lord are upon it, from the beginning of the year until its end." (Deuteronomy: 11:10–12) In other words, in the place you lived until now, God sent you water to make the crops grow whether you deserved it or not. But in the future, you will be rewarded only if you deserve it. The eyes of God will be upon your society, to see if you live up to His expectations.   26

For me, the one thing that defines us as human beings is this metaphor of the eyes of God being upon us. I don't literally believe that God has eyes with which He watches us. . . . Rather, I take it to mean that God makes moral demands on us, that there are standards by which God summons us to live. For me, that verse from Deuteronomy is bad meteorology—I have no reason to believe that the rain falls only on the farms of the virtuous; but it is good theology—we are summoned to live at a higher level by the notion that our behavior matters to God. □

Thinking about the Reading

TRUE/FALSE QUESTIONS

In the space provided, write T if the sentence is true, and F if the sentence is false, based on your reading of the preceding selection.

_____ 1. What Hitler and the Nazis did in Germany was illegal.
_____ 2. In a system of many gods, it is not clear what is good and what is evil.
_____ 3. Kushner thought that the Clint Eastwood movie he saw was excellent.
_____ 4. Edmund Cahn believes that people have a "sense of injustice."
_____ 5. In the television drama seen by minister G. Peter Fleck, a man chooses the door to heaven.

COMPREHENSION QUESTIONS

In answering the following comprehension questions, *paraphrase* the selection—that is, restate it in your own words without copying phrases of more than three or four words from the reading. (See Appendix A for more on how to answer comprehension questions.) Here is an example:

Sample question
What made Kushner's students angry?

Sample answer (words and phrases from the reading are italicized):
The students were angry because the *victims* of the *Nazis* during *the Holocaust* were *helpless*, and because they were killed only because they were *Jewish*.
Here are the questions:

1. According to Kushner, why was Hitler wrong?
2. Why are right and wrong less clearly distinguished in a religious system of many gods?
3. Why should morality not be determined by individual conscience or majority vote?
4. According to Kushner, what does the biblical saying "the eyes of the Lord are [on your land]" mean?

OUTLINE

Complete the following outline of Kushner's selection by listing the topics he discusses in the space provided.

Paragraph(s) 1: The Holocaust

    2–8: _____

     9: Monotheism versus many gods

    10: _____

11–12: Two possibilities for defining morality

13–14: _____

15–17: Our sense of injustice

18–24: _____

    25: The story of Kushner's grandfather

26–27: _____

SUMMARY

Use the preceding outline to write a summary of the reading. In the first sentence of your summary, mention the title, the author, and the main topic of the selection. Paraphrase the writer's points in your own words. (See Appendix B for more on how to write a summary.)

Making Connections

REACTING TO THE READING

Write about your personal reaction to the reading. Some possible topics include your agreement or disagreement with a specific issue; a relevant personal experience; an idea that is new to you; a related idea from another source (such as a book, a movie, or a television program); or why you like or dislike the selection.

1. Find a picture related to one of the following topics: belief in God, sense of injustice, or another topic discussed in the reading. In writing, describe the picture and relate your thoughts and feelings about it. Discuss the picture and your writing with your classmates.
2. Find a passage in a book, magazine, or newspaper that is related to the reading. In writing, summarize the passage and describe how it is related. Discuss the passage and your writing with your classmates.

Getting Ready to Write

PREWRITING ACTIVITIES

Using the topic *belief in God, sense of injustice,* or *good versus evil,* or another topic from the reading, spend 10 minutes on *one* of the following prewriting activities: freewriting, clustering, listing, or cubing. (See Appendix C.) Then discuss your prewriting with your classmates.

DISCUSSION AND COMPOSITION QUESTIONS

Choose one or more of the following questions to discuss with your classmates in preparation for writing.

On Peacemaking Issues
1. What issues raised in the reading are related to the goal of achieving world peace?
2. How might a "sense of injustice" be related to world peace? Discuss.
3. Describe a person who has either a strong or a weak sense of injustice.
4. Do you possess a sense of injustice? Discuss.
5. Explain why people acquire or do not acquire a sense of injustice.
6. What are we currently doing to develop a sense of injustice among people of the world?
7. How might we encourage people to develop a better sense of injustice?
8. In your opinion, will more people acquire a sense of injustice in the future? Why or why not?
9. Could you (on your own or with others) do anything to help develop a sense of injustice among people? If so, what? If not, why not?

On Related Issues

10. Describe the Holocaust or another event involving a nation's immoral behavior.
11. Do you believe that a sense of injustice comes from God? Discuss.
12. If people have a sense of injustice, why does injustice continue to exist in the world?
13. Tell about an example of injustice that you saw or read about. Was the injustice corrected? Why or why not?
14. Do you believe in God? Why or why not?
15. Why might people who do not believe in God still behave in moral ways?

PLANNING TO WRITE

Choose one of the preceding Composition Questions as your writing topic. Begin to plan your paragraph or essay by identifying the topic and listing your thoughts on that topic.

Example: If people have a sense of injustice, why does injustice continue to exist in the world?

Topic: Why injustice exists

—Some people do not have a true sense of injustice, or their sense of injustice is blocked.
—Some people justify their beliefs and actions even if these are unjust.

Then write the first draft of your paragraph or essay. (See Appendixes D and E for more on how to write paragraphs and essays.)

Revising and Editing Your Writing

REVISING YOUR WRITING

Use the Revision Checklist in Appendix F (p. 271) to evaluate the first draft of your (or your classmate's) writing in terms of content and organization. After deciding how your paragraph or essay can be improved, write a second

draft incorporating the changes. On the checklist identify the areas in which you had difficulty so you can doublecheck these areas in later writings.

EDITING YOUR WRITING

After you are satisfied with content and organization, use the Editing Checklist in Appendix G (p. 272) to reevaluate your (or your classmate's) writing. On the checklist identify the areas in which you had difficulty so you can doublecheck these areas in later writings.

From *Freedom from Fear*

AUNG SAN SUU KYI

Aung San Suu Kyi, daughter of the Burmese revolutionary leader Aung San, won the 1991 Nobel Peace Prize for her work for democracy in Burma. In this selection from her book *Freedom from Fear* (1991), the writer stresses the importance of not giving in to fear if we hope to work effectively for social change.

Getting Ready to Read

THINKING ABOUT THE TITLE

Is it possible to be free of fear? What does the selection title mean to you?

KEY VOCABULARY/CONCEPTS

Discuss with your classmates what you know about some of the following words and concepts.

corruption	impartial punishment	reform
spite	human dignity	apathy
ignorance	harmony	the opposition
avarice	justice	inspiration
totalitarian	dominate	authoritarian rule
courage	ethics	torture
oppression	human rights	compassion
intrepidity	revolution	ruthless power

Before reading the selection, ask yourself and/or discuss with your class-mates the following questions.

1. Are you a fearful or a courageous person? Explain.
2. How is freedom from fear related to instituting political change?

It is not power that corrupts but fear. Fear of losing power corrupts those   1
who wield it, and fear of the scourge of power corrupts those who are sub-ject to it. Most Burmese are familiar with the four *a-gati*, the four kinds of corruption. *Chanda-gati*, corruption induced by desire, is deviation from the right path in pursuit of bribes or for the sake of those one loves. *Dosa-gati* is taking the wrong path to spite those against whom one bears ill will, and *Moga-gati* is aberration due to ignorance. But perhaps the worst of the four is *bhaya-gati*, for not only does *bhaya*, fear, stifle and slowly destroy all sense of right and wrong, it so often lies at the root of the other three kinds of cor-ruption.

Just as *chanda-gati*, when not the result of sheer avarice, can be caused by   2
fear of want or fear of losing the goodwill of those one loves, so fear of be-ing surpassed, humiliated or injured in some way can provide the impetus for ill will. And it would be difficult to dispel ignorance unless there is free-dom to pursue the truth unfettered by fear. With so close a relationship be-tween fear and corruption, it is little wonder that in any society where fear is rife, corruption in all forms becomes deeply entrenched.

Public dissatisfaction with economic hardships has been seen as the chief   3
cause of the movement for democracy in Burma, sparked off by the student demonstrations of 1988. It is true that years of incoherent policies, inept official measures, burgeoning inflation and falling real income had turned the country into an economic shambles. But it was more than the difficul-ties of eking out a barely acceptable standard of living that had eroded the patience of a traditionally good-natured, quiescent people—it was also the humiliation of a way of life disfigured by corruption and fear. The students were protesting not just against the death of their comrades but against the denial of their right to life by a totalitarian regime which deprived the pres-ent of meaningfulness and held out no hope for the future. And because the students' protests articulated the frustrations of the people at large, the demonstrations quickly grew into a nationwide movement. Some of its

keenest supporters were businessmen who had developed the skills and the contacts necessary not only to survive but to prosper within the system. But their affluence offered them no genuine sense of security or fulfilment, and they could not but see that if they and their fellow citizens, regardless of economic status, were to achieve a worthwhile existence, an accountable administration was at least a necessary if not a sufficient condition. The people of Burma had wearied of a precarious state of passive apprehension where they were "as water in the cupped hands" of the powers that be.

Emerald cool we may be
As water in cupped hands
But oh that we might be
As splinters of glass
In cupped hands.

Glass splinters, the smallest with its sharp, glinting power to defend itself against hands that try to crush, could be seen as a vivid symbol of the spark of courage that is an essential attribute of those who would free themselves from the grip of oppression. Bogyoke Aung San regarded himself as a revolutionary and searched tirelessly for answers to the problems that beset Burma during her time of trial. He exhorted the people to develop courage: "Don't just depend on the courage and intrepidity of others. Each and every one of you must make sacrifices to become a hero possessed of courage and intrepidity. Then only shall we all be able to enjoy true freedom."

The effort necessary to remain uncorrupted in an environment where fear is an integral part of everyday existence is not immediately apparent to those fortunate enough to live in states governed by the rule of law. Just laws do not merely prevent corruption by meting out impartial punishment to offenders. They also help to create a society in which people can fulfil the basic requirements necessary for the preservation of human dignity without recourse to corrupt practices. Where there are no such laws, the burden of upholding the principles of justice and common decency falls on the ordinary people. It is the cumulative effect of their sustained effort and steady endurance which will change a nation where reason and conscience are warped by fear into one where legal rules exist to promote man's desire for harmony and justice while restraining the less desirable destructive traits in his nature.

In an age when immense technological advances have created lethal weapons which could be, and are, used by the powerful and the unprincipled to dominate the weak and the helpless, there is a compelling need for a closer relationship between politics and ethics at both the national and international levels. The Universal Declaration of Human Rights of the United Nations proclaims that "every individual and every organ of society" should strive to promote the basic rights and freedoms to which all human beings regardless of race, nationality or religion are entitled. But as long as there are governments whose authority is founded on coercion rather than on the mandate of the people, and interest groups which place short-term profits above long-term peace and prosperity, concerted international action to protect and promote human rights will remain at best a partially realized struggle. There will continue to be arenas of struggle where victims of oppression have to draw on their own inner resources to defend their inalienable rights as members of the human family.

The quintessential revolution is that of the spirit, born of an intellectual conviction of the need for change in those mental attitudes and values which shape the course of a nation's development. A revolution which aims merely at changing official policies and institutions with a view to an improvement in material conditions has little chance of genuine success. Without a revolution of the spirit, the forces which produced the iniquities of the old order would continue to be operative, posing a constant threat to the process of reform and regeneration. It is not enough merely to call for freedom, democracy and human rights. There has to be a united determination to persevere in the struggle, to make sacrifices in the name of enduring truths, to resist the corrupting influences of desire, ill will, ignorance and fear. 6

Saints, it has been said, are the sinners who go on trying. So free men are the oppressed who go on trying and who in the process make themselves fit to bear the responsibilities and to uphold the disciplines which will maintain a free society. Among the basic freedoms to which men aspire that their lives might be full and uncramped, freedom from fear stands out as both a means and an end. A people who would build a nation in which strong, democratic institutions are firmly established as a guarantee against state-induced power must first learn to liberate their own minds from apathy and fear. 7

Always one to practice what he preached, Aung San himself constantly demonstrated courage—not just the physical sort but the kind that enabled him to speak the truth, to stand by his work, to accept criticism, to admit his faults, to correct his mistakes, to respect the opposition, to parley with 8 the enemy and to let people be the judge of his worthiness as a leader. It is for such moral courage that he will always be loved and respected in Burma—not merely as a warrior hero but as the inspiration and conscience of the nation. The words used by Jawaharlal Nehru to describe Mahatma Gandhi could well be applied to Aung San: "The essence of his teaching was fearlessness and truth, and action allied to these, always keeping the welfare of the masses in view."

Gandhi, that great apostle of non-violence, and Aung San, the founder of a national army, were very different personalities, but as there is an inevitable sameness about the challenges of authoritarian rule anywhere at any time, so there is a similarity in the intrinsic qualities of those who rise up to meet the challenge. Nehru, who considered the instillation of courage in the people of India one of Gandhi's greatest achievements, was a political modernist, but as he assessed the needs for a twentieth-century movement for independence, he found himself looking back to the philosophy of ancient India: "The greatest gift for an individual or a nation . . . was *abhaya*, fearlessness, not merely bodily courage but absence of fear from the mind." 9

Fearlessness may be a gift but perhaps more precious is the courage acquired through endeavour,* courage that comes from cultivating the habit of refusing to let fear dictate one's actions, courage that could be described as "grace under pressure"—grace which is renewed repeatedly in the face of harsh, unremitting pressure. 10

Within a system which denies the existence of basic human rights, fear tends to be the order of the day. Fear of imprisonment, fear of torture, fear of death, fear of losing friends, family, property or means of livelihood, fear of poverty, fear of isolation, fear of failure. A most insidious form of fear is that which masquerades as common sense or even wisdom, condemning as foolish, reckless, insignificant or futile the small, daily acts of courage which help to preserve man's self-respect and inherent human dignity. It is not easy for a people conditioned by fear under the iron rule of the principle that might is right to free themselves from the enervating miasma of fear. Yet even under the most crushing state machinery, courage rises up again and again, for fear is not the natural state of civilized man. 11

The wellspring of courage and endurance in the face of unbridled power is generally a firm belief in the sanctity of ethical principles combined with a historical sense that despite all setbacks, the condition of man is set on an 12

*British spelling.

ultimate course for both spiritual and material advancement. It is his capacity for self-improvement and self-redemption which most distinguishes man from the mere brute. At the root of human responsibility is the concept of perfection, the urge to achieve it, the intelligence to find a path towards it, and the will to follow that path if not to the end at least the distance needed to rise above individual limitations and environmental impediments. It is man's vision of a world fit for rational, civilized humanity which leads him to dare and to suffer to build societies free from want and fear. Concepts such as truth, justice and compassion cannot be dismissed as trite when these are often the only bulwarks which stand against ruthless power. □

Thinking about the Reading

TRUE/FALSE QUESTIONS

In the space provided, write T if the sentence is true and F if the sentence is false, based on your reading of the preceding selection.

_____ 1. Fear can lead to ignorance.
_____ 2. Most people in Burma did not support the student protests of 1988.
_____ 3. Politics and ethics must be related today.
_____ 4. Freedom from fear must come before democracy can be realized.
_____ 5. Fear is never seen as similar to common sense.

COMPREHENSION QUESTIONS

In answering the following comprehension questions, *paraphrase* the selection—that is, restate it in your own words without copying phrases of more than three or four words from the reading. (See Appendix A for more on how to answer comprehension questions.) Here is an example:

Sample question:
According to the writer, what are the four kinds of corruption?

Sample answer (words and phrases from the reading are italicized):
Chanda-gati comes from *desire*, *dosa-gati* from *spite*, *moga-gati* from *ignorance*, and *bhaya-gati* from *fear*.

Here are the questions:

1. What has caused dissatisfaction in Burma?
2. What did Aung San (the writer's father) tell the Burmese people to do?
3. What does Aung San Suu Kyi mean by a "revolution of the spirit"?
4. How were Gandhi and the writer's father similar?

OUTLINE

Complete the following outline of Aung San Suu Kyi's selection by listing the topics she discusses in the space provided.

Paragraph(s) 1–2: Fear corrupts

3: _____

4: Advantages of the rule of law

5: _____

6: Revolution of the spirit

7: _____

8: Aung San's courage

9: _____

10: The nature of courage

11: _____

12: The source of courage

SUMMARY

Use the preceding outline to write a summary of the reading. In the first sentence of your summary, mention the title, the author, and the main topic of the selection. Paraphrase the writer's points in your own words. (See Appendix B for more on how to write a summary.)

Making Connections

REACTING TO THE READING

Write about your personal reaction to the reading. Some possible topics include your agreement or disagreement with a specific issue; a relevant personal experience; an idea that is new to you; a related idea from another source (such as a book, a movie, or a television program); or why you like or dislike the selection.

FINDING RELATED SOURCES

1. Find a picture related to one of the following topics: fear, courage, or another topic discussed in the reading. In writing, describe the picture and relate your thoughts and feelings about it. Discuss the picture and your writing with your classmates.

2. Interview someone you know about fear, courage, or another topic from the reading. Ask the person to describe his or her thoughts, feelings, and experiences. Take notes during the interview. Then, using your notes, write a summary of the interview that includes your reaction as well. Discuss the interview and your summary with your classmates.

Getting Ready to Write

PREWRITING ACTIVITIES

Using the topic *fear, courage,* or *human rights,* or another topic from the reading, spend 10 minutes on *one* of the following prewriting activities: freewriting, clustering, listing, or cubing. (See Appendix C.) Then discuss your prewriting with your classmates.

DISCUSSION AND COMPREHENSION QUESTIONS

Choose one or more of the following questions to discuss with your classmates in preparation for writing.

On Peacemaking Issues

1. What issues raised in the reading are related to the goal of achieving world peace?
2. Is fear related to world peace? Discuss.
3. Describe a time when you felt afraid of something or someone.
4. Describe a time when you reacted to a frightening situation with courage.
5. Tell about someone (other than yourself) who reacted to a frightening situation with courage.
6. Compare two frightening situations and how the people involved responded.
7. What causes fear?
8. What causes people to act with courage?

9. How can fear be overcome?

10. Are most people capable of overcoming fear? Discuss.

11. In the future, do you think people will act with courage to create a more peaceful world? Why or why not?

12. Could you (on your own or with others) use courage to create a more peaceful world? If so, how? If not, why?

On Related Issues

13. What is a "revolution of the spirit"?

14. Explain why Gandhi, Aung San, or another historical figure was a great political leader.

15. Why is apathy a bad thing?

16. Compare Aung San Suu Kyi's definition of "right action" with that of Kushner in "From *Who Needs God?*" (Chapter 17).

PLANNING TO WRITE

Choose one of the preceding Composition Questions as your writing topic. Begin to plan your paragraph or essay by identifying the topic and listing your thoughts on that topic.

Example: How can fear be overcome?

Topic: My attempt to overcome my fear of protesting the exploitation of part-time teachers in higher education

—Studying in order to understand the situation
—Finding others willing to work with me

Then write the first draft of your paragraph or essay. (See Appendixes D and E for more on how to write paragraphs and essays.)

Revising and Editing Your Writing

REVISING YOUR WRITING

Use the Revision Checklist in Appendix F (p. 271) to evaluate the first draft of your (or your classmate's) writing in terms of content and organization. After deciding how your paragraph or essay can be improved, write a second

draft incorporating the changes. On the checklist identify the areas in which you had difficulty so you can doublecheck these areas in later writings.

EDITING YOUR WRITING

After you are satisfied with content and organization, use the Editing Checklist in Appendix G (p. 272) to reevaluate your (or your classmate's) writing. On the checklist identify the areas in which you had difficulty so you can doublecheck these areas in later writings.

19

The Simplicity of Love

J. KRISHNAMURTI

J. Krishnamurti was a religious leader from India who, in the 1960s and 1970s, frequently lectured in the United States about Eastern religion and philosophy. After presenting his speech to an audience, he would often respond to questions, as he does in the following selection. "The Simplicity of Love," taken from Krishnamurti's book *Think on These Things* (1964), examines a kind of love that he believes is a key to meaningful change in the world.

Getting Ready to Read

THINKING ABOUT THE TITLE

"What is love?" is not an easy question to answer. There are many different types of love: romantic love, love of family, love of friends, love of country, among others. What kind of love might change the world?

KEY VOCABULARY/CONCEPTS

Discuss with your classmates what you know about some of the following words and concepts.

love	transform	a pleasurable habit
greed	an important man	awake
disrespect	institution	nonviolence
consideration	corruption	envy
gentle	a true Brahmin	ambition

insensitivity	villagers	lust
extraordinary	philosophize	poisonous
doctorate	rationalize	deadly

PREREADING QUESTIONS

Before reading the selection, ask yourself and/or discuss with your class-mates the following questions.

1. How do you define *love?*
2. What are some of the different kinds of love?
3. How do people express love?

A man in religious robes used to come every morning to pick flowers 　　　1
from the trees in a nearby garden. His hands and eyes were greedy for the
flowers, and he picked every flower within reach. He was clearly going to
offer them to some dead god image, a thing made of stone. The flowers
were lovely things, just opening to the morning sun, and he did not pick
them gently, but tore them off, cruelly taking away what the garden held.
His god demanded lots of flowers—lots of living things for a dead stone
image.

Another day I watched some young boys picking flowers. They were not 　　　2
going to offer the flowers to any god; they were talking and thoughtlessly
tearing off the flowers and throwing them away. Have you ever observed
yourself doing this? I wonder why you do it. As you walk along, you will
break off a branch, tear off the leaves and drop it. Have you not noticed this
thoughtless action on your part? The grown-up people do it too; they have
their own way of showing disrespect for living things. They talk about not
doing harm, yet everything they do is destructive.

One can understand your picking a flower or two to put in your hair, or 　　　3
to give to somebody with love, but why do you just tear at the flowers?

The other day I was out walking with a boy and we saw a stone lying on 　　　4
the road. When I removed it, he asked, "Why did you do that?" What does
this question indicate? Is it not a lack of consideration, respect? You show
respect out of fear, do you not? You quickly get up when an older person
comes into the room, but that is not respect; it is fear. Because if you really
felt respect, you would not destroy the flowers, you would remove a stone
from the road, you would take care of the trees and the garden. But,

whether we are old or young, we have no real feeling of consideration. Why? Is it that we don't know what love is?

Do you understand what simple love is? Not complex sexual love, nor the love of God, but just love—being considerate, really gentle in one's whole approach to all things. At home you don't always get this simple love. Your parents are too busy. At home there may be no real affection, no gentleness, so you come to school with that background of insensitivity and you behave like everybody else. And how is one to develop sensitivity? Not that you must have rules against picking the flowers; for when you are only controlled by rules, there is fear. But how can we create this sensitivity which makes you careful not to do any harm to people, to animals, to flowers?   5

Are you interested in all this? You should be. If you are not interested in being sensitive, you might as well be dead—and most people are. Though they eat three meals a day, have jobs, produce children, drive cars, wear fine clothes, most people are as good as dead.   6

Do you know what it means to be sensitive? It means, surely, to have a tender feeling for things: to see an animal in pain and do something about it, to remove a stone from the path because so many bare feet walk there, to pick up a nail on the road because somebody's car might get a punctured tire. To be sensitive is to feel for people, for birds, for flowers, for trees— not because they are yours, but just because you are awake to the extraordinary beauty of things, and how is this sensitivity to be developed?   7

The moment you are deeply sensitive, you naturally do not pick the flowers; there is a natural desire not to destroy things, not to hurt people, which means having real respect, love. To love is the most important thing in life. But what do we mean by love? When you love someone because that person loves you in return, surely that is not love. To love is to have that extraordinary feeling of affection, without asking anything in return. You may be very smart; you may pass all your examinations, get a doctorate and achieve a high position, but if you do not have this sensitivity, this feeling of simple love, your heart will be empty and you will be miserable for the rest of your life.   8

So it is very important for the heart to be filled with this sense of affection, for then you won't destroy, you won't be cruel, and there won't be wars any more. Then you will be happy human beings; and because you are happy, you won't pray, you won't look for God, for that happiness itself is God.   9

Now, how is this love to happen? Surely, love must begin with the educator, the teacher. If, besides giving you information about mathematics, geography, or history, the teacher has this feeling of love in his heart and talks   10 about it; if he removes the stone from the road and does not allow his servant to do all the dirty jobs; if in his conversation, in his work, in his play, when he eats, when he is with you or by himself, he has this feeling and shows it to you often; then you will also know what it is to love.

You may have clear skin, a nice face; you may wear a lovely sari or be a great athlete; but without love in your heart, you are an ugly human being; and when you love, whether your face is ugly or beautiful, it has a light. To love is the greatest thing in life; and it is very important to talk about love, to feel it, to encourage it, to value it; otherwise it soon goes away, for the world is very cruel. If while you are young you don't feel love, if you don't look with love at people, at animals, at flowers, when you grow up, you will find that your life is empty; you will be very lonely, and fear will follow you always. But the moment you have in your heart this extraordinary thing called love and feel the depth, the joy, the excitement of it, you will discover that for you the world is transformed. 11

Questioner: Why is it that so many rich and important people are invited to school events? 12

Krishnamurti: What do you think? Don't you want your father to be an important man? Are you not proud if he becomes a member of parliament and is mentioned in the newspapers? If he takes you to live in a big house, if he goes to Europe and comes back smoking a cigar, are you not pleased? 13

You see, the wealthy and those in power are useful to institutions. The institution says nice things about them and they do something for the institution, so it works both ways. But the question is not just why the school invites the important people to its events: it is why you also want to be an important person; or why women want to marry the richest, the best known, or the most handsome man. Don't you all want to be a big something or other? And when you have those desires, you have in you already the seed of corruption. Do you understand what I am saying? 14

Forget for the moment the question of why the school invites the wealthy, because there are also poor people at these events. But do any of you sit near the poor people, near the villagers? Do you? And have you noticed another extraordinary thing: how the religious leaders want to be seated in important places, how they push their way up to the front? We all want to have importance, recognition. The true Brahmin is one who does not ask anything from anyone, not because he is proud, but because he is a light unto himself. But we have lost all that. 15

You know, there is a story about Alexander, the great conqueror, when he came to India. After he had conquered the country, he wanted to meet the prime minister who had created such order in the land and had developed such honesty among the people. When the king explained that the prime minister was a Brahmin who had returned to his village, Alexander asked that he come to see him. The king sent for his prime minister, but he would not come because he did not care to show himself off to anyone. Unfortunately, we have lost that spirit. Since we are in ourselves empty, we are psychological beggars, seeking someone or something to feed us, to give us hope, to support us, and that is why we make normal things ugly. 16

It is all right for some important official to come to lay the cornerstone of a building; what harm is there in that? But what is bad is the whole spirit behind it. You never go to visit the villagers, do you? You never talk to them, feel with them, see for yourself how little they have to eat, how endlessly they work day after day without rest; but because I have pointed out to you certain things, you are ready to criticize others. Don't sit around and criticize; that is empty. But go and find out for yourself what the conditions are in the villages and do something there: plant a tree, talk to the villagers, invite them here, play with their children. Then you will find out that a different kind of society will exist, because there will be love in the land. A society without love is like a land without rivers; it is like a desert. But where there are rivers, the land is rich; it has beauty. Most of us grow up without love, and that is why we have created a society as bad as the people who live in it. 17

Questioner: What is the difference between need and greed? 18

Krishnamurti: Don't you know? Don't you know when you have what you need? And does not something tell you when you are greedy? Begin with simple things, and you will see that this is so. You know that when you have enough clothes, jewels, or whatever it is, you don't have to philosophize about it. But the moment need moves into the area of greed, it is then that you begin to philosophize, to rationalize, to explain away your greed. A good hospital, for example, requires so many beds, a certain standard of cleanliness, certain medicines, this and that. A travelling man must perhaps have a car, a coat, and so on. That is need. You need certain knowledge and skill to do your job. If you are an engineer, you must know certain things— but the knowledge can become connected to greed. Through greed the mind uses the objects of need to make itself more important. It is a very simple process if you observe it. If you are aware of your real needs and you 19 see how greed comes in, how the mind uses objects to make itself important, then it is not difficult to see the difference between need and greed.

Questioner: If the mind and the brain are one, then why is it that when a thought or a desire arises which the brain tells us is ugly, the mind so often likes this thought?

20

Krishnamurti: Actually what happens? If a pin pricks your arm, the nerves carry the sensation to your brain, the brain identifies the pain, then the mind wants to stop the pain, and you take away the pin or otherwise do something about it. But there are some things that the mind goes on with, even though it knows them to be ugly or stupid. It knows how stupid it is to smoke, and yet one goes on smoking. Why? Because it likes the sensation of smoking, and that is all. If the mind were as aware of the stupidity of smoking as it is of the pain of a pinprick, it would stop smoking. But it doesn't want to see that clearly because smoking has become a pleasurable habit. It is the same with greed or violence. If greed were as painful to you as the pinprick in your arm, you would stop being greedy; you wouldn't philosophize about it. And if you were really awake to the full meaning of violence, you wouldn't write books about non-violence—which is all nonsense, because you don't feel it; you just talk about it. If you eat something which gives you a bad stomach-ache, you don't continue to eat it, do you? You throw it away. Similarly, if you once realized that envy and ambition are poisonous, cruel, as deadly as the bite of a cobra snake, you would awaken to them. But, you see, the mind does not want to look at these things too closely; in this area, it has special interests, and it refuses to admit that ambition, envy, greed, lust are poisonous. Therefore it says, "Let us discuss non-greed, non-violence, let us have ideals"—and in the meantime it continues with its evil actions. So find out for yourself how corrupting, how destructive and poisonous these things are, and you will soon move away from them; but if you only say, "I must not" and continue as before, you are being dishonest. Be one thing or the other, hot or cold. ☐

21

Thinking about the Reading

TRUE/FALSE QUESTIONS

In the space provided, write T if the sentence is true and F if the sentence is false, based on your reading of the preceding selection.

_____ 1. The young boys were going to offer flowers to a god.
_____ 2. If you felt respect, you would remove a stone from the road.
_____ 3. People who are not sensitive are as good as dead.
_____ 4. To love is to return the feeling of someone who loves you.
_____ 5. Religious leaders like to sit with the poor people.

COMPREHENSION QUESTIONS

In answering the following comprehension questions, *paraphrase* the selection—that is, restate it in your own words without copying phrases of more than three or four words from the reading. (See Appendix A for more on how to answer comprehension questions.) Here is an example:

Sample question:
What does it mean to be sensitive?

Sample answer (phrases from the reading are italicized):
To be sensitive is to care about people and things, to want to help an *animal in pain*, to pick up a *stone from the path* so that it doesn't hurt anyone, to be aware of the *beauty of things*.
Here are the questions:

1. What does the writer mean by "simple love"?
2. What should a teacher do to teach the meaning of love?
3. Why do people want to be viewed by others as important?
4. Why does the human mind tend not to look at evil too closely?

OUTLINE

Complete the following outline of Krishnamurti's selection by listing the topics he discusses in the space provided.

Paragraph(s) 1–3: The tearing of flowers
    4: _____
  5–7: Sensitivity
  8–9: _____
   10: Teaching love
   11: _____
12–17: "Important" people's behavior
18–19: _____
20–21: The mind's evil ways.

SUMMARY

Use the preceding outline to write a summary of the reading. In the first sentence of your summary, mention the title, the author, and the main topic of the selection. Paraphrase the writer's points in your own words. (See Appendix B for more on how to write a summary.)

Making Connections

REACTING TO THE READING

Write about your personal reaction to the reading. Some of the possible topics include your agreement or disagreement with a specific issue; a relevant personal experience; an idea that is new to you; a related idea from another source (such as a book, a movie, or a television program); or why you like or dislike the selection.

FINDING RELATED SOURCES

1. Find a picture related to one of the following topics: the feeling of love, sensitivity, or another topic discussed in the reading. In writing, describe the picture and relate your thoughts and feelings about it. Discuss the picture and your writing with your classmates.
2. Find a passage in a book, magazine, or newspaper that is related to the reading. In writing, summarize the passage and describe how it is related. Discuss the passage and your writing with your classmates.

Getting Ready to Write

PREWRITING ACTIVITIES

Using the topic *the feeling of love, sensitivity,* or *ambition,* or another topic from the reading, spend 10 minutes on *one* of the following prewriting activities: freewriting, clustering, listing, or cubing. (See Appendix C.) Then discuss your prewriting with your classmates.

DISCUSSION AND COMPOSITION QUESTIONS

Choose one or more of the following questions to discuss with your classmates in preparation for writing.

On Peacemaking Issues

1. What issues raised in the reading are related to the goal of achieving world peace?
2. Is love related to world peace? Discuss.
3. Describe someone who feels love strongly. How does that person express love?
4. Describe someone who does not feel love strongly. How does that person act?
5. To what extent do you feel love? How do you express it?
6. Compare the extent to which two individuals feel and express love.
7. Are people in your native country (or in the United States) encouraged to feel and express love? If so, how are they encouraged? If not, how does this affect their relations with others?
8. Compare the extent to which people in two different places or cultures are encouraged (or not encouraged) to feel and express love.
9. How might people who find it hard to feel and express love be encouraged to do so?
10. In your opinion, will more people be better able to feel and express love in the future? Why or why not?
11. Could you (on your own or with others) do anything to help people feel and express love? If so, what? If not, why?

On Related Issues

12. Is it true, as mentioned in the text, that women want to marry "the richest, the best known, or the most handsome man"? Discuss.
13. Do men want to marry the richest, the best known, or the most beautiful woman? Discuss.
14. Do you sometimes want to be seen by others as important? Discuss.
15. Do you agree or disagree with Krishnamurti's ideas about interaction between the rich and poor? Why?
16. Are you a greedy person? Discuss.
17. Is ambition necessarily a bad thing? Why or why not?
18. Is envy necessarily a bad thing? Why or why not?

PLANNING TO WRITE

Choose one of the preceding Composition Questions as your writing topic. Begin to plan your paragraph or essay by identifying the topic and listing your thoughts on that topic.

Example: Are you a greedy person? Discuss.

Topic: Am I greedy?

—Ways in which I am greedy or materialistic
—Ways in which I am not greedy

Then write the first draft of your paragraph or essay. (See Appendixes D and E for more on how to write paragraphs and essays.)

Revising and Editing Your Writing

REVISING YOUR WRITING

Use the Revision Checklist in Appendix F (p. 271) to evaluate the first draft of your (or your classmate's) writing in terms of content and organization. After deciding how your paragraph or essay can be improved, write a second draft incorporating the changes. On the checklist identify the areas in which you had difficulty so you can doublecheck these areas in later writings.

EDITING YOUR WRITING

After you are satisfied with content and organization, use the Editing Checklist in Appendix G (p. 272) to reevaluate your (or your classmate's) writing. On the checklist identify the areas in which you had difficulty so you can doublecheck these areas in later writings.

20

Environmentalism of the Spirit

AL GORE

Al Gore, elected to the vice presidency in 1992, has been a leading American defender of the environment for more than twenty years. In *Earth in the Balance* (1993), from which the following selection is taken, he criticizes the reluctance of the U.S. government at the 1992 United Nations Earth Summit in Rio de Janeiro to support environmental protection, and calls for a change in policy.

Getting Ready to Read

THINKING ABOUT THE TITLE

For centuries religious writings have made a connection between spirituality in human beings and respect for the environment. How are environmentalism and the spirit connected?

KEY VOCABULARY/CONCEPTS

Discuss with your classmates what you know about some of the following words and concepts.

stewardship	monotheism	instant gratification
accountability	spiritual	indifferent
abuse	universalist	prophetic
sacred	transformation	transgression

207

baptize	reform	God's will
fertilize	moderation	literal truth
Nirvana	ecological crisis	disrupting
atmosphere	initiative	

PREREADING QUESTIONS

Before reading the selection, ask yourself and/or discuss with your class-mates the following questions.

1. Do you believe in a religion? If so, what does your religion teach about the environment?
2. From what nonreligious sources have you learned respect for the environment?

Virtually all current world religions have much to say about the relationship between humankind and the earth. Islam, for example, offers familiar themes. The Prophet Mohammed said, "The world is green and beautiful and God has appointed you His stewards over it." The central concepts of Islam taught by the Qu'ran—*tawheed* (unity), *chalifa* (trusteeship), and *akhrah* (accountability)—also serve as the pillars of the Islamic environmental ethic. The earth is the sacred creation of Allah, and among Mohammed's many instructions about it is: "Whoever plants a tree and diligently looks after it until it matures and bears fruit is rewarded." The first Muslim caliph, Abu-Baker, drew upon the Qu'ran and the *hadith* (oral traditions of the Prophet) when he ordered his troops: "Do not cut down a tree, do not abuse a river, do not harm animals, and be always kind and human to God's creation, even to your enemies."

A common thread in many religions is the sacred quality of water. Christians are baptized in water, as a sign of purification. The Qu'ran declares that "we have created everything from water." In the Lotus "Sutra," Buddha is presented metaphorically as a "rain cloud," covering, permeating, fertilizing, and enriching "all parched living beings, to free them from their misery to attain the joy of peace, joy of the present world, and joy of Nirvana . . . everywhere impartially without distinction of persons . . . ever to all beings I preach the Law equally . . . equally I rain the Law—rain untiringly."

The sacredness of water receives perhaps the greatest emphasis in Hinduism. According to its teachings, the "waters of life" are believed to bring to humankind the life force itself. One modern Hindu environmentalist, Dr. Karan Singh, regularly cites the ancient Hindu dictum: "The earth is our mother, and we are all her children." And in the Atharvaveda, the prayer for peace emphasizes the links between humankind and all creation: "Supreme Lord, let there be peace in the sky and in the atmosphere, peace in the plant world and in the forests; let the cosmic powers be peaceful; let Brahma be peaceful; let there be undiluted and fulfilling peace everywhere."

Sikhism, the northern Indian monotheistic offshoot of Hinduism that was founded around 1500, places a great deal of spiritual significance on the lessons we can learn directly from nature. Its founder, Guru Nanak, said "Air is the Vital Force, Water the Progenitor, the Vast Earth the Mother of All: Day and Night are nurses, fondling all creation in their lap." According to the Sikh seer, Guru Granth Sahib, human beings are composed of five elements of nature, which teach lessons and inspire strength in the formulation of our character: "Earth teaches us patience, love; Air teaches us mobility, liberty; Fire teaches us warmth, courage. Sky teaches us equality, broad-mindedness; Water teaches us purity, cleanliness."

One of the newest of the great universalist religions, Baha'i, founded in 1863 in Persia by Mirza Husayn Ali, warns us not only to properly regard the relationship between humankind and nature but also the one between civilization and the environment. Perhaps because its guiding visions were formed during the period of accelerating industrialism, Baha'i seems to dwell on the spiritual implications of the great transformation to which it bore fresh witness: "We cannot segregate the human heart from the environment outside us and say that once one of these is reformed, everything will be improved. Man is organic with the world. His inner life molds the environment and is itself deeply affected by it. The one acts upon the other and every abiding change in the life of man is the result of these mutual reactions." And, again, from the Baha'i sacred writings comes this: "Civilization, so often vaunted by the learned exponents of arts and sciences will, if allowed to overleap the bound of moderation, bring great evil upon men."

This sensitivity to the changes wrought by civilization on the earth is also evident in new statements from the leaders of Western religions. Pope John Paul II, for example, in his message of December 8, 1989, on humankind's responsibility for the ecological crisis, said: "Faced with the widespread destruction of the environment, people everywhere are coming to understand that we cannot continue to use the goods of the earth as we have in the past . . . a new ecological awareness is beginning to emerge which, rather than being downplayed, ought to be encouraged to develop into concrete programs and initiatives." In concluding, the Pope directly addressed his "brothers and sisters in the Catholic church, in order to remind them of their serious obligation to care for all of creation. . . . Respect for life and for the dignity of the human person extends also to the rest of creation, which is called to join man in praising God."

Many environmental theorists who think of the Catholic church only long enough to complain bitterly about its opposition to birth control (which many Catholics, in fact, use) might be surprised to read the Pope's powerful and penetrating analysis of the ecological crisis and recognize him as an ally: "Modern society will find no solution to the ecological problem unless it takes a serious look at its lifestyle. In many parts of the world, society is given to instant gratification and consumerism while remaining indifferent to the damage which these cause. As I have already stated, the seriousness of the ecological issue lays bare the depth of man's moral crisis."

7

The Judeo-Christian tradition has always presented a prophetic vision, from Joseph's warnings to Pharaoh about the seven lean years to John's jubilant promise in Revelations: "We will praise the Lamb, Triumphant, with all creatures." Many prophecies use the images of environmental destruction to warn of transgressions against God's will. For example, for those who believe in the literal truth of the Bible, it is hard to read about the predictions of hurricanes 50 percent stronger than the worst ones today, due to the accumulation of greenhouse gases that we have fostered, without recalling the prophecy of Hosea: "They have sown the wind, and they shall reap the whirlwind. . . ."

8

Nevertheless, there is no doubt that many believers and non-believers alike share a deep uneasiness about the future, sensing that our civilization may be running out of time. The religious ethic of stewardship is indeed harder to accept if one believes the world is in danger of being destroyed— by either God or humankind. This point was made by the Catholic theologian Teilhard de Chardin when he said, "The fate of mankind, as well as of religion, depends upon the emergence of a new faith in the future." Armed with such a faith, we might find it possible to resanctify the earth, identify it as God's creation, and accept our responsibility to protect and defend it.

9

We might even begin to contemplate decisions based on long-term considerations, not short-term calculations.

And if we could find a way to understand our own connection to the earth—all the earth—we might recognize the danger of destroying so many living species and disrupting the climate balance. James Lovelock, the originator of the Caia hypothesis, maintains that the entire complex earth system behaves in a self-regulating manner characteristic of something alive, that it has managed to maintain critical components of the earth's life support systems in perfect balance over eons of time—until the unprecedented interference of modern civilization: "We now see that the air, the ocean and the soil are much more than a mere environment for life; they are a part of life itself. Thus the air is to life just as is the fur to a cat or the nest for a bird. Not living but something made by living things to protect against an otherwise hostile world. For life on earth, the air is our protection against the cold depths and fierce radiations of space."

Lovelock insists that this view of the relationship between life and the nonliving elements of the earth system does not require a spiritual explanation; even so, it evokes a spiritual response in many of those who hear it. It cannot be accidental, one is tempted to conclude, that the percentage of salt in our bloodstreams is roughly the same as the percentage of salt in the oceans of the world. The long and intricate process by which evolution helped to shape the complex interrelationship of all living and nonliving things may be explicable in purely scientific terms, but the simple fact of the living world and our place in it evokes awe, wonder, a sense of mystery—a spiritual response—when one reflects on its deeper meaning.

We are not used to seeing God in the world because we assume from the scientific and philosophical rules that govern us that the physical world is made up of inanimate matter whirling in accordance with mathematical laws and bearing no relation to life, much less ourselves. Why does it feel faintly heretical to a Christian to suppose that God is in us as human beings? Why do our children believe that the Kingdom of God is up, somewhere in the ethereal reaches of space, far removed from this planet? Are we still unconsciously following the direction of Plato's finger, looking for the sacred everywhere except in the real world?

It is my own belief that the image of God can be seen in every corner of creation, even in us, but only faintly. By gathering in the mind's eye all of creation, one can perceive the image of the Creator vividly. □

Thinking about the Reading

TRUE/FALSE QUESTIONS

In the space provided, write T if the sentence is true and F if the sentence is false, based on your reading of the preceding selection.

_____ 1. Buddha is viewed as similar to a rain cloud.

_____ 2. Sikhism places the greatest emphasis on water.

_____ 3. Baha'i is an ancient religion.

_____ 4. The Catholic church does not support birth control.

_____ 5. The fact that hurricanes may become stronger in the future seems related to biblical prophesies.

COMPREHENSION QUESTIONS

In answering the following comprehension questions, *paraphrase* the selection—that is, restate it in your own words without copying phrases of more than three or four words from the reading. (See Appendix A for more on how to answer comprehension questions.) Here is an example:

Sample question:
What does Islam teach about the earth?

Sample answer (words from the reading are italicized):
Islam teaches that the world is one, that humankind is responsible for it, and that humankind is *accountable* to God.

Here are the questions:

1. According to Sikhism, what lessons can we learn from the five elements of nature?
2. How might industrialism have affected Baha'i?
3. What did Pope John Paul II call for humankind to do?
4. What Judeo-Christian prophecies are related to the environment?

OUTLINE

Complete the following outline of Gore's selection by listing the topics he discusses in the space provided.

Paragraph(s) 1: Religious connections between humans and the earth

    2–3: _____

      4: Sikh teachings

      5: _____

    6–7: Teachings of the Pope

    8–9: _____

     10: Lovelock's theory about the earth system

     11: _____

 12–13: Seeing God in the world

SUMMARY

Use the preceding outline to write a summary of the reading. In the first sentence of your summary, mention the title, the author, and the main topic of the selection. Paraphrase the writer's points in your own words. (See Appendix B for more on how to write a summary.)

Making Connections

REACTING TO THE READING

Write about your personal reaction to the reading. Some possible topics include your agreement or disagreement with a specific issue; a relevant personal experience; an idea that is new to you; a related idea from another source (such as a book, a movie, or a television program); or why you like or dislike the selection.

FINDING RELATED SOURCES

1. Find a picture related to one of the following topics: spirituality and the environment, an image of God, or another topic discussed in the reading. In writing, describe the picture and relate your thoughts and feelings about it. Discuss the picture and your writing with your classmates.

2. Find a passage in a book, magazine, or newspaper that is related to the reading. In writing, summarize the passage and describe how it is related. Discuss the passage and your writing with your classmates.

Getting Ready to Write

PREWRITING ACTIVITIES

Using the topic *spirituality and the environment* or *an image of God*, or another topic from the reading, spend 10 minutes on *one* of the following prewriting activities: freewriting, clustering, listing, or cubing. (See Appendix C.) Then discuss your prewriting with your classmates.

DISCUSSION AND COMPOSITION QUESTIONS

Choose one or more of the following questions to discuss with your classmates in preparation for writing.

On Peacemaking Issues

1. What issues raised in the reading are related to the goal of achieving world peace?
2. Are spirituality and the environment related to world peace? Discuss.
3. How do you feel about the environment?
4. Describe how someone you know feels about the environment.
5. Compare and contrast how two people you know feel about the environment.
6. Do you believe in God? If so, do you think God wants you to do certain things? What things? Does God want you to do anything about the environment? Discuss.
7. Would it be good for people to have spiritual feelings about the environment? Why or why not?
8. Should we teach people to have spiritual feelings about the environment? If so, how could we do this?
9. Why is it dangerous to not care about the environment?
10. In your opinion, will people's spiritual feelings about the environment increase in the future? Why or why not?
11. Could you (on your own or with others) do anything to help people develop a spiritual connection to the environment? If so, what? If not, why?

On Related Issues

12. Describe a particular religion's or religious leader's teachings about the environment.
13. How do you view prophecies—predictions of the future—biblical and others?

14. Why do many people feel uneasy about the future?

15. Do you agree with Gore that the earth is like a living thing? Discuss.

16. Do you share Gore's opinion that the image of God can be seen in "all of creation"? Discuss.

PLANNING TO WRITE

Choose one of the preceding Composition Questions as your writing topic. Begin to plan your paragraph or essay by identifying the topic and listing some thoughts on that topic.

Example: How do you feel about the environment?

Topic: My feelings about the environment

—Sometimes I don't think about the environment and act carelessly.
—Sometimes I appreciate its beauty and realize the need to take better care of it.

Then write the first draft of your paragraph or essay. (See Appendixes D and E for more on how to write paragraphs and essays.)

Revising and Editing Your Writing

REVISING YOUR WRITING

Use the Revision Checklist in Appendix F (p. 271) to evaluate the first draft of your (or your classmate's) writing in terms of content and organization. After deciding how your paragraph or essay can be improved, write a second draft incorporating the changes. On the checklist identify the areas in which you had difficulty so you can doublecheck these areas in later writings.

EDITING YOUR WRITING

After you are satisfied with content and organization, use the Editing Checklist in Appendix G (p. 272) to reevaluate your (or your classmate's) writing. On the checklist identify the areas in which you had difficulty so you can doublecheck these areas in later writings.

PART V: RESEARCH TOPICS

Choose one of the following topics on spiritual values for research. Refer to Appendix H for specific assignments. In addition, you may find it helpful to consult the list of Suggested Further Reading (at the end of this book) for sources related to your topic.

belief in God	American Indians/Native Americans
sense of injustice	a minority group
a religion	the American Indian movement
religious persecution	a political movement
a case of injustice	sense of identity
fear	the human potential movement
courage	humanistic psychology
political leadership	honesty
apathy	skepticism
political corruption	spiritual values
spiritual traditions	images of God

WORLD PEACE can only be realized if people feel able to achieve that goal through effective action. The writers in Part VI discuss various ways of promoting world peace.

In "Stages of Community Making," M. Scott Peck, author of *The Road Less Traveled*, discusses his activities as a consultant to groups wishing to create a spirit of community. Benjamin B. Ferencz, chief prosecutor for the United States during the post–World War II Nuremberg War Crimes trials and an advocate for international law, discusses the benefits of an international government in "Understand What Needs to Be Done." Aung San Suu Kyi in "The Need for Solidarity" urges people to overcome fear, apathy, and ethnic barriers so that they may join the struggle to create a more democratic, more just, and more peaceful society. Finally, in "Political Activity," Rigoberta Menchu discusses the personal barriers she had to overcome in order to work effectively for social justice and peace.

21

Stages of Community Making

M. SCOTT PECK

In *The Different Drum* (1987), from which this selection is taken, psychologist M. Scott Peck discusses his experiences as a consultant to organizations and groups seeking to develop a spirit of community. He observes that these groups typically experience four stages of development.

Getting Ready to Read

THINKING ABOUT THE TITLE

What "stages" might be involved in developing a spirit of community?

KEY VOCABULARY/CONCEPTS

Discuss with your classmates what you know about some of the following words and concepts.

community	conflict-avoidance	rugged individualism
chaos	heal	expectation
crisis	convert	prejudice
"faking it"	sensitivity group	ideology
pretense	emptiness	theology
lies	mystical	overcontrolling

Before reading the selection, ask yourself and/or discuss with your class-mates the following questions.

1. Have you ever felt like part of a real community? If so, tell about it.
2. What characteristics must a group have in order to be a real community?

Communities, like individuals, are unique. Still we all share the human condition. So it is that groups that try to form themselves into community usually go through certain stages. These stages, in order, are:

Pseudocommunity

Chaos

Emptiness

Community

Not every group that becomes a community follows this process exactly. Communities that temporarily form in response to a crisis, for example, may not go through all these stages. But in the process of community making by plan, this is the natural, usual order.

Pseudocommunity

The first response of a group in trying to form a community is most often to try to fake it. The members try to be an instant community by being very nice with one another and avoiding all disagreement. This attempt is what I call "pseudocommunity." It never works.

In pseudocommunity a group tries to get community easily by pretense. It is not an evil, conscious pretense of lies. Rather it is an unconscious process by which people who want to be loving attempt to do so by not telling the truth about themselves and their feelings in order to avoid conflict. But it is still a pretense. It is a tempting but nonproductive shortcut to nowhere.

The main aim of pseudocommunity is conflict-avoidance. The lack of conflict in a group is not by itself a problem. Genuine communities may experience long periods of time free from conflict. But that is because they have learned how to deal with conflict rather than avoid it. Pseudocommunity is conflict-avoiding; true community is conflict-resolving.

Once individual differences are not only allowed but encouraged to ap- pear, the group moves to the second stage of community development: chaos. 5

Chaos

The chaos is related to attempts to heal and convert. For example, after a period of silence, a member will say, "Well, the reason I came to this work-shop is that I have such and such a problem, and I thought I might find a solution to it here." 6

"I had that problem once," a second member will answer. "I did such and such, and it took care of the difficulty." 7

"Well, I tried that," the first member answers, "but it didn't solve any-thing." 8

"When I accepted that Jesus was my Lord and Savior," a third member says, "it took care of that problem and every other problem I had." 9

"I'm sorry," says the first member, "but that Jesus Lord and Savior stuff won't help me. I'm not interested in that." 10

"No," says a fourth member. "As a matter of fact, it makes me sick." 11

"But it's *true*," says a fifth member. 12

And so they're off. 13

In general, people resist change. So the healers and converters try harder to heal and convert, until finally their victims get angry and start trying to heal the healers and convert the converters. It is indeed chaos. 14

The stage of chaos is a time of disagreement. But that is not the main thing. Frequently, real communities will be required to disagree. Only they have learned to do so productively. The disagreement during chaos is chaotic. It is not only noisy, it is uncreative, unproductive. The disagree-ment that occurs from time to time in a real community is loving and re-spectful and usually quiet—even peaceful—as the members work hard to listen to each other. Still, sometimes in a real community, people may be-come angry. Yet even then one has a feeling that an agreement will be achieved. Not so in chaos. If anything, chaos, like pseudocommunity, is boring, as the members disagree with each other with no result. Indeed, the main feeling an observer is likely to have in response to a group in the chaotic stage of development is hopelessness. The fighting is going nowhere, achieving nothing. It is no fun. 15

How long the chaotic stage will last depends on the nature of the leader and the nature of the group. Some groups will leave it behind almost as soon as I point the way out. Even though chaos is unpleasant, other groups will stay in it for hours. Back in the sensitivity-group days there were a number of groups that stayed in unproductive chaos for their entire existence.

Emptiness

"There are only two ways out of chaos," I will explain to a group after it has spent enough time arguing and getting nowhere. "One is into organization—but organization is never community. The only other way is into and through emptiness."

Often the group will simply ignore me and go on arguing. Then after a while I will say, "I suggested to you that the only way from chaos to community is into and through emptiness. But you were not interested in my suggestion." More arguing, but finally a member will ask with some annoyance, "Well, what is this emptiness anyway?"

It is no accident that groups are not generally eager to take my suggestion of emptiness. The fact that "emptiness" is a mystical sort of word is not the problem. People are smart, and often deep in their consciousness they know more than they want to know. As soon as I mention "emptiness," they have an idea of what is to come. And they are in no hurry to accept it.

Emptiness is the hard part. It is also the most important stage of community development. It is the bridge between chaos and community.

When the members of a group finally ask me to explain what I mean by emptiness, I tell them simply that they need to empty themselves of barriers to communication. And I am able to use their behavior during chaos to show them specific things—feelings, assumptions, ideas, and motives—that have filled their minds and made them closed. The process of emptying themselves of these things is the key to the change from "rugged" to "soft" individualism. The most common barriers to communication that people need to empty themselves of before they can enter real community are:

Expectations and preconceptions. Until we can empty ourselves of expectations and stop trying to fit others and our relationships with them into a preconceived form, we cannot really listen, hear, or experience. "Life is what hap-

16

17

18

19

20

21

22

pens when you've planned something else," someone once wisely put it. But despite this wisdom, we still do not go easily into new situations with an open (and empty) mind.

Prejudices. Prejudice, which is probably more often unconscious than conscious, comes in two forms. One is the judgments we make about people without any experience of them at all, as when you or I might say to ourselves on meeting a stranger, "He is too feminine. I bet he's a real creep." Or "My God, she looks like she's ninety—probably not very smart." Even more common are the judgments we make about people on the basis of very brief, limited experience. Not a workshop goes by when I don't quickly conclude that some member is a real "nerd," only to discover later that that person has great gifts. 23

Ideology, theology, and solutions. Obviously we cannot move very far toward community with our fellow human beings when we are thinking and feeling, "She has clearly no appreciation of Christian ideas; she has a long way to go before she will be saved like me." Or else, "Well it's clear he's a Republican businessman conservative. I hope there'll be someone here worth talking to." It is not only such ideological and theological thoughts that we need to put away; it is any idea that seems to us "the one and only right way." 24

The need to heal, convert, fix, or solve. My most basic desire when I try to heal is to feel good myself. But there are several problems here. One is that my suggested cure may not work for my friend. Indeed, offering someone my cure usually only makes that person feel worse. So it was that all the advice that Job's friends (in the Bible) gave him in his time of trouble only made him more miserable. The fact is that often the most loving thing we can do when a friend is in pain is to *share* that pain—to be there even when we have nothing to offer except our presence and even when being there is painful to ourselves. 25

The need to control. This barrier to community is my own main problem. As the leader of a workshop, I am supposed to be sure that the group does not get out of control—that it comes to no harm. Furthermore, even though I have told the group that each member is no more and no less responsible than any other member for the success of the group, I don't really feel that way in my heart. If the workshop fails, I feel, I'm the one who is going to look bad. Consequently, I am tempted to *do* things that will lead to the desired results. But the desired result—community—cannot be achieved by a 26 leader who tells everyone what to do. It must be created by the group as a whole. Paradoxically, then, to be a good leader, I must spend most of the time sitting back, *doing nothing*, waiting, letting it happen. As a basically over-controlling person, I don't do that very easily.

Community

When the members become open and empty, the group enters community.   27

What happens next? Where does the group go from here? What, then, is its task?   28

There is no one answer to those questions. For the group that has gotten together for a short experience of community, its main task may be to simply enjoy that experience—and benefit from the healing that accompanies it. It will have the additional task, however, of ending itself. Women and men who have come to care for each other deeply need time to say good-bye. People need to discuss the pain of returning to an everyday world without community. It is important for short-term communities to give themselves the time for ending. This may involve a formal ritual, with special words being said.   29

If the group has gotten together to solve a problem—related to a community, church, or business—then it should go on with that task. But only after it has had the time to enjoy the experience of community for itself. Groups should always keep in mind the rule: "Community-building first, problem-solving second." ☐   30

Thinking about the Reading

TRUE/FALSE QUESTIONS

In the space provided, write T if the sentence is true and F if the sentence is false, based on your reading of the preceding selection.

_____ 1. Genuine communities do not experience conflict.

_____ 2. Chaos is an interesting stage.

_____ 3. Organization is different from community.

_____ 4. Expectations prevent one from listening.

_____ 5. Peck does not feel prejudice during group meetings.

COMPREHENSION QUESTIONS

In answering the following comprehension questions, *paraphrase* the selection—that is, restate it in your own words without copying phrases of more than three or four words from the reading. (See Appendix A for more on how to answer comprehension questions.) Here is an example:

Sample question:
What do people do in the "pseudocommunity" stage of community formation?

Sample answer (words from the reading are italicized):
The members are *nice* to each other but they do not honestly express their real thoughts and feelings. They are pretending that they have no problems or *disagreements*.

Here are the questions:

1. What happens during the "chaos" stage?
2. How is fighting different in the "chaos" and "community" stages?
3. Why are group members often not interested in the "emptiness" stage at first?
4. Why does Peck feel that, as a leader, he must not control a group too much?

OUTLINE

Complete the following outline of Peck's selection by listing the topics he discusses in the space provided.

Paragraph(s) 1: The stages of community
    2–5: _____
    6–16: The "chaos" stage
   17–20: _____
   21–26: Barriers to communication
   27–30: _____

SUMMARY

Use the preceding outline to write a summary of the reading. In the first sentence of your summary, mention the title, the author, and the main topic of the selection. Paraphrase the writer's points in your own words. (See Appendix B for more on how to write a summary.)

Making Connections

REACTING TO THE READING

Write about your personal reaction to the reading. Some possible topics include your agreement or disagreement with a specific issue; a relevant personal experience; an idea that is new to you; a related idea from another source (such as a book, a movie, or a television program); or why you like or dislike the selection.

FINDING RELATED SOURCES

1. Find a picture related to one of the following topics: community, openness, expectations, or another topic discussed in the reading. In writing, describe the picture and relate your thoughts and feelings about it. Discuss the picture and your writing with your classmates.
2. Interview someone you know about community, openness, or another topic discussed in the reading. Ask that person to describe his or her thoughts, feelings, and experiences. Take notes during the interview. Then, using your notes, write a summary of the interview that includes your reaction. Discuss the interview and your summary with your classmates.

Getting Ready to Write

PREWRITING ACTIVITIES

Using the topic *community, openness,* or *expectations,* or another topic from the reading, spend 10 minutes on *one* of the following prewriting activities: freewriting, clustering, listing, or cubing. (See Appendix C.) Then discuss your prewriting with your classmates.

DISCUSSION AND COMPOSITION QUESTIONS

Choose one or more of the following questions to discuss with your classmates in preparation for writing.

On Peacemaking Issues

1. What issues raised in the reading are related to the goal of achieving world peace?
2. Is community related to world peace? Discuss.
3. Tell about your own experience with a certain place that was (or was not) a good community.
4. Compare two places in terms of the "spirit of community" felt by the people who live there.
5. Is it important to develop a spirit of community? Why or why not?
6. How might people develop a spirit of community?
7. In your opinion, will people be better able to develop a spirit of community in the future? Why or why not?
8. Could you (on your own or with others) do something to help promote a spirit of community in a certain place? If so, what? If not, why?

On Related Issues

9. Describe your experience with a group in the "pseudocommunity" stage.
10. Describe your experience with a group in the "chaos" stage.
11. Tell of a time when expectations, preconceptions, prejudices, ideology, theology, or a need to convert presented a difficulty for you.
12. Tell of a time when you experienced the type of "emptiness" described by Peck (that is, when you needed to "empty" yourself of certain expectations, prejudices, feelings, or beliefs).
13. Is conflict a good thing? Discuss.
14. Describe someone you know who always tries to convert others to his or her way of thinking.
15. Is it good to have a need to control others? Discuss.
16. Tell about a group that successfully solved a problem. How did the group do it? Did the group go through Peck's stages?

PLANNING TO WRITE

Choose one of the preceding Composition Questions as your writing topic. Begin to plan your paragraph or essay by identifying the topic and listing your thoughts on that topic.

Example: Could you (on your own or with others) do something to help promote a spirit of community in a certain place? If so, what? If not, why?

Topic: The Brooklyn College Multicultural Action Committee's efforts to create a stronger spirit of community at the college

—Efforts to improve the campus atmosphere
—Efforts to revise course curricula

Then write the first draft of your paragraph or essay. (See Appendixes D and E for more on how to write paragraphs and essays.)

Revising and Editing Your Writing

REVISING YOUR WRITING

Use the Revision Checklist in Appendix F (p. 271) to evaluate the first draft of your (or your classmate's) writing in terms of content and organization. After deciding how your paragraph or essay can be improved, write a second draft incorporating the changes. On the checklist identify the areas in which you had difficulty so you can doublecheck these areas in later writings.

EDITING YOUR WRITING

After you are satisfied with content and organization, use the Editing Checklist in Appendix G (p. 272) to reevaluate your (or your classmate's) writing. On the checklist identify the areas in which you had difficulty so you can doublecheck these areas in later writings.

22

Understand What Needs to Be Done

BENJAMIN B. FERENCZ

Benjamin B. Ferencz was chief prosecutor for the United States during the Nuremberg War Crimes trials following World War II and has worked as an advocate for international law. In the following selection from *Planethood* (1991), Ferencz argues in favor of an international government, one that could effectively resolve political disputes and thereby prevent war.

Getting Ready to Read

THINKING ABOUT THE TITLE

What do you think the term "planethood" could mean?

KEY VOCABULARY/CONCEPTS

Discuss with your classmates what you know about some of the following words and concepts.

lawlessness	executioner	civil war
world prosperity	mass murder	the Constitution
arms race	international law	the Union
law enforcement	American colonies	creative thinking
courts	independence	diversity
elected representatives	tariffs	the Founding Fathers

executive   customs   anarchy

the Wild West   credit

PREREADING QUESTIONS

Before reading the selection, ask yourself and/or discuss with your classmates the following questions.

1. Would a system of international government be beneficial? Why or why not?
2. Would it be possible to create a system of international government? Why or why not?

There will always be a bad guy in the international neighborhood as long 1
as we have a world of lawlessness. This book describes the way to save humanity from the warfare that forces us to pay for killing machines and takes away world prosperity. And it doesn't depend on everyone becoming nice and kind by tomorrow!

Unless we change our way, humanity seems to be moving toward death. 2
A new way of doing things is needed to give our children a future. How do we move from an arms race to a peace race? What can we do about the present world crisis?

Solving the Problem of War

The only way to permanently solve the problem of war between nations 3
is to replace the LAW OF FORCE with the FORCE OF LAW.

Aside from problems with our politicians, we still have systems of gov- 4
erning ourselves that work. You slept peacefully in your bed last night because your city has a system of laws, enforcement, and courts that make you relatively safe. (Of course, nothing is perfect, but this is at least partly true.) Similarly, the state in which you live has a political structure with the three elements needed for good government: elected representatives to make laws, an executive branch with police to enforce the laws, and courts to resolve disagreements, decide who is guilty, who has broken the law, and what their punishment will be.

Without these three elements—laws, enforcement, and courts—lawless- 5
ness will take control. You might have to kill or risk being killed just to get less safety than your city, county, and state governments are now giving you. Remember the Wild West of the last century in which anyone with a

gun could be a lawmaker, enforcer, judge, jury, and executioner—sometimes all within one minute. The bloodshed of the Wild West days finally forced us to introduce law and order. Similarly, the killing and danger of nuclear war can force the nations of this earth to go beyond today's way of resolving disagreements by mass murder.

Just One More Layer

Today in the United States, we have four layers of government: city, county, state, and national. We have these four layers because we need them to have order within our nation. Adding only one more layer of government will enable us to have a prosperous future on this planet.

6

International governance—something like a United Nations of the World—will rescue us from our present crisis. U.S. President Harry S. Truman said, "When Kansas and Colorado have a disagreement over water in the Arkansas River, they don't call out the National Guard in each state and go to war over it. They go to the Supreme Court of the United States and accept the decision. There isn't a reason why we cannot do that internationally. . . ." It will be just as easy for nations to get along in a republic of the world as it is for you to get along in the republic of the United States."

7

The growth of international law and cooperation over the past century has prepared us to create a permanent peace with world-wide prosperity. Let's look at the progress we have made in replacing the law of force with the force of law. Louis Sohn, Professor in International Law, Emeritus, Harvard Law School, has shown that in the last forty years, more international agreements have been reached than during the previous four thousand years; that the International Court of Justice after a slow period now has more cases than it can handle (including several cases brought by African countries and other new members of the international community); that several regional courts are dealing with an increasing number of cases; and that more than two hundred international organizations deal with matters of daily concern to the majority of mankind in an effective and acceptable way.

8

The First Attempt

In 1776 the American colonies wanted independence from England. Under the leadership of George Washington, we fought the Revolutionary War, defeated England, and the United States had begun as a great nation. Right? No, wrong!

9

Except for a few students of history, most people do not realize that after   10
winning the War of Independence from England, there was no government
of the United States of America. There were only thirteen nation-states.
They got together to write the "Articles of Confederation" to agree on the
rules for relating to each other.

Increasing Chaos and Anarchy

Since each of the thirteen nation-states did not have to follow the rules of   11
the Articles, it is not surprising that the United States of America began to
fall apart. New York collected tariffs on goods from Connecticut and New
Jersey—even though such tariffs were forbidden under the Articles. Every
"Yankee" (New England) ship and New Jersey market boat had to pay entrance fees at New York customs just like ships from London or Hamburg.
States would ignore the Congress when they did not get their way. The Congress often did not have enough representatives present to do business, it
usually did not have money in its bank account, and its credit was bad so it
could not borrow money.

After four years of trouble in all parts of the country, with soldiers called   12
out in several states to deal with disagreements, and with civil war nar-
rowly avoided at least half a dozen times, the future looked dark. George
Washington was deeply concerned that the United States after winning the
war would tear itself apart in peace. He wrote to John Jay in June 1786, "I
am uneasy and apprehensive, more so than during the war."

The Constitutional Convention

Disturbed by conflicts, Virginia proposed a meeting in Annapolis in Sep-   13
tember 1786 to discuss trade among the states. The representatives were unable to agree on anything except to meet again in Philadelphia on the
second Monday of the following May. This was to be the famous Constitutional Convention of 1787. The Continental Congress agreed that the representatives would meet for "the sole purpose of revising the Articles of
Confederation, and reporting to Congress and the several Legislatures, such
alterations and provisions therein, as shall, when agreed to in Congress, and
confirmed by the states, render the Federal Constitution adequate to the exi-
gencies of Government, and the preservation of the Union."

Difficult Issues

There was disagreement on almost every issue. It took patience and an ability to listen to each other to understand opposing views. The delegates were careful to control their emotions and did not try to make decisions on issues that would tear the convention apart. They worked day by day, living with disagreement. They were determined to achieve a unified government. *The Great Rehearsal* by Carl Van Doren describes the interaction of interests that the Constitutional delegates had to deal with. Van Doren considers the Convention a "great rehearsal" of the process that we need today to create a final layer of world governance that will give humanity a future on this planet. 14

The Convention almost fell apart over the demand of small states to have an equal voice in Congress, and the demand of large states to have greater representation. New York had over 300,000 residents while Delaware had less than 60,000. And Delaware did not want to be outvoted! 15

The solution seems obvious now, but at the time it took creative thinking and a willingness to compromise. After all, how could you empower both the large states and the small states at the same time—and still have an effective government? Roger Sherman of Connecticut suggested that there be two houses of Congress. It was decided that the number of Representatives in the House was to be related to each state's population, and the Senate was to have two Senators from each state regardless of size—which makes all states equal. The "impossible" had been accomplished by compromise. 16

Our Way Is Clear

The challenges that faced America back then must have seemed as great to them as ours do to us. Patriot Tom Paine noted that the thirteen colonies were "made up of people from different nations, accustomed to different forms and habits of government, speaking different languages, and more different in their models of worship." Pennsylvania and Delaware had religious freedom for Christians; in Rhode Island Catholics could not vote; and in Massachusetts, Catholic priests could be put in prison for life! They had no common money or system of taxation, and there were trade and travel restrictions between the states. They were divided into liberals and conservatives. Some depended upon slavery for their existence, and others considered it a terrible evil. It was North vs. South, East vs. West, planter vs. 17

merchant, and one religion against another. Some of the states were talking about war with each other.

Yet with all this diversity, two centuries ago the patriots put the Constitution together in about 100 working days (May 25 to September 17). From the beginning on September 17, 1787, to official birth on June 21, 1788, our federal republic only took nine months! And in those days it took three weeks to travel from Philadelphia to Atlanta! And no telephones, either! 18

The Federal Solution

The Founding Fathers achieved this great union by designing a government that respected and included the thirteen separate nation-states instead of putting itself in opposition to them as disorderly criminals to be punished when they broke the law. They did this by leaving each nation-state in control of almost all of the decisions that affect its own citizens. Since the people of each state had their own state legislatures, it was up to the voters to make sure they were getting the state government they wanted. Then by creating an added layer of Federal government that would handle national problems that could not be solved by individual states, they had a system that would usually avoid interstate conflict. The national government could make and enforce decisions that required states to cooperate with each other and to support activities that served the common good. 19

This is the next step we must achieve for the world to survive the international anarchy and lawlessness of today. This political invention has been tested by the U.S. for over 200 years—and it has been copied by dozens of other nations throughout the world. □ 20

Thinking about the Reading

TRUE/FALSE QUESTIONS

In the space provided, write T if the sentence is true and F if the sentence is false, based on your reading of the preceding selection.

_____ 1. President Harry S. Truman said we should have an international system of laws similar to our national system.

_____ 2. We have not made much progress in international law in the last forty years.

_____ 3. The Articles of Confederation were not effective in establishing national law and order.

_____ 4. It was agreed that the large states would have more votes in the Senate than the small states.

_____ 5. The federal government took over all the decisions affecting all citizens.

COMPREHENSION QUESTIONS

In answering the following comprehension questions, *paraphrase* the selection—that is, restate it in your own words without copying phrases of more than three or four words from the reading. (See Appendix A for more on how to answer comprehension questions.) Here is an example:

Sample question:
What does Ferencz mean by the "force of law"?

Sample answer (words from the reading are italicized):
We have a *system* of laws that forces people to behave in a responsible way toward each other. The system includes *elected representatives* to make laws, an *executive* to enforce the laws, and *courts* to resolve disagreements.

Here are the questions:

1. What used to happen in the Wild West?
2. Why was the United States not a great nation immediately after the Revolutionary War?
3. What did the small and large nation-states disagree about?
4. How were the people of the thirteen states different?

OUTLINE

Complete the following outline of Ferencz's selection by listing the topics he discusses in the space provided.

Paragraph(s) 1–2: The way to save humanity

    3–5: _____

    6–8: The need for international law

    9–10: _____

11–12: Political chaos

    13: _____

14–16: The dispute between small and large states

17–18: _____

19: The Founding Fathers' solution to the problem

20: _____

SUMMARY

Use the preceding outline to write a summary of the reading. In the first sentence of your summary, mention the title, the author, and the main topic of the selection. Paraphrase the writer's points in your own words. (See Appendix B for more on how to write a summary.)

Making Connections

REACTING TO THE READING

Write about your personal reaction to the reading. Some possible topics include your agreement or disagreement with a specific issue; a relevant personal experience; an idea that is new to you; a related idea from another source (such as a book, a movie, or a television program); or why you like or dislike the selection.

FINDING RELATED SOURCES

1. Find a picture related to one of the following topics: international law, war, or another topic discussed in the reading. In writing, describe the picture and relate your thoughts and feelings about it. Discuss the picture and your writing with your classmates.
2. Find a passage in a book, magazine, or newspaper that is related to the reading. In writing, summarize the passage and describe how it is related. Discuss the passage and your summary with your classmates.

Getting Ready to Write

PREWRITING ACTIVITIES

Using the topic *international law*, *war*, or *arms race*, or another topic from the reading, spend 10 minutes on one of the following prewriting activities: freewriting, clustering, listing, or cubing. (See Appendix C.) Then discuss your prewriting with your classmates.

DISCUSSION AND COMPOSITION QUESTIONS

Choose one or more of the following questions to discuss with your class-mates in preparation for writing.

On Peacemaking Issues

1. What issues raised in the reading are related to the goal of achieving world peace?
2. Is international law related to world peace? Discuss.
3. What might a world governed by international law be like?
4. To what extent do we already have a system of international law?
5. Is our system of international law more effective today than in the past? Discuss.
6. Do we need a more effective system of international law? Why or why not?
7. Is it possible to create a true international government? Why or why not?
8. Why might we want to develop a better system of international law?
9. Do you think we will have a more effective system of international law in the future? Why or why not?
10. Could you (on your own or with others) do anything to help develop a more effective system of international law? If so, what? If not, why?

On Related Issues

11. Describe a past example of international lawlessness.
12. Describe a past example of an international conflict resolved by international law.
13. Is the situation of nations today similar to that of the thirteen American nation-states in 1787? Why or why not?
14. Does the government of the United States or of your native country usually follow international laws? Discuss with examples.
15. Tell about a particular conflict between nations or between groups within one nation. Was it resolved peacefully or violently? Why?
16. Compare Ferencz's views in this selection with Peck's in "Stages of Community Making" (Chapter 21) on how groups can form a community to resolve conflict.

Choose one of the preceding Composition Questions as your writing topic. Begin to plan your paragraph or essay by identifying the topic and listing your thoughts on that topic.

Example: Is it possible to create a true international government? Why or why not?

Topic: It would be difficult but possible to have an international government.

—Reasons why it would be difficult to develop
—Reasons why it would be possible to create

Then write the first draft of your paragraph or essay. (See Appendixes D and E for more on how to write paragraphs and essays.)

Revising and Editing Your Writing

REVISING YOUR WRITING

Use the Revision Checklist in Appendix F (p. 271) to evaluate the first draft of your (or your classmate's) writing in terms of content and organization. After deciding how your paragraph or essay can be improved, write a second draft incorporating the changes. On the checklist identify the areas in which you had difficulty so you can doublecheck these areas in later writings.

EDITING YOUR WRITING

After you are satisfied with content and organization, use the Editing Checklist in Appendix G (p. 272) to reevaluate your (or your classmate's) writing. On the checklist identify the areas in which you had difficulty so you can doublecheck these areas in later writings.

23

The Need for Solidarity

AUNG SAN SUU KYI

In 1991, Aung San Suu Kyi received the Nobel Peace Prize for her work in attaining civil rights for the people of Burma. The following selection is a speech she gave in 1989. In it she speaks of a need to bring together the diverse ethnic groups of Burma in the struggle for democracy.

Getting Ready to Read

THINKING ABOUT THE TITLE

What is *solidarity*? Many common expressions speak of the need for solidarity: "United we stand; divided we fall"; "A house divided against itself cannot stand"; "In unity there is strength."

KEY VOCABULARY/CONCEPTS

Discuss with your classmates what you know about some of the following words and concepts.

democracy	a movement	sympathy
ethnic group	political rights	progress
unified	oppression	equitable
harmony	threats	fascism
broad-minded	intimidation	self-disciplined
prosperity	justice	popular government
sacrifice	compassion	independence
courage	a "clean slate"	decline

Before reading the selection, ask yourself and/or discuss with your class-mates the following questions.

1. Is it possible for different groups of people (whether of different races, religions, languages, classes, or cultures) to work together for social change? Why or why not?
2. Cite an example of two or more different groups of people that either suc-ceeded or failed in their attempt to work together for social change.

We should like to thank you very much for coming and supporting us. We of the National League for Democracy believe very strongly that it is im-portant in our movement for democracy that all ethnic groups in the coun-try work together. It is in trying to help bring together all ethnic groups, all peoples, that we go on these organizational tours and try to visit as many places as possible. In the Kachin State there are many different peoples. Be-cause of this ethnic variety, I think that you already know what problems there are in creating a unified country, what problems must be overcome.

We must all work together if we are all to live together in unity and har-mony. I don't think I need to tell the people of the Kachin State how impor-tant it is for us all to be broad-minded and observe good political values. We must have as our goal the building of a real and lasting Union. Only af-ter building this Union can we really work towards peace and prosperity for all. We must all sacrifice our own needs for the needs of others. Without this, it will be impossible to build the kind of Union that we need.

I have heard many times on this trip that people are afraid to become in-volved in politics, but this has been nowhere true in all of the Kachin State. In some areas people are joining the movement with great courage. In these areas I have seen that the local people are enjoying more political rights. What we have seen on our organizational tours is that in those areas where people are daring to be politically active, they enjoy more rights. Where people are fearful, however, they suffer more oppression. Because of this, if we want democracy, we need to show courage. By this I don't mean the courage to cause trouble.

I must often remind people of this. By courage I mean the courage to do what one knows is right, even if one is afraid. We should do what we be-

lieve is right, even if we are afraid. Of course, we cannot help being afraid;
we just have to work to control our fear.

In Burma we have a tendency to use threats in raising our children. I
should like to ask you kindly not to do this. In our country we threaten children in teaching them to do or not do something, rather than explaining to
them so that they understand themselves. This kind of teaching by intimidation is now so prevalent that the rulers who govern us don't try to explain
things to ordinary people, but, instead, use threats to control them. This is
part of our culture, one that we should change. Let us teach our children by
explaining to them. This is our responsibility; we have a duty to teach the
children a sense of justice and compassion. Our young people are very important to me. We need to do more to look after them.

Children's minds are like a clean slate. That's why we have a great responsibility in raising them. We must not teach them things that will divide
them because of linguistic or ethnic differences; we must teach them so that
they understand the idea of the Union. In the Kachin State, for instance, we
have Jungpaw, Lisu, Shan, Burmans and other peoples. For all of them to
live together in harmony we must teach our children from earliest childhood the concept of national unity, of nationhood.

From my earliest childhood my mother taught me this idea of national
unity, not by merely talking about it but by including it in everyday work.
For example, we always had people from various ethnic groups living with
us. At that time my mother was working with nurses. Nurses from all over
the country would come to Rangoon to attend classes on child care. She
would invite those from ethnic minorities to stay at our home. Since my
youth, then, I was taught to live closely with people from other ethnic
groups.

In this way we need to give thought to ethnic groups other than our
own. We need to show sympathy and understanding. Without this, progress
for the country will be impossible.

Not thinking only of our own interests can also be applied to economic
issues. Not just in the Kachin State, but all over the country, there are people
who value their own businesses more than politics. Actually, though, only if
there is a good political system will it be possible to reach economic goals.
Even if business is doing well, if the political system is unjust, the nation
will not prosper. For example, during the era of the BSPP (Burma Socialist
Programme Party) there were some people who were very successful in
business, but what could they do with their money? In a country like

Burma, where the situation was constantly worsening, how could they find prosperity with their money? Quite a few of them sent their children abroad with the money. Just think of how much money the country lost with these young people! What is important is using this money for the good of the whole country, not just for one's own interest or the interests of one's family. Please, then, don't place economics above politics, for it is a fact that all nations that prosper economically are those that also have an equitable political system.

During the Second World War, Germany and Japan practiced fascism. At that time, too, the Germans and Japanese were very disciplined people. They were brave and they valued education. Yet however disciplined, however brave, however educated they were, because of their political philosophy and their political systems their countries were really not able to develop. Despite initial victories in the war, they eventually lost. Fascism is not an ideology that benefits the majority. With this kind of ideology a country can never truly develop over the long run. 10

After the war, both Germany and Japan adopted democratic institutions. By introducing democracy, these countries have also gone on to become two of the most prosperous nations in the world. This shows clearly that only with an effective government and equitable political system can a country really progress. We as citizens still need to be more self-disciplined; we still need to be more courageous, but in addition, we also need a proper form of government. So far we haven't even reached the zero level. If we want democracy, we need to reach that zero level. Only by so doing can we begin our work. Now, though, however hard we try, we cannot really work for our country freely. 11

There are those who say they would rather not be involved in the movement for democracy, but when the elections come, they will vote on the side of democracy. This is not enough. We still need to work towards free and fair elections. We have to work hard if we want our basic freedoms. Only if we have these freedoms can we continue to progress after achieving democracy. Will people who are not involved now become involved after we gain democracy? If people are still unwilling to take part in public life after we achieve a democratic government, that government will not be a stable one. 12

But let me ask about the real meaning of democracy. Those who want popular government should also become involved in politics. They should have individual political ideas. They should have positive attitudes and a willingness to sacrifice. Without this there is no way we can win. It has 13

242   *Working for a Better World*

been more than forty years since Burma gained independence. If we ask what progress has been made in these more than forty years, only depressing answers appear. When I visited Myitkyina over thirty years ago, there was no problem of electricity—it was always available. Now there is not even enough electricity and we find power in short supply. So we see that in these past thirty years and more there has been not only no progress but actual decline. We must ask ourselves, then: Why has this decline occurred? Most will answer that it is because the BSPP was bad. I won't argue with that, but we must ask again: Why was the BSPP able to last so long, then? I think the answer to this has to do with the people at large. Because we, the citizens, simply stood by and watched, the system was able to last as long as it did. When the time came to take up independence, I think that the BSPP gained control of the government because the citizens failed to carry out the duties of citizenship. If we want a stable democracy in the future, every single one of us must bear this responsibility conscientiously. We must be willing to sacrifice. We must all understand that there is great merit in sacrificing for others and that by so doing we live the full life. □

Thinking about the Reading

TRUE/FALSE QUESTIONS

In the space provided, write T if the sentence is true and F if the sentence is false, based on your reading of the preceding selection.

_____ 1. Prosperity in Burma will come only after a Union is created.
_____ 2. Courage means not being afraid.
_____ 3. By meeting people from different ethnic groups, Aung San Suu Kyi learned about national unity.
_____ 4. In the past, wealthy businesspeople in Burma were happy with the social conditions.
_____ 5. Democracy is necessary to ensure social progress.

COMPREHENSION QUESTIONS

In answering the following comprehension questions, *paraphrase* the selection—that is, restate it in your own words without copying phrases of more than three or four words from the reading. (See Appendix A for more on how to answer comprehension questions.) Here is an example:

Sample question:

According to Aung San Suu Kyi, what must the Burmese people do to build a real Union?

Sample answer (words from the reading are italicized):

They must be willing to make individual *sacrifices* so that conditions will improve for everybody.

Here are the questions:

1. What is the result of people's involvement in politics?
2. Why should parents use explanation rather than intimidation when disciplining children?
3. What does the recent history of Germany and Japan show?
4. What must people do to ensure social progress?

OUTLINE

Complete the following outline of Aung San Suu Kyi's selection by listing the topics she discusses in the space provided.

Paragraph(s) 1–2: Importance of working together

    3–4: _____

      5: Using explanation with children

    6–8: _____

      9: Economic issues

  10–11: _____

    12: Effects of noninvolvement

    13: _____

SUMMARY

Use the preceding outline to write a summary of the reading. In the first sentence of your summary, mention the title, the author, and the main topic of the selection. Paraphrase the writer's points in your own words without copying phrases of more than three or four words from the reading. (See Appendix B for more on how to write a summary.)

Making Connections

Write about your personal reaction to the reading. Some possible topics include your agreement or disagreement with a specific issue; a relevant personal experience; an idea that is new to you; a related idea from another source (such as a book, a movie, or a television program); or why you like or dislike the selection.

FINDING RELATED SOURCES

1. Find a picture related to one of the following topics: working together, national unity, or another topic discussed in the reading. In writing, describe the picture and relate your thoughts and feelings about it. Discuss the picture and your writing with your classmates.
2. Find a passage in a book, magazine, or newspaper that is related to the reading. In writing, summarize the passage and describe how it is related. Discuss the passage and your summary with your classmates.

Getting Ready to Write

PREWRITING ACTIVITIES

Using the topic *working together, national unity, solidarity,* or *democracy,* or another topic from the reading, spend 10 minutes on *one* of the following prewriting activities: freewriting, clustering, listing, or cubing. (See Appendix C.) Then discuss your prewriting with your classmates.

DISCUSSION AND COMPOSITION QUESTIONS

Choose one or more of the following questions to discuss with your classmates in preparation for writing.

On Peacemaking Issues

1. What issues raised in the reading are related to the goal of achieving world peace?
2. Is working together related to world peace? Discuss.

3. Tell about an example of two or more diverse groups that succeeded or failed in working together. What caused them to succeed or fail?
4. Is it important for diverse groups of people to work together? Why or why not?
5. How might people succeed in working together?
6. Do you think that people (in a particular place or throughout the world) will work together more successfully in the future? Why or why not?
7. Could you (on your own or with others) do anything to help diverse groups of people work together more successfully? If so, what? If not, why?

On Related Issues
8. Tell about your own or someone else's involvement in a political movement.
9. Is it good for people to get involved in political movements? Why or why not?
10. Why are some people afraid of getting involved in politics?
11. Why are some people uninterested in political involvement?
12. Compare two political movements and their degrees of success.
13. How can people cause political change?
14. Do you think people will be more effective in causing political change in the future? Why or why not?
15. What kinds of political change would you like to see in a particular place? Why?

PLANNING TO WRITE

Choose one of the preceding Composition Questions as your writing topic. Begin to plan your paragraph or essay by identifying the topic and listing some thoughts on that topic.

Example: Why are some people afraid of getting involved in politics?

Topic: Why some people are afraid of political involvement

—Fear of retribution
—Fear that it is a waste of their time

Then write the first draft of your paragraph or essay. (See Appendixes D and E for more on how to write paragraphs and essays.)

Revising and Editing Your Writing

REVISING YOUR WRITING

Use the Revision Checklist in Appendix F (p. 271) to evaluate the first draft of your (or your classmate's) writing in terms of content and organization. After deciding how your paragraph or essay can be improved, write a second draft incorporating the changes. On the checklist identify the areas in which you had difficulty so you can doublecheck these areas in later writings.

EDITING YOUR WRITING

After you are satisfied with content and organization, use the Editing Checklist in Appendix G (p. 272) to reevaluate your (or your classmate's) writing. On the checklist identify the areas in which you had difficulty so you can doublecheck these areas in later writings.

24

Political Activity

RIGOBERTA MENCHU

Rigoberta Menchu won the Nobel Peace Prize in 1992 for her leadership role in the struggle of the Guatemalan people for social, economic, and political rights. In the following selection from her autobiography, *I, Rigoberta Menchu* (1984), she describes how her work with a peasant workers' union (the CUC) helped her to become a more effective political activist.

Getting Ready to Read

THINKING ABOUT THE TITLE

Political means related to politics and government. What do you think is possible to achieve through political activity?

KEY VOCABULARY/CONCEPTS

Discuss with your classmates what you know about some of the following words and concepts.

organize	strike	united
finca (plantation)	criticism	middle class
fugitive	constructive	peasant
compañero (comrade)	humiliated	intellectual
Indians	insult	discrimination
ladino	ashamed	exploitation
linguistic barriers	Indianist	

Before reading the selection, ask yourself and/or discuss with your class-mates the following questions.

1. Have you ever been involved in political activity of any sort? If so, describe it.
2. Can individuals change the structure of society through political activity? Discuss.

We went on organizing our people in 1979. I remember that I hadn't   1
heard anything of my parents since the farewell in the community. I didn't
know where they were. They had no news of me either. We didn't see
them for a long time. I went to the plantations, I went to other areas, but
I couldn't go back to my village because I was a fugitive like my parents. We
lived with other people, with *compañeros* from other Indian groups, and with
the many friends I made in the organization. It was almost as if I were living
with my brothers and sister, with my parents. Everyone showed me so much
affection. So we organized the majority of workers on the South coast, in
the sugar, coffee and cotton plantations. And they agreed to carry on the political work when they returned to the Altiplano so that everybody would be
organized. Most of the workers were Indians and poor ladinos,* and we
didn't need to hold courses explaining the situation since it was all around
us. Our work went very well. And soon there just wasn't enough time for
everything; we had to rush from one place to another, carrying documents,
carrying everything. The reason for this was so that others wouldn't put
themselves at risk; we were already in danger; the enemy knew us. I traveled
from region to region, sleeping in different houses.

All this gave me a lot to think about, a lot, because I came across the lin-   2
guistic barriers over and over again. We couldn't understand each other and
I wanted so much to talk to everybody and feel close to many of the women
as I was to my mother. But I couldn't talk to them because they didn't understand me and I didn't understand them. So I said: "We can't possibly go
on like this. We must work to help people understand their own people, and
be able to talk to one another." From then on I concentrated on getting to
know my *compañeros* closely and teaching them the little I knew, so that they

*In Latin America, people of mixed American Indian (Native American) and European ancestry.

too could become leaders of their communities. I remember we talked of many things: of our role as women, our role as young people. We all came to the conclusion that we hadn't had a childhood, nor had we ever really been young because, as we were growing up we'd had the responsibility of feeding little brothers and sisters—it was like having a lot of children ourselves. I sometimes stayed with other Indians in their houses.

I remember the village of Huehuetenango very well, where I stayed in the house of a *compañero* who had ten children. I made a mistake there. It was something that I hadn't realized, thinking that we'd all had the same experiences. The mistake was not to have brought a blanket with me for this journey. I only had a sheet with me for the night. I arrived at that village in the Altiplano, and it was so cold, so incredibly cold. You can't believe how cold it was. So I hoped these people would lend me some clothes or a shawl to put over me. But at night I saw that they didn't even have anything for themselves and it made me very sad. How were we going to sleep? It was so cold! The dogs came in and out of the little house all the time because it was open. I asked: "Tell me, are we going to stay here?" I thought we could get leaves from the mountain to warm ourselves with. It was rather late to think of that but they collected quite a lot of leaves. . . . And so they all lay down round the fire; they were all sleeping and I wondered, well, where should I go? And I lay down next to them. By midnight it was so cold that we were almost frozen! The cold woke the parents up. "How cold it is," they said. "Yes," I said, and my jaw was almost stiff with cold. I'd never felt so cold before. Although my home is in the Altiplano too, the cold there doesn't compare with this. The parents got up for a while and then went to sleep again. I began to wonder how human beings can stand so much. We often say we can't bear something but we do bear it. The children were all right, quiet on the floor. Since the parents were very fond of me and thought of me as a leader, they said: "Look, here is a mat. Sit on this." But for my part, I couldn't use the mat because I was too ashamed, and also because I felt we were all equal and that they had as much right to the mat as I had. I told my host that I was ashamed by the special treatment they gave me because I was poor too, I was from the mountains too, from the same conditions, and that if we are fighting for equality for everyone, we must begin by sharing everything we have. I didn't mind sharing the mat with the children but I didn't deserve the mat for myself. It made me think a great deal, because I said: "In our house we have a mat each." This meant that I'd never suffered as they had here. And I began to discover many things that I hadn't experienced. So many rich people wasting even whole beds—one mattress isn't enough for them; they have two or three on their beds. And here there isn't even a mat to sleep on. This gave me a lot to think about. This happened with many people. I used to sleep one, two, three nights in one place, then I'd move on to another place for my work. I was happy.

Something I want to tell you is that I had a friend. He was the man who taught me Spanish. He was a ladino, a teacher, who worked with the CUC. He taught me Spanish and helped me with many things. We used to meet secretly because we couldn't meet openly where he lived. That *compañero* taught me many things, one of which was to love ladinos a lot. He taught me to think more clearly about some of my ideas which were wrong, like saying all ladinos are bad. He didn't teach me through ideas; he showed me by his actions, by the way he behaved towards me. At that time, we used to talk through the night. It was when we began supporting the struggle of peasants in general, and carrying out coordinated actions. For instance, if we call a strike, it's for all workers. If we call an assembly, we listen to the views of all the masses. It was my job to sound out the views of all the *compañeros* I was in contact with in the area I happened to be in, and send them to the regional coordinating body. Then they'd be sent to the national coordinating body to discuss with the *compañeros* there. Anyway, the example of my *compañero* ladino made me really understand the barrier which has been put up between the Indian and the ladino, and that because of this same system which tries to divide us, we haven't understood that ladinos also live in terrible conditions, the same as we do.

That's when I became very attached to my *compañero* ladinos and we began to talk a lot. Our organization includes Indians and poor ladinos, so we began putting this into practice. I remember having lengthy discussions with ladinos. I especially remember the times for criticism and the self-criticism which, I think, all revolutionary struggles go through to make the change more profound. The first time I pointed out an error by one of the ladinos, I felt terrible. Well, I'd never ever criticized a ladino before. I know deep inside what it is to feel humiliated, to have always been called "dirty Indian." "She's an Indian," they'd say as an insult. So for me criticizing a ladino was like putting on a mask and doing something shamelessly. Nevertheless, my criticism was constructive. I criticized the *compañero* but accepted his criticism too. These were the first things I found difficult to accept in our struggle.

As I was saying, I'm an Indianist, not just an Indian. I'm an Indianist to my fingertips and I defend everything to do with my ancestors. But I didn't understand this in the proper way, because we can only understand when we start talking to each other. And this is the only way we can correct our ideas. Little by little, I discovered many ways in which we had to be understanding towards our ladino friends and in which they had to show us understanding too. Because I also know *compañeros* ladinos with whom we shared the worst conditions, but who still felt ladino, and as ladinos, they didn't see that our poverty united us. But little by little, both they and I began discussing many very important things and saw that the root of our problems lay in the ownership of the land. All our country's riches are in the hands of the few.

My friend was a *compañero* who had taken the side of the poor, although I have to say that he was middle class. He was someone who'd been able to study, who had a profession and everything. But he also understood clearly that he had to share these things with the poor, especially his knowledge. He preferred to help the CUC rather than become a member because he said: "I don't deserve to be called a peasant. I'm an intellectual." He recognized his inability to do or know many things that peasants know, or the things poor people know. He said: "I can't talk about hunger the way a peasant can." I remember that when we said the root of our problems was the land, that we were exploited, I felt that being an Indian was an extra dimension because I suffered discrimination as well as suffering exploitation. □

Thinking about the Reading

TRUE/FALSE QUESTIONS

In the space provided, write T if the sentence is true and F if the sentence is false, based on your reading of the preceding selection.

_____ 1. Menchu did not need to explain the working situation to the peasants.

_____ 2. Menchu and her *compañeros* had had a good childhood.

_____ 3. In Huehuetenango, Menchu was ashamed to use the only mat.

_____ 4. Poor ladinos and Indians in Guatemala live in similar conditions.

_____ 5. Menchu's ladino friend was a member of the CUC.

COMPREHENSION QUESTIONS

In answering the following comprehension questions, *paraphrase* the selection—that is, restate it in your own words without copying phrases of more than three or four words from the reading. (See Appendix A for more on how to answer comprehension questions.) Here is an example:

Sample question:
Why couldn't Menchu go back to her village?

Sample answer (words from the reading are italicized):
Menchu was a *fugitive*. She had to stay away from the police, who would have arrested her for her political activities.

Here are the questions:

1. Why was Menchu upset by linguistic barriers?
2. What did she realize in Huehuetenango?
3. What did Menchu's ladino friend teach her?
4. Why was it hard for Menchu to criticize a ladino?

OUTLINE

Complete the following outline of Menchu's selection by listing the topics she discusses in the space provided.

Paragraph(s) 1: Organizing *compañeros*

    2: _____

    3: An experience in Huehuetenango

    4: _____

5–6: Changing attitude toward ladinos

    7: _____

SUMMARY

Use the preceding outline to write a summary of the reading. In the first sentence of your summary, mention the title, the author, and the main topic of the selection. Paraphrase the writer's points in your own words. (See Appendix B for more on how to write a summary.)

Making Connections

REACTING TO THE READING

Write about your personal reaction to the reading. Some possible topics include your agreement or disagreement with a specific issue; a relevant personal experience; an idea that is new to you; a related idea from another source (such as a book, a movie, or a television program); or why you like or dislike the selection.

FINDING RELATED SOURCES

1. Find a picture related to one of the following topics: political activity, social consciousness raising, or another topic discussed in the reading. In writing, describe the picture and relate your thoughts and feelings about it. Discuss the picture and your writing with your classmates.
2. Interview someone you know about political activity, social consciousness raising, or another topic discussed in the reading. Ask that person to describe his or her thoughts, feelings, and experiences. Take notes during the interview. Then, using your notes, write a summary of the interview that includes your reaction. Discuss the interview and your summary with your classmates.

Getting Ready to Write

PREWRITING ACTIVITIES

Using the topic *political activity, social consciousness raising,* or *linguistic barriers,* or another topic from the reading, spend 10 minutes on *one* of the following prewriting activities: freewriting, clustering, listing, or cubing. (See Appendix C.) Then discuss your prewriting with your classmates.

DISCUSSION AND COMPOSITION QUESTIONS

Choose one or more of the following questions to discuss with your classmates in preparation for writing.

On Peacemaking Issues

1. What issues raised in the reading are related to the goal of achieving world peace?
2. Is political activity related to world peace? Discuss.
3. Tell of a time when you (or someone you know) worked for some kind of social change.
4. Tell about a situation involving a group of people who worked together for social change. Did they succeed or fail? Why?
5. Compare how two groups of people are working for social change (in two places or in the present versus the past).
6. What causes people to work (or not to work) for social change?
7. What can people do to create social change?
8. Think of a particular place where unjust social conditions exist. Do you think those conditions will improve in the future? Why or why not?
9. Could you (on your own or with others) do anything to bring about social change? If so, what? If not, why?

On Related Issues

10. What difficulties did Menchu face in her attempt to organize people?
11. Tell about someone (other than Menchu) who attempted to organize people and the difficulties he or she faced.
12. Describe your own experience with linguistic barriers.
13. Relate an experience that improved your understanding of social conditions.
14. Tell about a friend who taught you something important.
15. Discuss an example of divisiveness among people that turned into unity as a result of common interests.

PLANNING TO WRITE

Choose one of the preceding Composition Questions as your writing topic. Begin to plan your paragraph or essay by identifying the topic and listing some thoughts on that topic.

Example: Tell about someone (other than Menchu) who attempted to organize people and the difficulties he or she faced.

Topic: Difficulties faced by Bishop Tutu in South Africa

  —Hostility between blacks and whites
  —Hostility between different black factions

Then write the first draft of your paragraph or essay. (See Appendixes D and E for more on how to write paragraphs and essays.)

Revising and Editing Your Writing

REVISING YOUR WRITING

Use the Revision Checklist in Appendix F (p. 271) to evaluate the first draft of your (or your classmate's) writing in terms of content and organization. After deciding how your paragraph or essay can be improved, write a second draft incorporating the changes. On the checklist identify the areas in which you had difficulty so you can doublecheck these areas in later writings.

EDITING YOUR WRITING

After you are satisfied with content and organization, use the Editing Checklist in Appendix G (p. 272) to reevaluate your (or your classmate's) writing. On the checklist identify the areas in which you had difficulty so you can doublecheck these areas in later writings.

PART VI: RESEARCH TOPICS

Choose one of the following topics on working for a better world for research. Refer to Appendix H for specific assignments. In addition, you may find it helpful to consult the list of Suggested Further Reading (at the end of this book) for sources related to your topic.

women's liberation

unions

workers' rights

women's rights

community

prejudice

open-mindedness

conflict

conflict resolution

international law

war/a particular war

United Nations

cold war

arms race

new world order

World War III

nuclear war

world peace

political coalitions

political change

social change

economic change

a political conflict

the future world

Appendix A: Answering Comprehension Questions

Appendix B: Writing Summaries

Appendix C: Prewriting Activities

Appendix D: Writing Paragraphs

Appendix E: Writing Essays

Appendix F: Revision Checklist

Appendix G: Editing Checklist

Appendix H: Research Assignments

APPENDIX A

Answering Comprehension Questions

In answering comprehension questions, you should do the following: (1) Make sure that you understand the question. (2) Find the section of the reading that gives the answer. (3) Paraphrase the writer's point; do not copy sentences exactly from the reading. (However, you may use key words or phrases from the reading in your answer.)

Consider the following example:

1. How has the world made progress since World War II?

The topic of the question is *world progress since World War II*. The answer can be found in paragraphs 1 and 2 of "The Illusion of Progress" by Lester R. Brown (Chapter 1).

The following answer is unacceptable because it is almost entirely copied from the reading (as the italicized words show):

Unacceptable:
The world has made progress because *the global economic production is about five times larger than it was in 1950 and world food production has also increased a great deal.* This *was made possible by modern technology.*

The following answer is acceptable because it uses a few key words without copying sentences word-for-word from the reading:

Acceptable:
The world has made progress because *global economic production* has increased a lot and more *food* has also been produced. *Modern technology* has allowed this to occur.

It is also acceptable to answer without using key words from the reading:

Acceptable:
We have made progress because we produce more and better products. The lives and work of many people are easier due to the development of such things as computers, video recorders, better televisions and telephones, and so on.

APPENDIX B

Writing Summaries

A summary should state (in your own words) the main points of the reading. The main points of the readings in this book are identified in the "Outline" exercise. When writing your summary, begin with a sentence stating the title, the author, and the main topic of the reading. After rereading the appropriate paragraphs of the selection as necessary, write one sentence for each topic identified in the outline. Clarify the relationships between sentences by using appropriate connecting expressions or transitions (such as *on the one hand ... on the other hand, moreover, however,* and *therefore*) or by referring to previously mentioned words or ideas (this problem, this idea of progress).

Here are a sample outline and summary for the reading in Chapter 1, "The Illusion of Progress":

OUTLINE

Paragraphs 1–2: Global economic progress since World War II

3–4: A sense of illusion

5–8: Negative effects of environment on economy

9–10: Problems in Africa and Latin America

11–13: Importance of croplands, forests, grasslands

14–16: Decrease in available land

17–18: GNP does not account for loss of natural resources

19–21: Repetto's new system of accounting

SUMMARY

In "The Illusion of Progress," Lester R. Brown questions the extent to which we are making progress in the world. On the one hand, a great deal of economic growth has occurred since World War II, and many people are living a good life. On the other hand, many people are not living a good life, and we are destroying our natural resources, which may make it difficult for us to have a good future. Due to environmental damage, the rate of growth in food production is slowing down. This problem is particularly apparent in Africa and South America. The three biological systems that support the world economy—croplands, forests, and grasslands—are all being harmed by our careless treatment of the environment. Since 1981, there has been a decrease in productive land area. Our way of measuring economic progress does not take this loss of natural resources into account. Economist Robert Repetto has suggested a new way of calculating GNP (gross national product) that would consider natural resources. If we used his system, we might begin to treat our natural resources in a more responsible way.

APPENDIX C

Prewriting Activities

FREEWRITING

Freewriting is a prewriting exercise that involves writing down whatever comes into your mind on a particular topic. When freewriting, you write nonstop without worrying about grammatical errors, incomplete sentences, or other surface errors. You should focus on generating ideas for writing.

The following example of freewriting is on the topic *global environmental damage*.

> Garbage in the street. Gas fumes in the air. Water maybe not so germ-filled as in some Third World countries but not healthy either. Probably will get worse. Maybe we'll all be drinking bottled water soon—okay for those who can afford it! Maybe some college students should go into the bottled water business—a growth industry? . . . The ozone layer—a big hole in the atmosphere, letting in cancercausing rays. Because we like our convenient spray deodorants. Won't be so "convenient" if we get skin cancer . . .

CLUSTERING

Clustering involves making a diagram to generate ideas for writing. Begin by circling your topic in the middle of a blank sheet of paper. Then draw lines from the topic and write associated words and phrases. These secondary ideas are circled, too. Next, write down more associated ideas until you have created a "cluster" of many related ideas. The accompanying example of clustering is on the topic poverty.

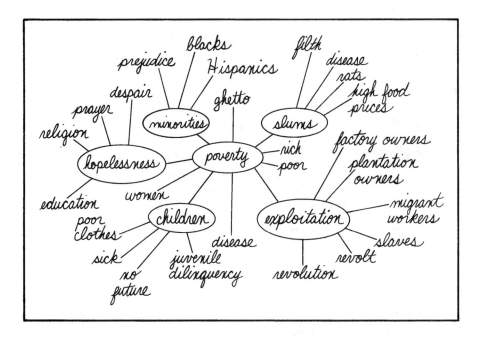

LISTING

Listing is another way of generating ideas for writing. Begin by identifying and underlining the main topic. Beneath it list as many related ideas as possible as they come to mind. The following example of listing is on the topic *overpopulation*.

---

overpopulation

disease	overcrowded schools
hunger	world health organizations
children	religion
abortion / legal?	social habits
early death	fear
high death rate	large families
no jobs	macho attitudes
no housing	responsibility

CUBING

Cubing involves drawing a cube around the main topic and labeling the sides *associated, describe, compare, argue, explain,* and *solve* (see the accompanying example on page 267). These labels refer to rhetorical patterns that can be used to generate ideas about a topic. You then choose one of these labels to write about. The sample cubing shown here is on the topic *political activity*.

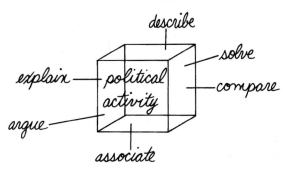

Associate – My experiences

Describe – In my country

Compare – Now and in the past

Argue – Is it good to get involved?

Explain – Why people do or don't do it

Solve – Attempts to solve a particular problem

<u>Describe</u>

In the late 1960's and early 1970s a lot of young people in the United States were politically active. A major reason was the Vietnam War. There was also a "counterculture" that was protesting our general life-style—turning away from materialism, living in communes, joining consciousness-raising and sensitivity groups. We seemed to be moving in a positive direction. But then we seemed to turn back toward selfish goals: the "me" generation, the 1980s and its money scandals. Where has idealism gone? I hope it's not dead.

APPENDIX D

Writing Paragraphs

A *paragraph* usually contains certain elements. In general, the first or second sentence of a paragraph mentions the paragraph's topic. This sentence is called the *topic sentence*. The middle sentences of a paragraph go on to support or explain the topic sentence, perhaps by including an example, relevant details and information, or an explanatory story. The last sentence of a paragraph usually restates or summarizes the main point, or in some other way brings the paragraph to a smooth close while also leading into the next paragraph. However, it is important to remember that not all paragraphs need always be written exactly like this. By adding variety to your writing you also make it more interesting.

The following paragraph answers a question relating to Lester R. Brown's "The Illusion of Progress" (Chapter 1): "Has the world become a better place since the 1950s? Why or why not?"

Although many people believe that we are making continual progress toward a better world, this may be an "illusion." **Topic sentence**

As Brown indicates, we produce a lot more goods now than we did in 1950. But let's look at some of the things we have produced. The United States has produced a lot of products for military use. We have a lot of nuclear bombs. We have also developed computer-driven "smart bombs." I question whether these types of goods make the world a better place. Part of our consumer mentality is that we always want to buy more of the latest products. So we feel that we need a lot of money to purchase them. But do we really need to buy a new car every two or three years? Perhaps if we thought less about having money and more about developing good relations with the people around us, we would do more to improve our quality of life. **Middle sentences support topic sentence with examples.**

In other words, even though we produce more goods today, this may not mean that the world is a better place than it was in 1950. **Closing sentence restates main point.**

Writing Essays

An *essay* is made up of several types of paragraphs that serve different functions. It usually begins with an *introductory paragraph* that states the essay's topic and *thesis* (main point). The thesis may appear at any point in the introduction, although it is most commonly stated in the final sentence.

Following the introduction are the *middle paragraphs* or *body* of the essay. Here you discuss and support your thesis with examples, facts, relevant details, and so on. Some essays may have only one long middle paragraph (such as one in which a brief story is told or an event is described). Most essays, however, have two, three, or more middle paragraphs, depending on how many main points need to be presented in support of the thesis. Each middle paragraph should focus on only one main point. This main point should be stated in the topic sentence and supported by an example, details, explanation, or information, rather than by vague or general comments.

An essay ends with the *concluding paragraph*. In it, you restate the thesis (in new words) and make a final statement about your topic to bring the essay to a satisfying close.

The following brief sample essay is written in response to a question relating to Lester R. Brown's "The Illusion of Progress" (Chapter 1): "Has the world become a better place since the 1950s? Why or why not?"

Introduction	In "The Illusion of Progress," Lester R. Brown gives impressive data about the economic progress that we have made since 1950. Yet, despite this progress, one might wonder if the world has really become a better place. } **Thesis statement**
First middle paragraph	One way of describing our progress is to note that we produce a lot more goods. But let's look at some of the goods that we produce. The United States, for example, has produced a lot of goods for military use. We have enormous numbers of nuclear bombs. I'm not sure, however, that these bombs improve our lives. And, of course, we then have to get rid of the nuclear waste that comes from producing those bombs. Such waste has seriously polluted our world environment and has caused a great deal of disease in human beings. We would be better off trying to work with other people in the world to create a situation where war seemed less likely to occur and less money needed to be devoted to producing weapons of war. } **Topic Sentence** · **Discussion and support of first main point**
Second middle paragraph	We have a consumer mentality that tells us we must spend a great deal of money to buy new goods. Although I admit that a microwave oven is convenient, I'm not sure that everybody needs to have one. Some Americans feel they need to buy a new car every few years. Perhaps we would be better off making cars that lasted longer so that we would not have to spend so much money on cars. Perhaps we would be better off spending less money on things in general. Then we would not have to be so concerned about having so much money. We might be better off being more concerned about our relations with other people—family, friends, and neighbors. That would probably do more to improve our quality of life than all the goods we can buy. } **Topic sentence** · **Discussion and support of second main point**
Conclusion	We certainly have made a lot of progress since 1950 in certain ways. Yet I believe that if we think more carefully about what is most important to leading a good life, we will come to the conclusion that to a great extent we have been going in the wrong direction. } **Thesis restated**

Revision Checklist

_____ 1. Does the opening sentence or paragraph present the topic and state the thesis?

_____ 2. Is the writer's main point clearly stated?

_____ 3. Is everything in the paragraph or essay related to the topic?

_____ 4. Is the paragraph or essay organized in a clear and logical way?

_____ 5. In an essay, is the main point presented in a new paragraph and stated in a topic sentence?

_____ 6. Are the main points supported by relevant details, examples, personal experiences, facts, or other types of evidence? Is this evidence interesting?

_____ 7. Does the paragraph or essay have an effective conclusion that brings it to a satisfying end?

_____ 8. What do I like most about this writing?

_____ 9. What do I like least about this writing?

_____10. How can the writer improve the paragraph or essay? What can be added, omitted, or clarified in revision to make it more effective?

APPENDIX G

Editing Checklist

_____ 1. Has the writer indented at the beginning of paragraphs?

_____ 2. Has the writer used correct punctuation (a period at the end of each sentence, commas where appropriate, and so on)?

_____ 3. Has the writer used articles correctly (for example, _a_ or _the_ with singular count nouns but not with plural or noncount nouns with general meaning, _the_ to refer to one or more definite things)?

_____ 4. Has the writer used singular and plural nouns and pronouns correctly?

_____ 5. Has the writer used verb forms correctly (for example, singular or plural as appropriate, correct verb tenses, active or passive voice as appropriate, and so on)?

_____ 6. Has the writer used word forms (noun, verb, adjective, adverb) correctly? (If you are not sure of a particular word's correct form, check a dictionary.)

_____ 7. Has the writer made any spelling errors? (If you are not sure of a particular word's spelling, check a dictionary.)

_____ 8. Has the writer used words and expressions that clearly express the intended meaning?

_____ 9. Has the writer used correct sentence construction? Do sentences clearly convey meaning?

Research Assignments

Here are some research assignments for the topics at the end of each part. Choose your topic before proceeding. Then do one or more of the following assignments. All of the reference books mentioned here can be found in the library.

1. Look up your topic in an encyclopedia. Summarize some of the main points mentioned in the encyclopedia article. Then describe your own ideas and opinions on one or more of the ideas you came across in the encyclopedia article.

2. Look up your topic in the *Reader's Guide to Periodical Literature* (which indexes articles in popular magazines) or in the *New York Times Index* to find relevant articles. Choose an interesting article and ask the librarian to help you locate it. After reading the article, summarize it and react to one or more of the ideas expressed in the article. (You might instead read two articles and discuss the similarities and differences in the writers' views as well as your own reaction.)

3. List a few questions related to your topic. Then, using those questions, interview one or more people about your topic. Take notes during the interview. Afterwards, write a summary of the ideas expressed by the interviewees and state your reaction to those ideas.

4. Read one of the sources listed in Suggested Further Reading (following Appendix H). Write a summary of the book. Include also your reactions—your thoughts and feelings, your personal experience, your agreement or disagreement.

5. After doing library research on your topic, write a paper in which you summarize the views of two or more sources and compare or contrast them with your own ideas. A formal research paper usually includes a title page, footnotes or endnotes, and a bibliography. (Check with your instructor to see whether these items should accompany your research paper.)

Suggested Further Reading

Allen, Paula Gunn. (1986) *The Sacred Hoop: Recovering the Feminine in American Indian Traditions*. Boston: Beacon Press. (NATIVE AMERICANS/WOMEN)

Aung San, Suu Kyi. (1991) *Freedom from Fear*. New York: Penguin. (POLITICAL ACTIVISM)

Baldwin, James. (1962) *The Fire Next Time*. New York: Dell. (U.S. RACE RELATIONS)

Bell, Derrick. (1992) *Faces at the Bottom of the Well: The Permanence of Racism*. New York: Basic. (U.S. RACE RELATIONS)

Bok, Sissela. (1990) *A Strategy for Peace: Human Values and the Threat of War*. New York: Vintage. (WAR/PEACE)

Boothby, Neil. (1987) "Children and War," in A. Cohen and L. Leach, eds., *Generations: A Universal Family Album*. New York: Pantheon. (BIRTH/CULTURAL CONTINUITY/HUMAN INTERRELATEDNESS)

Brown, Lester R., ed. (1991) *The Worldwatch Reader on Global Environmental Issues*. New York: Norton. (ENVIRONMENT)

———, Christopher Flavin, and Sandra Postel, eds. (1984–present) *The State of the World*. New York: Norton. (ENVIRONMENT)

Caldicott, Helen. (1986) *Missile Envy: The Arms Race and Nuclear War*. New York: Bantam. (WAR/PEACE)

Carson, Rachel. (1962) *Silent Spring*. Boston: Houghton Mifflin. (ENVIRONMENT)

Crow Dog, Mary. (1990) *Lakota Woman*. New York: Harper Perennial. (NATIVE AMERICANS/POLITICAL ACTIVISM)

Hall, Edward T. (1959) *The Silent Language*. New York: Doubleday. (CROSS-CULTURAL COMMUNICATION)

———. (1966) *The Hidden Dimension*. New York: Doubleday. (CROSS-CULTURAL COMMUNICATION)

———. (1976) *Beyond Culture*. New York: Doubleday. (CROSS-CULTURAL PERCEPTION)

Hansson, Carola, and Karin Liden. (1983) "Liza and Family," in George Blecher and Lore Blecher, eds., *Moscow Women: Thirteen Interviews*. New York: Pantheon/Random House. (SOVIET WORKING WOMEN)

Harrison, Paul. (1981) *Inside the Third World: The Anatomy of Poverty*. London: Penguin. (WORLD POVERTY)

Houston, Jeanne Wakatsuki, and James Houston. (1973) *Farewell to Manzanar*. Boston: Houghton Mifflin. (JAPANESE AMERICANS)

Keen, Sam. (1991) *Fire in the Belly: On Being a Man*. New York: Bantam. (MALE ROLE)

King, Martin Luther, Jr. (1958) *Stride toward Freedom*. New York: Harper & Row. (NONVIOLENT RESISTANCE)

Kingston, Maxine Hong. (1975) *The Woman Warrior*. New York: Vintage. (IMMIGRANTS)

Krishnamurti, J. (1964) *Think on These Things*. New York: Harper & Row. (RELIGIOUS/SPIRITUAL VALUES)

Kushner, Harold. (1989) *Who Needs God?* New York: Pocket Books. (RELIGIOUS/SPIRITUAL VALUES)

Laqueur, Walter, and Barry Rubin, eds. (1979) *The Human Rights Reader*. New York: Meridian. (HUMAN RIGHTS)

Menchu, Rigoberta. (1984) *I, Rigoberta Menchu*. New York: Verso. (POLITICAL ACTIVISM)

Merton, Thomas. (1985) *Love and Living*. New York: Harvest/Harcourt (RELIGIOUS/SPIRITUAL VALUES)

Miles, Rosalind. (1990) *The Women's History of the World*. New York: Harper Perennial. (WOMEN'S RIGHTS)

Montagu, Ashley. (1952) *The American Way of Life*. New York: Putnam. (AMERICANS)

Neihardt, John. (1981) *Black Elk Speaks*. Lincoln, Nebr.: University of Nebraska Press. (NATIVE AMERICANS/RELIGIOUS AND SPIRITUAL VALUES)

Nieto, Sonia. (1992) *Affirming Diversity: The Socio-Political Context of Multicultural Education*. New York: Longman. (MULTICULTURALISM/EDUCATION/IMMIGRANTS)

Peck, M. Scott. (1978) *The Road Less Traveled*. New York: Touchstone. (RELIGIOUS/SPIRITUAL VALUES)

———. (1989) *The Different Drum: Community Making and Peace*. New York: Touchstone. (COMMUNITY/PEACE)

Rodriguez, Richard. (1982) *Hunger of Memory*. New York: Bantam. (MEXICAN AMERICANS/LANGUAGE)

Tannen, Deborah. (1990) *You Just Don't Understand*. New York: Ballantine. (MEN AND WOMEN/CROSS-CULTURAL COMMUNICATION)

Terkel, Studs. (1992) *Race*. New York: New Press. (U.S. RACE RELATIONS)

West, Cornell. (1993) *Race Matters*. Boston: Beacon Press. (U.S. RACE RELA-TIONS)

Wheeler, Thomas C. (1972) *The Immigrant Experience*. New York: Dial Press. (IMMIGRANTS)

About the Authors

ELAINE BROOKS is associate professor of ESL at Brooklyn College, City University of New York. She has taught a variety of college-level ESL courses, primarily intermediate/advanced reading and writing. Journal articles growing out of her research on the relationships among ESL students' reading, writing, and first- and second-language literacy levels have been published in *ESL and Beyond ESL*, *Ending Remediation*, and *Practical Research*. Professor Brooks holds a Ph.D. in applied linguistics from New York University and an M.A. in TESOL from Teachers College, Columbia University.

LEN FOX is associate professor of ESL at Brooklyn College, City University of New York. He began his ESL teaching career in the U.S. Peace Corps, working in Tunisia, North Africa, from 1966 to 1968. He has written extensively about ESL teaching, peace education, and global community for a variety of journals including *College Composition and Communication*, *Teaching ESL at CUNY*, *Resource*, and *Journal of Basic Writing*. An editor of the *Brooklyn College Multicultural Newsletter* and a member of the multicultural committee at Brooklyn College, Professor Fox has been active in the planning and organization of anti-bigotry teach-ins and various other events aimed at promoting positive attitudes toward multiculturalism. He holds a Ph.D. in applied linguistics and an M.A. in TESOL from New York University.

Acknowledgments

Excerpts from "The Illusion of Progress" by Lester R. Brown and from "Picturing a Sustainable Society" by Lester R. Brown, Christopher Flavin, and Sandra Postel are reprinted from *State of the World 1990*, A Worldwatch Institute Report on Progress Toward a Sustainable Society, Project Director: Lester R. Brown. By permission of W. W. Norton & Company, Inc. ©1990 by Worldwatch Institute.

Excerpts from "Land Hunger in Asia" by Paul Harrison are reprinted by permission of the Peters Fraser & Dunlop Group Ltd.

Excerpt from *Missile Envy* by Helen Caldicott. Copyright ©1984 by Helen Caldicott. Reprinted by permission of William Morrow & Company, Inc., and International Creative Management, Inc.

"Where I Come From Is Like This" by Paula Gunn Allen is reprinted from *The Sacred Hoop* by Paula Gunn Allen. Copyright ©1986, 1992 by Paula Gunn Allen. Reprinted by permission of Beacon Press.

"Liza and Family" by Carola Hansson and Karin Liden is reprinted from *Moscow Women: Thirteen Interviews* by Carola Hansson and Karin Liden. Copyright ©1983 by Random House, Inc. Reprinted by permission of Pantheon Books, a division of Random House, Inc.

"American Men Don't Cry" by Ashley Montagu. Permission granted by copyright owner Ashley Montagu.

"Machismo in Washington" by I. F. Stone. Permission granted by Jeremy J. Stone.

"Grandparents Have Copped Out" by Margaret Mead, June 12, 1971 Op-ed. Copyright ©1971/78 by The New York Times Company. Reprinted by permission.

"Hoang Vinh" case study reprinted from *Affirming Diversity: The Sociopolitical Context of Multicultural Education* by Sonia Nieto. Copyright ©1992 by Longman Publishing Group.

"An Education in Language" by Richard Rodriguez. Excerpt from *State of the Language* by Leonard Michaels and Christopher Ricks. Reprinted by permission of the University of California Press.

"Children and War" by Neil Boothby is reprinted from *Generations: A Universal Family Album* by Smithsonian Institution, ed. by Anna Cohen and Lucinda Leach. Copyright ©1987 by Smithsonian Institution. Reprinted by permission of Pantheon Books, a division of Random House, Inc.

"The Arab World" from *The Hidden Dimension* by Edward T. Hall. Copyright ©1966, 1982 by Edward T. Hall. Used by permission of Doubleday, a division of Bantam Doubleday Dell Publishing Group, Inc., and by permission of Edward T. Hall.

"Anglo vs. Chicano" by Arthur L. Campa is reprinted with permission of Arthur Campa, Jr.

"Living in Two Cultures" by Jeanne Wakatsuki Houston is reprinted from *Farewell to Manzanar* by James D. Houston and Jeanne Wakatsuki Houston. Copyright ©1973 by James D. Houston. Reprinted by permission of Houghton Mifflin Co. All rights reserved.

"The Ways of Meeting Oppression" by Martin Luther King, Jr., is reprinted by arrangement with The Heirs to the Estate of Martin Luther King, Jr., c/o Joan Davis Agency as agent for the proprietor.

"Who Needs God?" by Harold Kushner. Copyright ©1989 by Harold S. Kushner. Reprinted by permission of Simon & Schuster, Inc.